AMERICAN POLITICS AND EVERYDAY LIFE

AMERICAN POLITICS AND EVERYDAY LIFE

ROBERT D. HOLSWORTH
Virginia Commonwealth University
J. HARRY WRAY
DePaul University

1807 1982

175 YEARS OF PUBLISHING

JOHN WILEY & SONS
New York • Chichester • Brisbane • Toronto • Singapore

Copyright © 1982 by John Wiley & Sons, Inc.

Library of Congress Cataloging in Publication Data:

Holsworth, Robert D.
  American politics and everyday life.

  Bibliography: p.
  Includes index.
  1. United States—Politics and government.
2. Consumption (Economics)—United States.
3. Quality of life—United States. 4. Social
values. I. Wray, J. Harry. II. Title.
JK274.H653   320.973   81-23171
ISBN 0-471-08645-2   AACR2

Printed in the United States of America

10 9 8 7 6 5 4 3 2 1

TO OUR PARENTS

ABOUT THE AUTHORS

Robert D. Holsworth is Assistant Professor of Political Science at Virginia Commonwealth University. He is the author of *Public Interest Liberalism and the Crisis of Affluence* and a number of articles on American politics and culture. He has also written columns and reviews for several newspapers across the nation.

J. Harry Wray is Assistant Professor of Political Science at DePaul University. He is the author of articles that have appeared in *The Journal of Politics* and the *Western Political Quarterly*. He also serves on the editorial board of *The Journal of Politics*. Both authors received their PhDs from the University of North Carolina in 1977.

PREFACE

Most books which introduce students to American politics seem to have been written according to a standard formula. There is a chapter on the Declaration of Independence and the Constitution, a chapter on the branches of government, a chapter on political parties and elections, one on public opinion and voting behavior, one on civil liberties, and another about the topic of political socialization. Books that summarize the conventional wisdom of political science may help students better understand the daily events detailed in newspapers. They may become more self-confident during political discussions with friends or with relatives. They may occasionally even be inspired to become more active and more thoughtful citizens.

It is our belief that the standard textbook treatment of American politics typically neglects to show how our nation's political values are connected to the conduct of our personal lives. One of the tacit standard messages is that politics is something which occurs in Washington, D.C., in the nation's statehouses, or in other corridors of power. In other words, politics is an activity external to us. We may participate in politics by voting, working in campaigns, or writing letters to politicians, but political life is also seen as something from which we can remove ourselves at will. If we decide not to soil our hands by active involvement, the political system will reciprocate by not exerting any influence over our lives.

As a consequence of this implicit message, the standard texts fail to raise, much less adequately discuss, some of the most fundamental questions about political life. Most books in the field of American politics are insufficiently attentive to the following set of questions.

1. How are our personal lives affected by America's economic and political priorities? How are our everyday actions, hopes, and fears shaped by our social order?
2. How is society's implicit definition of human beings reflected in the policies designed by our political institutions?
3. What strains and tensions emerge in both our personal lives and the political system because of the prevailing conception of human beings?
4. How are some important everyday concerns defined as insignificant and irrelevant according to the existing standards of political and economic life?
5. Is an alternative vision regarding people's needs, goals, and fears contained in contemporary movements for political change in America?

6. How could we create a society whose institutions reflect a different understanding of human beings than that which is presently evident?

From our point of view, these are important questions that everyone in a democratic society ought to think about. If a fundamental premise of democracy is that the people govern, it is surely critical that we come to understand the forces that influence us. Without such an understanding, we may be unwittingly governed by these forces, all the while thinking that we are free individuals in control of our destiny.

To consider seriously these six questions will require some people to examine their preconceptions about the meaning of a college education. We are fairly certain, from our own experience and from other sorts of evidence, that a significant number of students today consider a college education to be primarily a means for obtaining well-paying employment or simply as a good way to spend four years with some interesting friends. Given the state of American society today, it is certainly understandable that students hold these views. Yet one of the greatest opportunities of a college education is the chance for the student to think critically about his or her potential goals and to decide whether to spend a lifetime working to achieve those goals.

The benefits to be gained from using this opportunity to think seriously about the questions raised are, we think, ultimately more enduring than the benefits obtained from receiving a high grade or impressing relatives during a discussion. Ideally, students who confront the issues examined in the ensuing chapters should be able to understand why they hold certain political views or, equally important, why so many of us grow up believing that politics is insignificant and that the contours of the public world have little or no effect on our private lives. Students should be able to better understand the connections between a seemingly abstract and far-removed political order and our thoughts about work, leisure time activities, family life, and the worth of collective endeavors. To understand these connections is an important first step in deciding if we are satisfied with our lives or whether there are more appropriate, more desirable, and more humane ways of living.

This book offers a similar set of demands and rewards for teachers. In order to respond to the central questions one must examine the content of the political education we impart to our students every semester. We have to ask ourselves whether we should be satisfied with passing on the knowledge that a standard political science book calls "politics" or whether our vocation demands that we go further and try to explain the connections between our social and political values and the day-to-day existence of American citizens.

If we believe that it is part of our responsibility to offer this latter function, we may be confronted with a number of difficulties. First, since answers to the six questions are less precise than the subject matter of political science proper, our efforts will appear to be less scientific. Moreover, addressing these questions will cause some people to alter their established way of teaching and, in the process, cause them to abandon techniques that may have worked with other materials. Yet by taking these risks, we may actually explain more of the political universe than before and we may find it more rewarding also.

We take it for granted that particular methods of social, economic, and political organization foster the development of certain human characteristics and discourage the formation of others. In this book we try to illustrate how this assumption can be applied to the normal course of studying American politics. In so doing, we hope our argument will serve as a basis for discussion and further elaboration. The following statements summarize the principal elements of our position.

1. Human beings are considered in American society, for a number of reasons, to be primarily consumers of goods and services. It is thought that we realize our freedom, for the most part, not in our work or in our politics, but in our consumption.

2. This understanding is evident in policy decisions of major political institutions, in popular expressions of the "good life," in cultural institutions, in the mass media and, curiously enough, in both liberal and conservative reform movements.

3. A number of serious problems have begun to emerge because of this tendency to define the quality of life by the quantity of consumption. These problems include excessive anxiety and loneliness in personal life, popular dissatisfaction with some public institutions, and concern about whether the necessary resources exist to maintain an ever-expanding consumer lifestyle.

4. The potential for Americans to improve the quality of their existence cannot be reached solely by individual action. It requires collectively developing a stronger sense of economic justice, revitalizing our work lives and enlarging the opportunities for political action and public participation in decision making.

The first six chapters establish the main contours of our argument. We present an historical overview of American society since World War II and a general explanation of the values of a consumer society. We then show how these values exert a negative effect on our educational system, our work lives, the operation of the media and the public policies of our political order. Chapters 7 and 8 argue that neither conservative nor liberal reform movements can effectively improve American society because both ultimately are wed to the values of the consumer order. Chapters 9 and 10 depict some current strains we are experiencing and suggest directions to improve the quality of everyday life in America.

We would like to thank students, colleagues, and friends who read all or portions of early versions of this book and whose comments served to improve it.

These include James Block, Delma Bratvold, Anne DeLaney, Barbara Ericks, Nicholas Kass, Terry Lynch, Charles Menke, Cindy Tremback, and Judy Wray. We are especially indebted to Scott Keeter and David Yamada, both of whom offered extensive and extremely helpful advice. Wayne Anderson and Connie Rende of John Wiley & Sons have been encouraging and responsive. All of the above people, plus supportive friends too numerable to mention, have made this book better than it otherwise would have been. The faults which remain are our responsibility.

R.D.H.
J.H.W.

CONTENTS

CHAPTER 9   THE END OF CONSUMER SOCIETY?   158

CHAPTER 10   DEMOCRACY FOR AMERICA   176

CHAPTER 1

The Shattered Consensus

"Hey, hey LBJ, how many kids did you kill today."

Antiwar chant in the sixties.

"It's time to sweep that kind of garbage out of our society."

Vice-President Agnew on domestic opposition to the Vietnam War.

Alton Woods is 66 years old. He was born in Augusta, Georgia, and lived there until World War II when he joined the service. After leaving the army, Alton settled in New York City until his retirement in 1979. Despite having visited his home town only six times since he departed in 1942, Alton wants to buy some land outside Augusta and spend his remaining years in a small house he plans to have constructed. His motive for returning home is not, as one might expect, a desire to be near kinfolk and boyhood friends, for he says that he "hardly knows anyone there anymore." His rationale is simply that New York has become too dangerous a place for an elderly man. He remains indoors in the evening because "they haven't yet started coming into my house." Outside, the nighttime is, according to Alton, filled with terrors. "Kids, fourteen, fifteen, sometimes even younger knock you over and steal your wallet, junkies will take anything, and walk around the corner and you may not come back. An old man is never safe."

Asked how recently this problem has arisen, Alton responds that it is only in the past four or five years that it has reached crisis proportions. His neighborhood

1

has always been plagued by occasional crime, but never had the hoodlum element been so pervasive and so lacking in civility. Even little children are not protected as gang members "kick them off their bikes and ride away with them" for sport. Alton is so eager to leave the neighborhood that his plans have instigated a serious breach between him and his wife of 40 years. She hopes that they might weather the storm until the neighborhood enters a cycle of improvement, but Alton harbors no optimism about this ever occurring. At moments when he is beaten down by conditions to the point that callousness overwhelms his feelings of compassion and love, he can bring himself to exclaim that "no matter what she does, I'm leaving!" His expectations about relocating in Georgia are not particularly high, only that he believes it is a place where an "old man can live in peace."

Alton Woods is not a representative American in many respects. He is older than most of us, he is black, and he is currently exposed to crime more frequently than the average citizen. But in other respects, the troubles which he identifies and his responses to these problems strike a familiar chord. Alton's fears of "going outside" can serve as a metaphor to represent the systematic dislike and distrust of the public realm by the population at large. The world outside our homes and small circle of friends is commonly perceived as threatening or, at least, considered impersonal and unrewarding. We often find our work boring, our streets dangerous, our retailers exploitative, our corporations heartless, and our government insensitive. And, like Alton, we respond to this situation with a large measure of resignation. Since we cannot imagine effectively influencing this state of affairs, we devote our lives to finding a comfortable niche in the system that will enable us to live in peace. We seek to obtain some degree of freedom and power in a world that severely limits these possibilities.

This chapter traces the recent historical roots of the process by which individuals define their lives as a struggle against the outside world. We describe the set of beliefs and values that emerged in America after World War II, the challenges to these beliefs and values that occurred in the 1960s and the consequences of these challenges for our present condition. We argue that the retreat to private satisfaction which is so prevalent today is an understandable reaction to the state of our public life. But despite this apparent reasonableness, there are severe costs to pursuing this strategy; we diminish our sense of self; we diminish our capacity to see that community enrichment and political change are often preconditions of genuine personal development; and we actually fall prey to the very forces of public life which we are urgently striving to avoid. We become escape artists who, for the most part, only succeed in becoming further entangled in our chains.

THE POSTWAR CONSENSUS

When Franklin Delano Roosevelt was elected president in 1932, his immediate task was to grapple with the depression which had put a devastating end to the prosperity of the 1920s. Roosevelt's New Deal programs attempted to preserve the major elements of American capitalism through a judicious use of government intervention. Roosevelt decided that American business could only be saved if the government assumed a much greater role in the management of the economy. While this would call for the establishment of some measures of which business owners did not approve (such as a minimum wage, social security, and greater protection for labor unions), it was believed that in the long run these would be a fair price for business to pay. Roosevelt aided some businesses directly, and by putting some of the jobless on the government payroll, he infused the economy with money. This permitted businesses to sell their inventories, begin new production, and hire the workers that had been laid off as the result of business failures. When business owners turned against Roosevelt's policies, he often expressed astonishment. He compared these business owners to a person who had been saved from drowning at a public beach and then spent the rest of his life cursing the lifeguard for not saving his hat also.

While the New Deal made a dent in the depression, it is not at all clear that it rescued the American economy. At the end of the 1930s, unemployment was still high and the buying power of most Americans was limited. Prosperity came to America again during World War II. Roosevelt liked to express our commitment to victory against the Axis powers by saying that it was time for "Old Dr. New Deal to be replaced by Dr. Win the War." Properly speaking, however, it was Dr. Win the War which saved Dr. New Deal from a spate of malpractice suits. The war on Germany and the Axis powers also turned out to be the most successful war on poverty ever waged in America.

As World War II approached its end, Americans honored those who had died in the struggle, welcomed home the troops returning to their families, and celebrated the victory. But the coming of the peace brought some sobering questions to reflective Americans. Could the returning veterans honored in September be employed in December? Would the wartime prosperity continue in peacetime? Could the conflicts between labor and ownership be managed without the unity imposed by wartime? Was the American economy sufficiently stable to stand on its feet without war?

Perhaps a good way to understand this concern is to picture the American economy as a seriously injured individual. In the 1930s, this person only managed to survive, with the help of the New Deal, by crawling. With the advent of World War II, military spending and military conscription became the crutches that allowed the crippled person to walk. The central question after World War II centered on what would happen when the crutches were pulled away. Were the crutches the last step in a healing process? Or were they necessary props without which the individual would be again reduced to crawling?

Remarkably, the American economy not only remained standing after World War II, but it ran more efficiently than it had previously. It even began to shout how well it was doing. Most of the returning veterans were employed and many unions negotiated their best contracts. Ordinary workers were able to purchase single-family homes and sometimes even a second car. Suburbs were invented, promising to bring to the masses the economic benefits which had only been enjoyed by the few.[1]

Having emerged from World War II as the strongest military power in the world, it soon became apparent that we were the most prosperous economic entity also. By the 1950s, America was being labeled the affluent society. Rather than wondering whether America could manage to avoid the throes of a depression, we were confronted with the much less daunting problem of meeting the "challenge of abundance." Many professional economists basked in the glory of the unexpected prosperity and professed immodestly that they had solved the problems of boom and bust in the American economy. Using a metaphor which they had borrowed from television, itself a symbol of our newfound abundance, a number of economists claimed that the American economy was only in need for "fine tuning" and that any respectable group of professionals could handle the chore.

Victory in the war and the surprising economic development afterward helped to solidify a particular outlook on American society that has influenced our politics since that time. A consensus emerged about the worth of our economy, the nature of our political system, the quality of our personal life and the major threat to this way of life. The beliefs that comprised this consensus were shared by most citizens, whatever their political affiliation. This set of shared beliefs can be summarized by the following six points.

1. The American economy was basically sound. As mentioned, many prominent Americans assumed we had resolved the periodic disturbances to which the economic system had previously been liable. America was prosperous and becoming more so every day.

2. Our technology was fundamentally beneficent. American technological advances were either time-saving devices that expanded leisure time or gadgetry that enhanced the enjoyment of our leisure time. Perhaps the most explicit expression of our attitude toward technology was exhibited in what became known as the "kitchen debate" between the then vice-president Richard Nixon and the Soviet leader Nikita Khrushchev. The two men met at a trade fair in a kitchen which was supposedly representative of that found in an American home. Besides discussing issues of world peace, Nixon pointed to the utensils and appliances in the American kitchen not only to prove the American housemaker was competent, but to claim that a homemaker in Amerca was infinitely better off than one in the Soviet Union. The American washing machine became one more indication of our nation's superiority.

3. Our political system was about as laudable as one could practicably achieve. Admittedly, there were problems in American society and politicians, like politicians at all times, were occasionally rascals and

---

[1]Godfrey Hodgson, *America in Our Time* (New York: Vintage, 1976), 1978.

scoundrels. Yet when compared to the weakened democracies of Western Europe and especially when compared to the dictatorships under Soviet control, the American political system was certainly the most attractive model outside utopian speculation.

4. Most Americans could pursue their personal lives without major problems, other than the normal stresses to which people anywhere and everywhere are subjected. Indeed, at the time, the American "standard of living" was higher than that of most other nations. The basic component of this standard of living was the ability to purchase a wider array of consumer goods than could be bought by the average citizen of other countries. Serious discussion of whether this criterion was a valid indicator of a standard of living was simply not to be heard.

5. The internal problems that did remain in the affluent society—both economic and political—could be resolved without a major restructuring of the societal framework. For instance, the existence of poor people did not require a reevaluation of the set of premises by which economists operated. In fact, it was thought that by further growth in the economy, further expansion into areas untapped, the poor would be benefited. Solutions traditionally associated with socialism such as the redistribution of wealth were thought to have been made irrelevant by an economy that continued to grow. No political revolution was required in American society, only an effort to ensure that all Americans were able to enter the economy on equal terms.

6. The major threat to our economic prosperity and political freedom was the advance of communism, specifically the extension of Soviet influence throughout the world and inside America. Accordingly, Americans' primary political task, at home and abroad, was to protect ourselves and others from this threat. Our prosperity could not be undermined by inefficiency in the economic sphere, but only by laziness in the political arena. So convinced were we of the superiority of our emergent consensus, it was impossible to imagine another country freely opting for an alternative economic order. We thus developed a foreign policy committed to preventing communist subversion and a domestic policy which made explicit anticommunism the test of one's loyalty to America. The government was scrutinized for communist infiltrators, the movie industry was investigated for allegedly promoting the values of communism to unsuspecting audiences, schools were examined for any left-wing material in the curriculum, and grammar school students wrote essays on Americanism for contests sponsored by the American Legion.[2]

---

[2]Ibid., See pp. 67–98 for a similar though somewhat different list of the beliefs included in the postwar consensus.

BLOWS AGAINST THE CONSENSUS

The consensus that prevailed in American society in the late 1940s and throughout the 1950s was not to endure the 1960s. Events at home and abroad led many Americans to be less assured about the beliefs by which we had organized our national life and our personal lives also. A variety of people began to claim that American society was, in fact, beset by problems. Almost every component of the consensus was challenged and as a result America moved from being a relatively unified to being a divided society. Blacks marched in the streets, told President Kennedy that he was not moving fast enough on civil rights, raised their fists in the air and demanded "equality now." Young people accused their parents of living bankrupt lives and listened to folk singers such as Bob Dylan proclaim that the "times they are a'changing." They criticized American foreign policy, especially the raging war in Vietnam, and professed not to trust anyone over 30 years old. Professors rediscovered poverty, exposed students to literature criticizing the lives of "quiet desperation" led in modern times, and wrote books arguing that America was an imperialist power.

The first blow to the consensus was struck by the extremely active civil rights movement by the beginning of the 1960s. Dismayed by America's lack of progress toward achieving a genuinely integrated society and even more disheartened by the obstacles to equal rights, civil rights activists engaged in a series of imaginative political protests to publicize the existing discrimination and to mobilize support for their goals. Their strategy was designed to show that even the most minimal human rights were still denied to black Americans because of their color.

In 1960 a group of four black college students from Greensboro, North Carolina, entered a Woolworth's luncheonette and did not leave when they were refused service. Instead, they "sat in" and would not leave until they were either forced to do so or served as caucasians normally were. Although the waitress looked at the stubborn young men as if they were "from outer space," the sit-in proved to be an extremely effective short-term tactic. Who could possibly defend Woolworth's for only serving coffee to whites, especially when the same Woolworth's coffee was also served to blacks in New York City? Who could possibly condemn people who simply remained in an establishment sitting peacefully until served? Furthermore, when action was taken against the protestors, it only served to magnify the basic justness of their demands. Having proven to be an effective tactic, sit-ins spread and almost every major Southern city where public facilities were segregated was to experience civil rights agitation of this sort.

Civil rights activists employed strategies other than sit-ins to promote their goals. Freedom riders rode buses into segregated stations in Deep South cities with the intention of integrating the facilities at these stations. Marches and mass demonstrations were undertaken in those cities that had been particularly inhospitable to integration. Vigils and protests were made on behalf of blacks who were not allowed admission into all white schools and minority groups organized for the purpose of gaining political power themselves. The civil rights activists did not always find the political order responsive to their views. Until the death of President Kennedy, many politicians—including Kennedy—responded slowly and reluctantly to the demands for equal rights. There was a heated and frequently violent reaction from some white Southerners who were not happy with the prospect of equal rights for blacks. And there were divisions within the civil rights movement itself over such important themes as whether integration or separatism should be the ultimate goal of the movement, and whether it was justified to respond to the inequalities and unfairness of white society with violence. Despite the differences among the supporters of the civil rights movement and the difficulties which its supporters experienced in winning their demands, by 1965 it was no longer possible to suggest that the American political system was the self-evident champion of freedom and liberty in the world.[3]

The civil rights movement had wider effects than publicizing the inequities that remained under American law. It also prompted a reevaluation of the American economic system, a reevaluation that focused on the distribution of abundance. During the 1960s, writers increasingly noted the inexcusable amount of poverty that existed within the most affluent nation on the earth. In *The Other America,* a book that received nationwide attention, the young socialist writer Michael Harrington maintained that approximately one-quarter of our population lived in or on the brink of poverty, in rural slums and inner-city ghettos that affluent America conveniently ignored. In line with this analysis, more and more scholars began to question the influence of wealth and the major corporations on American politics and an entire generation of students was weaned on hearing about the "perverted priorities" of American politics.

Even activist Ralph Nader, who was not particularly known as a poverty fighter, began to mount an assault on the economic system. Having claimed at the beginning of the 1960s that the American automobile was "unsafe at any speed," Nader later expanded his criticism to include the normal operation of all corporate enterprise. By 1967, he was claiming that business crime was one of the two largest threats to life and limb in America. With chemical adulterants in our food, carcinogens where we worked, and death lurking on the highway, Nader contended that middle-class life in contemporary America was a continual risk due to the routine activity of American business. For those who were not convinced about conditions in the "other America" by Harrington, the professors, and Mr. Nader, the protests of the residents in many major American cities gave visible evidence of widespread dissatisfaction.

A second major blow to the consensus that emerged after World War II occurred with the popular reaction to the course of the Vietnam War in the 1960s. The United States had been a major force in Vietnam since 1947 when we had

[3]Ibid., pp. 179–224.

agreed to fund much of the French effort to retain their colony and oppose the war of national liberation being waged by many Vietnamese under the leadership of Ho Chi Minh. After the French departed in frustration in the mid-1950s, the United States decided that a unified Vietnam under the leadership of Ho Chi Minh was not in our interest. Consequently, Vietnam was divided into two nations, North Vietnam and South Vietnam. America's role in Southeast Asia was now enlarged as we became the principal supporter of the South Vietnamese government. The division of the country, however, was an artificial one and did not end the fighting. Neither Ho Chi Minh nor many people in the South were willing to recognize the government set up under American auspices and the war continued.

Our problem was that the government of South Vietnam could not even weather the attack from inside its own borders without extensive aid from the United States. By 1962, President Kennedy had received a recommendation from his advisors that American combat troops would be required if the supporters of Ho Chi Minh in the South were not to be victorious. Kennedy tried to stem the tide by sending only advisory troops, but his successor Lyndon Johnson realized that the stability of the South Vietnam regime necessitated a large commitment of fighting troops. But as Johnson escalated the American involvement, the North Vietnamese responded in kind. They entered the war in full strength, streaming down from the North into the South and putting an end to the American hopes of a quick victory.

As it became evident that Johnson was committed to fighting a massive war in Southeast Asia, opposition to the war began to increase and to assume a combative and vitriolic tone. The antiwar movement which was thought at one time to be inhabited only by "doves and other fairies" spread to the places where liberal opinion is formed in American society. Many newspapers and periodicals took up the antiwar cause in the mid-1960s and criticized politicians for leading us into a war that was not in the national interest. Many of our most prominent universities became seedbeds for youthful opposition to the war. A vocal group of religious leaders continually pointed to what they considered was the gross immorality of the war. The divisions across American society became more pronounced, best symbolized by the president's scorn for those who had, in his words, "gone dovish" on him and the corresponding disdain of the protestors who regularly stood outside the White House gates chanting, "Hey, hey LBJ, how many kids did you kill today?"

Eventually, the opposition to the war questioned not only this particular involvement, but the very premises that had guided American foreign policy since World War II. Exactly why, it was asked, was it our duty to stop communism everywhere it appeared? Could not a nation decide on its own to have that particular form of government? Many people argued that there were divisions within the communist world and that simply because a nation was communist in name did not mean that it was receiving marching orders from Peking or Moscow. The assumption of the postwar consensus that the biggest threat in our way of life was the expansion of communism was reversed to say that the biggest threat was the useless exhaustion of our people and resources by fighting wars 7000 miles from our homeland. Arguments like these helped to form one more crack in the consensus. When Johnson decided not to run for the presidency in 1968 because of opposition to his Vietnam policies, the crack became a gaping hole.

A third source of opposition to the assumptions of the consensus came from the actions undertaken by some highly visible young people during the 1960s. The youth movement was comprised by two logically distinct components that were difficult to separate in practice. One part was composed of those people who were interested in political change, occasionally even violent political change, and who desired to change America's public priorities. Perhaps the most striking manifestation of this group of politicized young people was evidenced in Eugene McCarthy's attempt to gain the Democratic presidential nomination in 1968. McCarthy's campaign attracted thousands of hard working antiwar college students who volunteered their services in the interests of a candidate who promised to make extrication from Vietnam his first priority. On some campuses, it was a badge of honor to have shaved one's beard or one's legs, cut one's hair and to have gone "clean for Gene."

Another segment of the youth movement remained apolitical and instead promoted a "cultural revolution" which opposed the competitive, materialistic values of American society, but maintained that change was the result of consciousness raising and not political action. Artie Sternlicht, a character in E.L. Doctorow's novel *The Book of Daniel,* provides a fine description of a cultural revolutionary. Talking to a reporter about the people in the peace movement, Sternlicht says "you mean those dudes who march down the street and think they're changing something. Peace marches are for the middle class to get its rocks off. The peace movement is part of the war. Heads or tails it's the same coin. The Indian or the buffalo, its the same nickel. Right? and they're both extinct."[4]

Although the emphasis placed on political action varied among elements of the youth movement, or the counterculture as it was later to be labeled, one similarity frequently outweighed the differences. This was the belief that the quality of American life, both public and private, would not be fully acceptable even if our foreign policy changed and even if disadvantaged minorities were given nondiscriminatory treatment. While they endorsed different ways of rectifying conditions, both components of the youth movement pointed to three similar problems within the dominant culture: (1) an economy not geared to the needs of workers; (2) a definition of a successful life that required an individual to adopt destructive personality traits; and (3) the difficulty of maintaining stable and rewarding relationships if one adopted the traits that seemed to be necessary for economic success. To be sure, the youth movement also attracted more than its share of

[4]E.L. Doctorow, *The Book of Daniel* (New York: Bantam, 1971), p. 213.

crazies and hypocrites as its eventual disintegration was to prove. At its height, however, it struck a very powerful blow against the operating consensus of American society.

By the summer of 1968, America was a fevered and divided society. While many people obviously still believed in the elements of the consensus, the truth of these were no longer self-evident to everyone. Martin Luther King and Robert Kennedy were dead. The National Democratic Convention in Chicago had turned into a pitched battle with bloodshed nationally televised as the police pummeled antiwar protesters and their supporters. George Wallace was running for president and doing surprisingly well on his platform of resentment. For many people, the guiding premises of American society did not make any sense and they were searching to organize the economy, foreign policy, and their personal lives differently. For many others, the guiding principles of American society were being attacked by a group of self-appointed revolutionaries who ought to be vanquished as quickly as possible. At this moment, Richard Nixon, the "new" Nixon, was elected president. He promised to bring us together.

A SOCIETY WITHOUT A PURPOSE

By 1968 Americans needed to be brought together in two ways. First, as the ordering consensus of American society evaporated, various segments of society directly opposed one another. The common ground between blacks and whites, students and workers, professors and politicians was becoming more difficult to find. America's image of a melting pot nation was giving way to the picture of a society populated by a number of warring camps. Second, as the consensus was shredded during the 1960s, more Americans began to doubt the meaning of their personal lives. Even many affluent people and a number of young adults raised with wealth questioned the purpose of life in America and began to look for a new way of restoring meaning to their lives.

Like other presidents, Nixon did not make good on his campaign pledge. In fact, the strategy Nixon followed in office was the exact opposite of what one would expect from a person supposedly committed to unifying the divergent elements of American society. He accented the existing divisions and tried to use these divisions to his own advantage.

Claiming that his presidency was being undermined by a conspiracy of freaks, revolutionaries, and the liberal establishment, Nixon instituted a series of measures designed to suppress his enemies. He attempted to turn popular opinion against those groups whom he maintained were undermining the peace effort and were overly critical of American policy at home. Nixon professed to be defending the values of traditional America, the values of the "silent majority," against the attacks of a vocal minority out to remake America in its own image. Having been elected on the promise to heal the divisions in American society, Nixon embarked on a policy labeled by one of his chief aides as "positive polarization."

Nixon, of course, was not entirely successful in his efforts. He was forced to resign in wake of the revelations about the illegal measures he used to suppress his enemies. Nor was Nixon successful in restoring the commitment of all Americans to the traditional values that made up the postwar consensus. While many people shared Nixon's suspicions of those who advocated major changes in American society, there was no longer one set of values which all good Americans would champion.

On the other hand, we cannot say that those people who opposed Nixon and the beliefs for which he stood were entirely successful either. Those people who were dissatisfied with the quality of American life certainly did make their views known. They were not able, however, to translate their dissatisfaction into an effective program for transforming American society. Throughout the 1960s and early 1970s, critics of American society claimed that our political and economic institutions did not deserve the confidence of the public. These critics suggested that our politicians were dishonest, our policies misguided, and our corporations corrupt. Such views became more popular. But what we ought to do about this and what consequences such beliefs held for the conduct of our personal lives were not at all obvious.

Besides Nixon's activity, another factor further complicated America's disarray in the 1970s. The energy crisis of 1973 not only put millions of Americans in gas lines at 6:00 AM in the morning, but also put us on notice that the era of American affluence might be approaching an end. Having based our entire economy on the premise of cheap and abundant energy, we were forced to realize that its underpinnings could be radically weakened at any moment.

We were not necessarily masters of our own fate, but part of an interdependent world, subject to the vagaries of Mid-East politics and the desire of the oil-producing countries to turn a nifty profit on the product to which the West had become addicted. Even those people who did not believe in the existence of an energy crisis, thinking it a conspiracy among the oil companies, did not act as if the American consumer could do much to cap the inevitable rise in fuel costs.

The challenges that had been issued against the prevailing consensus thus had a curious outcome in the 1970s. While the challengers had succeeded in casting doubt on the quality of American life and on our major public institutions, they had not succeeded in establishing new institutions or in reforming the old institutions so that these were now worthy of our respect. Many individual Americans were placed in a condition of limbo. No longer did they believe in the time-honored American values, but neither had they found a more attractive and rewarding way of living.

Scholars writing about American society during this period referred to the "crisis of legitimacy." Put simply, they were concerned that the average American had lost respect for and commitment to our major public institutions. One of the most critical questions became: How do individuals conduct their lives when they feel little or no commitment to and respect for the major institutions of their society?

By the end of the 1970s, our answer to this question had become clear. When we came into contact with our economic and political institutions, we would follow the rules and "play the game." Yet we would neither feel nor express any deep commitment to these institutions. We would go to work, but only for the money. We would perform well in school, but only for the grade. We might occasionally take part in politics, but only if we would benefit from it. At other times, we would express contempt for politicians, disrespect for the bureaucracy, and scorn for corporate America. Most of our commitments and most of our care would be lavished on the details of our personal life. The "me decade" was in full swing.

In some respects, the attention we lavished on ourselves was perfectly reasonable. Given how much of our everyday lives seemed fruitless and unrewarding, it is not surprising that we turned to more self-oriented concerns. Once we think of the threatening nature of life on the street, the prevalence of unrewarding work in our society, and the repulsiveness of what passes for business as usual in the political world, we can understand why many people believe that attending to themselves is the best available option.

In other respects, however, the selfishness of our time is not so reasonable. We want to suggest that it has harmful personal and social consequences. On a personal level, individuals do not necessarily become free by attending only to themselves. Indeed, it is possible that we become more controlled than we previously were. When we work only for the money, it means giving up the possibility of developing our skills and maturity by committing ourselves to a satisfying vocation. When we study only for the grade, we give up the opportunity of fully educating ourselves about our world and the forces and people within it. According to psychologists, people without an overriding purpose in life often experience more psychic strain than those who can maintain personal and social commitments.[5]

Because of the rejection of ethical obligations that it implies, the possible social consequences of the new selfishness are equally disturbing. It has always been evident to thoughtful people that no person is an island and that it is both foolish and dangerous to pretend that we have no responsibility toward others. It is foolish because we deny our basic need for the community which other people provide. It is dangerous because no society can remain peaceful for long if its members do not feel a sense of responsibility toward others. Crime, widespread irresponsibility in social and economic transactions, and random violence are only a few of the consequences that can be attributed, in part, to a lack of civility and community.

In this book, we plan to argue that the major public institutions in America—schools, the work place, the economy, and the political order—are doing very little to avert the harmful trends in American life. In fact, our major public institutions are often part of the problem. Our schools, work places, media, economy, and

[5]See, for instance, Erik H. Erikson, *Identity: Youth and Crisis* (New York: W.W. Norton and Company), 1968.

government prompt individuals to act in ways which prevent them from developing their talents as fully as they might and blind them to the social consequences of selfish action.

Obviously, this is an unhealthy situation. In making this assertion, we are not claiming that life today compares unfavorably with a lost paradise or a future golden age. Nor are we maintaining that all human beings are infinitely talented and, at bottom, thoughtful and considerate people. This has never been the case and we doubt that it ever will be. We are not trying to judge America by a self-imposed utopian standard. We are claiming that it is possible to use our talents more completely and to satisfy our needs in more fulfilling ways than we currently do. This book is written to persuade people that this might be the case if we organized our personal and public lives differently. We realize that not everyone will be persuaded, yet we hope that even the skeptical will be forced to grapple with the issues that we raise.

The rest of this chapter illustrates our argument by sketching some portraits of American life. We examine the ambitions of a college student, discuss the values underlying recent political movements to reduce taxes, and speak about the activity of a religious sect. In later chapters, we connect the experience of a diminished life to the explicit practices of our principal social institutions.

A DETERMINED WOMAN

The novelist Thomas Wolfe once explained the relationship between an individual's life and the broader influences on that life as:

> Each of us is all the sums he has not counted: subtract us into nakedness and night again, and you shall see begin in Crete four thousand years ago the love that ended yesterday in Texas.
>
> The seed of our destruction will blossom in the desert, the alexin of our cure grows by a mountain rock. . . . Each moment is the fruit of forty thousand years and every moment is a window on all time. (*Look Homeward, Angel,* 1029).

Our individual lives, as Wolfe so eloquently stated it, are repositories of our human heritage. Although we may not agree with him that every moment is a window on *all* time, it is certainly true that individual lives are windows on the time of a particular culture and a specific era.

In the struggles, ambitions, joys, and heartbreaks of each individual, we can see, if we look deeply enough, how people of that era deal with the themes of birth, development, work, love, growing old, and death. Our hopes, desires, fears, and ambitions are typically the end products of a complex interplay between our biological endowments, our particular upbringing, and the broader social forces that shape that upbringing and modify us from birth onward. While people always will differ in many ways, our private experiences nonetheless illuminate our public structures. In the following brief sketch of the ambitions expressed by a young college student, we think many of the questions that inevitably confront us can be discerned.

Karen Lant is a 21-year-old college student. A bright, alert person, she has worked for three years as a billing clerk before attending college full-time. While she is quiet in class and speaks only infrequently, she performs extremely well on exams. She not only exhibits a firm grasp of the class material, but also demonstrates that she has thought about it by presenting and defending a coherent viewpoint. Karen, a business major, says she might consider going into sales upon completion of her degree. While she is not quite certain of what she expects or wants out of life, Karen knows that clerking is not part of it and she abhors the thought of returning to her old job. She has, we might say, temporarily defined herself more by what she is not and does not want to be than by any positive identifications.

Talking to Karen, one would be moved by her dedication but also struck by the lack of content to her determination. A person is immediately made aware of her desire to obtain high grades, but when asked what motivates her, Karen does not even mention educational achievement. Nor does her tentative choice of a sales career appear to be related to positive goals which she herself has consciously selected and articulated. When asked about the attractions that a sales career might hold, Karen remarks that it can give her "freedom from a nosy boss, the money to live where I won't be attacked, and the salary to buy a good home and raise a family well." Her choice has more to do with avoiding the traps she felt as a billing clerk—inability to fend for herself, burdensome debts, and continual supervision by her boss—than it does with the intrinsic satisfactions of the work itself.

Karen Lant is, of course, a more complex woman than we have depicted in this brief sketch. She has a history of family relationships, associations with peers, and deep attachments to people that we have left unmentioned. She has unconscious fears that we have barely tapped and necessarily will leave unexplained. Nor, as with the sketch of Alton Woods at the beginning of this chapter, do we claim that everyone shares Karen's desires and motivations. Yet we still believe that this description gives us something important about which to think. Karen's experiences reflect decisions which most young people today will make, although they will make these decisions with varying degrees of consciousness.

Not everyone will enter business school, but most young people will have to determine their attitude toward education. Not everyone will become a salesperson, but most of us will have to decide what occupation to pursue or how to change the occupational structure in order to meet our vocational needs. Not everyone will be threatened by crime in the streets, but most people will have to decide how to tailor their living conditions to the real and imagined dangers of the world.

We believe Karen Lant's solutions to these dilemmas of life are reasonable ones. Who does not want to live with a decent amount of comfort? Who wants to be accused of not properly providing for their family? But despite the apparent reasonableness of Karen's answers, we can see how her choices are affected by outside social forces and how these choices may well reinforce the greater irrationality of the social order.

Is it not irrational for an educational system to be valuable only to the extent that it helps us to provide for our material sustenance? Surely, it speaks poorly for a society that students who know how to write clearly and think critically are not highly valued. Is it not irrational that our choice of occupation (insofar as we have a choice) is so dependent on considerations scarcely related to the intrinsic satisfactions of the employment? The poet Tom Wayman has written that we should ''honor each other'' by the labor we perform, and it is certainly a damning commentary that so many of us instead wind up ''degrading ourselves'' by the work we do. Is it not irrational that our choice of residence can spring from fear and be principally made according to the criterion of providing complete isolation? Surely, privacy is an important value but ideally we should be able to distinguish it from total disconnection with the outside world.

Karen's answers to these questions and her struggle to define her life illustrates familiar dilemmas. On one hand, her decision to quit the billing clerk job and attend school full time testifies to a desire for freedom that is not easily quelled and a determination to exert more of her talents and develop more of her skills than she had previously. On the other hand, it is questionable whether Karen's decisions will really bring her the freedom that she obviously seeks. Having accepted the necessity of living in strict isolation from others, having equated freedom with the level and style of consumption, and having neglected to consider how her family might be shaped by the social and economic forces outside it, Karen's freedom could be a diminished one. By escaping from the worst strictures of contemporary society exemplified by her job as a billing clerk, Karen may well be confined by fences not quite as visible.

TAX CUTTERS

The desires that impel Karen Lant are also, we believe, discernable on a larger scale in American society. One notable manifestation of this might be the tax revolt movement. In the late 1970s, a curmudgeonly 76-year-old Californian named Howard Jarvis proposed that property taxes be drastically reduced throughout the state. Although his idea was opposed by Jerry Brown, the governor of California, and by most liberal politicians because they felt it would work primarily to penalize the poor, it was placed on the ballot in 1978 as ''Proposition 13'' and won resounding popular approval.

The tax revolt was the generic name given to the political events in the late 1970s which were consistent with the assumptions and particulars of Proposition

13. Citizens were said to be disgusted with government inefficiency, fed up with spending programs for social welfare, and ready to embrace the ideas of conservative politicians. Prominent Republicans declared that the population had adopted the values which their party had been upholding for the past 20 years and the pages of political magazines were filled with articles purporting to explain the rightward turn of the American population.

Ronald Reagan in his 1980 presidential campaign criticized Jimmy Carter and the Democratic party for mismanaging the economy, permitting the expansion of Soviet influence throughout the world, and weakening the spiritual fiber of America. Reagan promised that he would restore economic prosperity, renew the American spirit, and control Soviet adventurism. During the campaign, the heaviest emphasis was placed on Reagan's economic program. Speaking the language of Howard Jarvis and the tax revolt, he maintained that the public was unfairly burdened by the existing tax system. He vowed to put the government on a diet so that we could retain more of our paycheck.

Reagan's endorsement of tax cuts appeared to spring from two related ideas. It was first grounded in the practical notion that economic recovery was dependent on reducing government spending and permitting taxpayers to keep more of their earnings. Aside from his ideas about economic recovery, Reagan expressed philosophical reasons for proposing a 25 percent or 30 percent tax cut to take effect over a three-year period. Reagan clearly felt that our current rate of taxation excessively limits our freedom. His vows to keep more money in our paychecks thus became part of a larger pledge to increase the amount of personal freedom in America. For instance, when Reagan debated Jimmy Carter during the campaign, he ended his remarks by asking Americans to cast their votes on the basis of whether their purchasing power had improved during the Carter presidency.

After the voting, many commentators argued that the election was more an indication that people disapproved of Carter than it was a mandate for Reagan's ideas. While it appeared to be true that most people wanted tax cuts and reduced government spending, it was also evident that many specific government programs had popular support—for example, social security benefits, tax breaks for homeowners, government support for local schools, aid to the disabled, higher pay for the military, benefits for veterans, and even food stamp programs. A few years prior, the journalist George Will in his attempt to explain the public's desire to cut government spending (but its support for particular programs), noted that the average American "has looked into his heart of hearts, prayed long and hard, and come to the conclusion that it is high time the government cut his *neighbor's* benefits."[6]

The conception of freedom that seems to underlie this mixed bag of citizen

---

[6]George F. Will, *The Pursuit of Happiness and Other Sobering Thoughts* (New York: Harper and Row, 1978), p. 186.

preferences is similar to Karen Lant's ideas about her life. Personal freedom is measured, in large part, by the amount of discretionary income at our disposal. We may express support of specific programs, yet we are also extremely attracted by appeals to improve our financial status. Since the end of World War II, to fulfill the American dream usually means to be able to purchase many consumer goods. As it becomes more difficult to translate this dream into reality, it is only to be expected that citizens will favor those government policies that will aid them economically. Given the unrewarding nature of our work and the lack of vitality in our public life, it is only natural that people look to consumer benefits as the redeeming feature of their existence. However, there are severe human costs to believing that consumer possessions really bring freedom.

American capitalism has often been criticized for having an imperialistic bent, an almost inherent need to search outside the borders of the country for markets for its products and natural resources for its manufacturers. In so doing, America has often been criticized for remaking the economy of other nations along lines detrimental to their development. American capitalism also engages, however, in a domestic imperialism in which its reach is not extended toward external economies but is instead directed toward remaking the American psyche according to the dictates of corporate profits. Domestic imperialism is intended to ensure our dependence on the corporate economy by defining happiness, freedom, rationality, and deviance according to its needs. We shall examine this process in detail in the next chapter. For now, we only want to say that putting more money in our pockets does not necessarily make us free.

A RELIGIOUS FAMILY

There are, of course, reactions to the strains and tensions of contemporary life opposed to the dominant tendencies of a consumer culture. One of the most widely publicized reactions to social disintegration is the emergence of religious sects among American youth and younger adults. Dissatisfied with their lives, unable to see the meaning and purpose of their existence, some have tried to find this elusive purpose in the discipline and community life of religious sects.

With the exception of Jim Jones and his followers in Jonestown, Guyana, the Reverend Moon's Unification Church has been the most publicized and controversial group. Popularly labeled as "Moonies," its members are recruited on the streets and asked to attend a workshop in which "intense indoctrination is combined with films, group discussion, sports, entertainment, prayer, and meditation."[7] After becoming a member of the church, the recruits devote almost their entire energies to

[7]Thomas Robbins, Dick Anthony, Madeline Doucas, and Thomas Curtis, "The Last Civil Religion: Reverend Moon and the Unification Church," in Irving L. Horowitz (ed.), *Science, Sin and Scholarship: The Politics of Reverend Moon and the Unification Church* (Cambridge: MIT Press, 1979), p. 53.

its pursuits. They live in a tightly disciplined, sexually segregated community and often spend their days "witnessing" on the streets and hawking various trinkets for the church. The church is swarming in controversy as it is alleged that recruits are brainwashed on weekend retreats, that the Reverend Moon is more interested in turning a profit than redeeming souls, and that the church functions as a front organization for the South Korean government.

Converts to the Unification Church who remain committed to its tenets testify to its capacity for mitigating the harshness of everyday existence. Explaining her initial attraction to the Church, one interviewee said: "It completely amazed me, the cleanliness of the people, the warm-heartedness of the people and the togetherness of heart and not just in the geographical sense, but actually in heart, really like a family."[8] We could probably safely change the last phrase to "like I think a family ought to be" for the church might be unneeded if the real family of the interviewee had fulfilled her desires.

Some members of the church join not only because of the familial security it provides but for its philosophy of interpersonal relations. More sensitive to the problems of relating to others in a consumer society that some of us considered perfectly normal, recruits find a pleasing alternative in church membership. One initiate reported joining because "I really wanted to develop my relationships with people to where I could really perfect my way of being with people, of loving people, of getting along with people. That was the most important thing to me."[9]

Most of us who come into contact with members of the Unification Church find their behavior irritating because their standard query about whether we believe that there is a spiritual crisis in the world quickly becomes tiresome. Yet it is not difficult to understand their commitment. Social psychologists are not required to tell us that initiates want to find security, a devoted group of friends, and meaning in life. While common-sense explanations are typically inaccurate when dealing with highly nuanced situations, the phenomenon of Reverend Moon can be understood because the needs his religion satisfies are so obviously left unmet by mainstream American culture.

If we can say that people like Karen Lant and tax cutters strive for freedom but do so in a way that is self-defeating and diminishing, most young people who join religious sects or look to serve somebody are searching for meaning, but also do so in a self-defeating and diminishing way. So long as community means the denial of our individualism this option will remain diminishing. The creation of rational communities, like the creation of genuine individualism, depends on modifying our way of working and living. Communities will only have a rational attraction when they are communities of accomplishment, places where free individuals decide in

[8]Ibid., pp. 55–56.
[9]Ibid., p. 57.

conjunction with each other what they are going to produce and how they are going to produce it, what the physical arrangement of their community is going to be and how honors, duties, and burdens are to be distributed.

We are nowhere near creating such communities today. To be sure, there are energies and sentiments which could be tapped in this regard, especially our resentments against the dependency and powerlessness in our lives. But there is no assurance that these resentments will be channeled in the direction of positive social construction; indeed, the danger exists that political leaders will mobilize these resentments in a manner that serves their interests well, but the public's welfare poorly. Political leaders, instead of attacking the causes of dependency and powerlessness, are constantly tempted to encourage psychological identification with their own adventures in their quest for power and reputation. The dilemma of contemporary America is that its citizens will oscillate between apathy and identification with the irrational pursuits of ambitious leaders. This is not a happy prospect to contemplate, but it is the logical outcome of a political and economic system that fosters diminished selves among the citizenry.

Perhaps Alton Woods will find peace by fleeing New York City and returning to Augusta, Georgia. Maybe his wife will accompany him and he will spend the rest of his life without his present fears. Who can blame him for trying to escape the terrors of his neighborhood? Resignation is occasionally more appropriate than valor. Yet this is surely not the proper response on a societywide scale to our problems. Whether we find peace by equating liberty with the style and quantity of consumption, or by identifying with political leaders, or by joining communities in which we acquiesce in the obliteration of our individualism, we impoverish ourselves in the process. We not only deny the importance of much of the world in which we exist, but we deny our capacity for shaping and changing the world in line with a vision of a nobler humanity.

Imagine how we would react if we visited a prison and despite the bars on the windows of the rooms, the barbed-wire fences surrounding the grounds, and the heavily armed guard towers rising over the premises, the inmates proclaimed to us that they were really free. Imagine if we were told that the prisoners were not affected by the conditions of living in a cage, but actually thrived in a controlled environment. Perhaps a few of us would believe this and leave to tell the world of these marvelous inmates who had freed themselves by an act of will from their oppressive conditions. Others might not be so easily persuaded. Some of us might simply argue that it is impossible to be free while living in a cell. Others might go further and attempt to show the prisoners how their lives were diminished by the objective conditions of their environment. We would try to show how the existence of the barbed-wire fences slashed and infected their personal lives, how the bars on the cellblock distorted their imagination, and how the machine guns on the guard towers deadened their relations with each other.

In much of this book, we try to depict the harmful constraints that American society currently imposes on us. These are not as visible as barbed-wire fences and machine guns, but they are harmful nonetheless. Fortunately, since these are not barbed-wire fences and machine guns, they might possibly be removed once we understand where they are located and how they function.

2

The Commandments of Consumer Society

Advertising ministers to the spiritual side of trade.

President Calvin Coolidge

I teach them how to jerk people around.

An Advertising Design Professor at an American University

It is often said that capitalism is as American as mom and apple pie. If this were really true, Hardee's would have a lot of explaining to do, for it is no secret that this restaurant chain does not think too highly of mom.

During the past 25 years, Americans have eaten their meals outside of the home in increasing numbers. The growth of fast-food restaurant franchises may perhaps be the most notable manifestation of this trend. Many of us feel that we have neither the time nor the money to patronize more traditional restaurants. We munch a whopper at Burger King, a leg and a thigh at Kentucky Fried, or a burrito at Taco Bell. We may not even like the food, but it is served quickly and it does get us through the day. Until recently, fast-food restaurants served only lunch, dinner, and between-meal snacks. No effort was made to obtain a breakfast trade and many franchises did not bother to open their doors until late morning. This is no longer the case. Drive up and down the main road of any mid-sized American town and you will surely find a number of banners streaming from the windows of Wendy's, Roy Rogers, and Burger Chef to remind you that the establishment now opens at 6:30 AM to serve breakfast.

Hardee's is one chain that has not rested content with hanging banners outside its windows. The company has developed an elaborate media campaign designed to gain a larger share of the growing breakfast trade. The theme of the campaign is that Hardee's makes biscuits as good, if not better, than those cooked at home. In one of its radio spots, a conversation takes place between a man and his grown-up son who live in the same town and meet, by accident, in Hardee's one morning. The conversation goes something like this.

Son: Dad, what are you doing here?

Dad: Getting one of Hardee's sausage biscuits.

Son: Doesn't mom still make her own biscuits?

Dad: Sure, but, ah, ah, they taste like they always have.

Son: (Voice dropping) Oh, I remember.

Dad: So whenever I want a really good breakfast, I just tell mom to sleep late and I come down to Hardee's for a sausage biscuit.

Son: Good idea.

Most of us are so accustomed to the appeals made by commercial advertisers that we rarely take the time to think about the assumptions contained in the messages we see and hear. If we did bother to think about what commercials tell us, we would not be surprised at Hardee's comments about mom's cooking. In a consumer society such as ours, an extraordinary amount of effort, inventiveness, and ingenuity is expended for the sole purpose of persuading us to buy. The cleverness of these pitches is frequently entertaining, but we might be better off if our ingenuity were put in the service of goals other than selling. Very little is held sacred by large corporations and there are few charges that advertisers will shy away from making if these might help to sell a product.

Anyone who is attentive to corporate America's messages will realize that they not only advertise particular products but promote an entire way of life. We are told what activities we ought to consider important and unimportant. We are informed about what we need to possess in order to become a worthwhile person. We are instructed how to act in our various social roles. And we are told which behaviors are considered unappealing. The way of life promoted in a consumer society might be summarized by the following rules which we call the Four Commandments of Consumer Society.

1. Do not expect to find your work intrinsically worthwhile. Work for what you can purchase after work.
2. Do not spend your leisure time developing your own talents. Make certain that you keep up with the latest trends and fashions.
3. Do not think that you can be an adequate person without acquiring the basic kit of consumer society.
4. Do not put off until tomorrow what you can purchase—by credit if necessary—today.

The purpose of this chapter is to explain and criticize these central tenets. We first describe capitalism's "great compromise" or how a consumer society developed in response to worker-employee problems in early American capitalism. Then we explain how a consumer economy attempts to control time so that there is a product for every moment of the day. How a consumer economy ties the fulfillment of our deepest needs and most powerful longing to the acquisition of goods and how politics in America is influenced by the values of the consumer economy are also explained. The conclusion speaks about the existing sources of opposition to these commandments.

We argue that the promise made by the modern corporate economy are both misleading and harmful. Corporate America misleads us when it implies that we can fulfill our most profound human needs by acquiring the products it sells. We suggest that it is more accurate to view the promises of corporate America as a form of teasing. Consumers are repeatedly promised fulfillment, only to discover that there is one more product, one more good that they must buy in order to obtain satisfaction. We suggest that consumer society is harmful because it encourages individuals to form character traits that are connected to fashionable behavior rather than the traditional virtues of personal integrity and social responsibility. Consumer society's values harm not only individuals but society at large insofar as we fail to develop the capacity to live and work with one another as humanely as we possibly could.

CAPITALISM'S "GREAT COMPROMISE"

One of the characteristic features of a capitalist economy is that the majority of workers do not work for themselves, but are in the employ of somebody else. Most of us do not directly sell the products we have made or the services we can offer; instead, we sell our ability to perform work to an organization that hires other workers. As of 1978, 95 percent of the U.S. working population worked for someone else. The worker is supposedly free to sell his or her labor time. In reality, there is little choice. Increasingly, a person chooses to work for someone else or not to work at all. The absence of effective choice permits the employer to make demands upon the laborer, but because the worker sells only time, there is no reason for the laborer to become totally involved in the work or loyal to the employer. This is not to suggest that workers are never loyal or that they never find their work interesting. It is just that there is no overriding reason why they should be loyal or interested. People who sell products directly maintain a keen interest in the work process as their livelihood may depend upon it. But there is no compelling reason for a shelf stocker at A&P to be concerned about maximum production.

It is important to understand that in a capitalist/worker relationship, the worker sells *time* for labor, not labor itself. The problem for the employer is to convert this time into effective work—the more the better. Workers often resist these efforts of employers because they feel that they have sold their time and not their souls. Both are interested in a fair day's work, yet both tend to define the term according to their own values. The workers resist the discipline and pace employers try to impose, while the employers try to eliminate what they consider laziness.

There is an inherent conflict at the root of a capitalist economy. Because the workers do not have a compelling interest in the labor process itself, they will likely desire to restrict output. Because the capitalists have a keen interest in the labor process, they are likely to attempt to push output to a maximum. Motivating the work force has been a continuing item of concern and a repeated source of problems for employers. In the history of capitalism, both sticks and carrots have been used to motivate workers. According to the needs of the moment and the political tone of the era, employers have used religious exhortation, physical compulsion, legal force, and higher wages to persuade workers to see a fair day's work in the same light as employers.

The conflict between the interests of employers and workers was most starkly apparent in the early days of industrial capitalism, for it seemed then that the miracles of capitalist development depended upon creating a mass of workers who lived in filth and were brutalized by the long and arduous labor they were compelled to perform. People who witnessed the origins of capitalist development in England were uniformly struck by the contrast between what the industry produced and the actual conditions of the laborers. The French social theorist Alexis de Tocqueville wrote that "from this foul drain the greatest strain of human industry flows out to fertilize the whole world. . . . Here humanity achieves its most complete development and civilized man is turned almost into a savage."[1]

Some nineteenth-century Americans thought that our nation could learn from England's mistakes and have capitalist development without the accompanying squalor. Yet experiments designed with this end in mind were notable failures. In Lowell, Massachusetts, for example, an ambitious effort to staff the mills with young women from the surrounding farms who would work for a few years and then return to the countryside was unsuccessful.[2] The factory system was eventually staffed by permanent help and nineteenth-century America was to experience the same problems that pocked the development of English capitalism. The work force was required to work long hours in horrible environments for subsistence wages. Living conditions were often no better than working conditions. Families were crowded into hovels, and company towns appeared in which the owners of the principal industry also controlled the prices and availability of housing, food and medical care.

At the inception of industrial capitalism in America, most employers required

---

[1] The Tocqueville quote is drawn from John F. Kasson, *Civilizing the Machine: Technology and Republican Values in America, 1776–1900* (New York: Penguin Books, 1976), p. 56. The next two paragraphs also draw from Kasson's work.

[2] Ibid., pp. 55–106.

their workers to labor for at least 12 hours per day. Capitalists knew that their profits were directly related to the amount of labor that their workers could be compelled to perform. They also felt that it was better to keep the workers in the factories, for they might use extended periods of leisure in a way that would negatively affect their ability and disposition to labor. As the historian John Kasson has written, American employers believed that leisure, in the hands of their operatives, "meant mischief; idleness at best, at worst vicious amusements, drink, gambling, and riot. Hence the resistance to shorter working hours throughout the nineteenth century and into the twentieth: work was a form of social control."[3]

Many workers believed, however, that the forms of social control exercised by the nineteenth-century capitalists were intolerable. They resented the arbitrary power of owners and foremen. They felt oppressed by working conditions and exploited by the wage scale. Nor did they see the urgent necessity for the discipline that their employers were so eager to impose. Workers and those reformers who agitated on their behalf commonly felt that they were being asked to perform more than a fair day's work. In fact, prior to the Civil War, some reformers went so far as to claim that employer-worker relations in the north were a more grievous wrong than slavery in the south. Orestes Brownson wrote that "wages is a cunning device of the devil, for the benefit of tender consciences, who would retain all the advantages of the slave system without the expense, trouble, and odium of being slaveholders."[4]

After the Civil War, opposition to the expanding industrial order continued to grow. This opposition was voiced not only by industrial workers, but by other groups who felt victimized by the capitalists. Many western farmers, for example, believed that eastern bankers were controlling the supply of money in order to keep farmers in perpetual debt to the banking interests. They opposed organizing the economy so as to reward private greed and attempted, with some success, to establish a system of cooperative purchasing and marketing. As a long-term goal, they sought the abolition of capitalism and the formation of a "cooperative commonwealth."[5]

Laborers in the direct employ of the capitalists began to organize in order to advance their interests. Some of these organizations were radical in intent as they desired to overturn the basic framework of the capitalist economy. In this vein, the writer Henry Demarest Lloyd asserted in the 1880s that the true spirit of American democracy included the "inalienable right of the people to own and operate, at their option, any or all of the wealth they create."[6] Other labor organizations, far less

[3]Ibid., p. 75.

[4]This quote is from Orestes Brownson, "The Laboring Classes," in Kenneth M. Dolbeare (ed.), *American Political Thought* (Monterey: Duxbury Press, 1981), p. 249.

[5]See Lawrence Goodwyn, *The Populist Movement* (New York: Oxford University Press, 1979).

[6]The quote is from Henry Demarest Lloyd, "Revolution: The Evolution of Socialism," in Dolbeare (ed.), *American Political Thought*, p. 376.

sweeping in their goals, were more concerned with benefits for their particular group than with the rights of workers in general or with the underlying structure of the capitalist economy. But whether radical or reformist in intent, few believed that workers were receiving a fair shake.

The labor movement in America was marked by a series of long and often bloody struggles. Few of the emerging corporate giants were readily willing to grant the rights which labor asserted. During the nineteenth and into the twentieth century, employers took a variety of action designed to stifle and break the back of the growing labor movement. Owners of industry asked the courts to declare labor legislation unconstitutional and to deny the right of union organizing. Union organizers were dismissed from their jobs and then blacklisted to prevent them from receiving employment elsewhere. Strikebreakers were employed during work stoppages and, if striking workers attempted to prevent their use, the government was called upon to subdue the workers with force.

In the long run, the employers and owners were not entirely successful. Capitalism was modified in America. While the more radical challenges to corporate America did not succeed, labor managed to obtain a degree of success. Workers received legal guarantees of their right to organize, laws establishing an eight-hour workday for many workers were passed, the government recognized the right of many workers to strike and a social security program was established. Workers did not obtain the upper hand and have not, to this day, obtained the upper hand in employer-labor relations. They did manage to temper some of the system's most inhumane excesses.

Capitalism's "great compromise" in the twentieth century attempted to solve the root conflict between workers and owners by giving many laborers more free time and by granting them more purchasing power. Workers were not able to own and operate their place of employment, but they became capable of purchasing more of the goods their plants were producing. After World War Two, as we mentioned in the previous chapter, many workers became able to purchase the basic kit of consumer society. In suburbs across the nation, workers owned their little piece of the system and, in some ways, became small capitalists themselves.

To be sure, this compromise was not extended to every working and poor American. Poverty was not eliminated and there remained areas of the economy where employee rights were nonexistent. Nor was the compromise so popular that workers everywhere became satisfied with their jobs and eager to meet all the imposed demands. Yet all of these matters are no longer the concern of all working Americans and this has made it that much more difficult to create a unified opposition to corporate America.

Eventually, even a few business owners who had bitterly opposed the compromise came to understand that the workers' gains played a conservative role and helped to stabilize the economy. In the first place, higher wages were a much less oppressive mechanism of social control than long working hours. Second, worker buying power aided the expansion of the economy for laborers and provided a new market for business' increased productive capacity. Finally, the economic divisions among the workforce could not help but give solace to those who had previously feared the overthrow of the entire economic order.

A PRODUCT FOR EVERY MOMENT

Having given many Americans the opportunity to join consumer society, American capitalists spared no effort to ensure that the populace would take full advantage of it. Instructions about how best to utilize our free time are heaped upon us daily. These instructions overwhelmingly encourage us to purchase the goods which the economy produces. Whether we are told to live life with gusto, to give ourselves a break today, or to help keep America rolling, the message always ends with an exhortation to buy. That leisure time can be productively spent in nonconsumption activities is a message rarely heard.

Going shopping has become a major form of recreation. The proliferation of shopping malls built since World War II is ample evidence of this. It is a rare American who has not attempted to relieve a fit of the blues or a moment of boredom by heading to the nearby mall. Many of us have even advised friends who appear to be in low spirits that they ought to go out and buy a record or a dress. Visit a mall on Saturday afternoon and you will see how deep the consumer ethos is embedded in the fabric of American life. The most notable feature of these malls is the omnipresent invitation to purchase something. We are invited to buy in honor of Abe Lincoln and George Washington, in order to get ready for Easter, to celebrate summer, and to prepare for returning to school.

A visitor to the mall will also note that activities previously held at churches, schools, and neighborhood gatherings are now located at shopping centers. On a random Saturday afternoon, the malls across America will have bake sales for the PTA, arts and crafts displays of local artists, fundraising drives for the high school band, a clown show, and an exhibition of dance aerobics by a Parents without Partners group. These activities do offer a welcome touch of variety to the monotonous urgings to consume. Yet the very fact that shopping centers have become the accepted locale for these activities indicates how traditional American culture has been entwined with the consumer ethos.

Advertising is probably the major practice by which the specific values of consumer society are conveyed. People connected with the industry often claim that it serves positive ends. Advertising is said to provide consumers with information about the availability of products, it is said to encourage product innovation, and it is said to foster competition throughout the economy. Advertising may possibly serve these functions. Yet it is also true that this description of advertising's functions is incomplete and does not go far enough in describing what it actually does. Advertising not only provides information about products, but it also attempts to control how we spend our time and how we evaluate our own personality.

From waking to sleeping, from conception through death, our lives are filled with messages from consumer society, telling us that we need what they have to sell. Mouthwash commercials tell husbands and wives not to kiss before gargling and pharmaceutical companies, with their array of sleeping pills, stomach remedies, beauty treatments, and overnight laxatives, have transformed going to sleep into a multibillion dollar industry. In between, the list of items which help prepare us for work, which we can wear or use at work, and which can give us relief when the day is completed proliferates endlessly. Messages for baby start long before birth and American funerals are typically the last fitting monument to the consumption ethic.

A second way that advertising connects certain time periods to various consumer pursuits is by the corporate economy's treatment of holidays. Throughout the year, there are numerous days when we are told to show someone special that we care by purchasing another item for them. Birthdays, father's day, or valentine's day are important dates on the consumer calendar. Special time periods, such as National Secretaries' Week, have been invented simply to benefit a particular industry.

The Christmas season has undoubtedly become the most noticeable example of advertising's impact. The season now begins in mid-October when stores trot out their decorations and begin their incantations to buy, builds to a frenzied climax the two weeks before December 25th, and stretches into January with post-Christmas sales. One waits with fear and loathing for the final desecration—perhaps the Virgin Mary sporting L'eggs or the Baby Jesus in Pampers. It is not uncommon these days to hear someone caught in the Christmas rush profess that they have given up hope of enjoying Christmas and are merely trying to survive it.

The attention paid to fashion is a third way that the corporate economy defines time in order to urge us to buy. Americans are continually told what activities and what dress are appropriate for the times and what activities and goods should be considered outdated. In a consumer society, there are apparently no limits to what can become an item of fashionable concern. Almost any part of our body and any item that we occasionally use can be placed under the category of fashion. Eyelashes, cigarette lighters, wastebaskets, and umbrellas are only a few of the items which currently have fashionable and unfashionable uses.

Goods which once served simple functional needs can suddenly move into the designer category. For years, Americans who wore jeans to school or put them on after work were adequately served by Levi's, Wranglers, and Plain Pockets. Twelve years ago, Charles Reich, the author of a best selling book, maintained that bluejeans expressed "profoundly democratic values. There are no distinctions of wealth or status, no elitism; people confront one another shorn of these distinctions."[7] Whether

---

[7] Charles Reich, *The Greening of America* (New York: Bantam, 1971), p. 256.

bluejeans were ever "profoundly" democratic is surely a matter of debate, but Reich was correct to note that they did not imply distinctions of wealth and status. Anyone who observed bluejean wearers today, however, would never think about making his statement because precisely the reverse has occurred. Calvin Klein and Gloria Vanderbilt have gone into the jeans business, raising prices and introducing distinctions of wealth and status that traditional American bluejeans avoided.

At times, the requirements for being fashionable are so demanding that people have to relearn how to perform fundamental human activities in order to remain stylish. A few years ago, shoe manufacturers introduced a line of merchandise which became known as platform shoes. It was hard to believe that a person could intentionally design a less worthwhile shoe. To a nonplatformed observer, the distinguishing characteristic of this shoe was that walking in it without stumbling seemed practically impossible. Yet since platform shoes were part of the so-called required uniform at American discos, young men and women across the land learned how to walk again at age 19.

For years, fashion was thought to be the province of women. A large industry devoted itself to instructing women on how they could become fashionable. A number of magazines— *Cosmopolitan, Glamour,* and *Mademoiselle*—had fashion instruction as their primary reason for existence. No respectable department store was without a cosmetics department and a make-up advisor who could counsel women on how best to enhance their natural appearance. Men often were thought to be less susceptible to the advertising appeals of the fashion industry. In the past 15 years, however, a concerted effort has been made to draw men into the world of glamour. American men used to go to barber shops. Today they make appointments with their hair stylists. They used to wear bluejeans. Today they have designer labels attached to their clothes. According to spokespersons for the fashion idustry, American life has become more "exciting" since men have become interested in glamour.

Capitalism is often defended on the grounds that it encourages hard work, thrift, and personal integrity. Although this may have been true at one time, it certainly is not the case today. A fashionable society does not reward thrift and those who make sacrifices for the sake of personal integrity. To be thrifty and ignore the demands of being in fashion may result in ridicule from peers. A person who might be impeccably tailored as to the fit and condition of his or her clothes may be the object of laughter because of the width of lapels or hem length.

Finally, think what it means to describe someone as a fashionable person. Does it mean that this person has any praiseworthy attributes such as integrity, courage, or the ability to care? Does it mean that this person has especially noteworthy talents? Does it mean that this person has become skilled at manipulating outward appearances, regardless of the personal qualities actually possessed? It might well be the case that someone who is a dedicated follower of fashion may be a person with no self at all, a figure bordering on the pathetic whose personality changes at the latest whim of Yves St. Laurent and Christian Dior.

OUR BODIES, OUR SELVES: THE LAST FRONTIER

The consumer society encourages us to think of ourselves as bundles of needs which must be fulfilled. The limits of these needs are defined only by the limits of the imaginations of advertising executives. Once identified, there is a tendency for these needs to be magnified. Thus the "need" for clean hair has grown into the need to avoid "itchiness" which may suggest the *possibility* of dandruff, and the "need" for clean dishes becomes magnified into the need to have dishes in which we can see our reflections. Of course people do have genuine needs and one of the greatest travesties of consumer society is that it deflects the satisfaction of these towards the consumption of irrelevant products.

If the creators of fashionable merchandise had to rely on the intrinsic worth of the products they market, many would not be as successful as they are. Nor would they be as successful if they simply informed us that "this is the current fashion in this line of goods" without attaching additional implications to their message. Creators of fashionable items succeed largely because they are able to persuade us that deep psychic and spiritual needs can be fulfilled by purchasing certain products.

One of the most vivid manifestations of this in our day can be seen in the behavior of teenagers. Parents and teachers complain of this age group that peer pressure is so strong as to make many of them immune to outside influence. The pressure varies from dating habits to decisions whether to use drugs, but it is especially influential in consumer purchasing decisions. Almost everyone who is acquainted with teenagers knows how important certain possessions are to gaining respect from others. We know of one parochial high school where students checked each other's jacket labels to see if their sport coats were purchased at a sufficiently prestigious clothing store. Teachers at middle class schools where there are no dress codes jokingly suggest that an Izod alligator shirt might as well be designated part of an official uniform.

There would be no reason to mention teenage behavior in this book if it were only a stage of personal development that adults normally overcame. In many ways, however, a consumer economy seeks to arrest everyone's mental development at the level of a thirteen year old. For every deep-seated human need, there is an advertiser to suggest that the need is best fulfilled by the purchase of its product. For almost every problem normally experienced in industrial society, a commercial advertiser promises a remedy. The range of associations is only limited by the imagination of the advertiser's copywriter. Does one feel alienated from work? Let AMF make week-ends. Is day-to-day life boring? Let Michelob put a little weekend in your weekday. Is your family under strain? Take the children to Disneyworld, Carowinds, King's Dominion, or Six Flags. Do you feel powerless? Try Marlboros. Are you worried that the tide of world events seems to be turning against the U.S.? Buy "tough, competitive" American cars. The problems and remedies appear endless.

Advertising appeals to adults and children imply that self-worth and status come with certain product purchases. A Mazda is for people who want an economical car with a "touch of class." Dewar's scotch whiskey is for the rising, hip capitalist. As is the case with fashion, almost any good can be associated with status. Even people who know better can at times fall prey to the strategems of advertisers. Persons who do not believe that there are significant differences among brands of aspirin may still purchase Bayer instead of their supermarket's house brand solely because they would be embarassed to give an A & P aspirin to a visitor who asks for a couple of tablets.

Another tactic frequently used by advertisers is to connect our desires for companionship, affection, and love to the purchase of their products. Most human beings cherish good friends and desire at least one deep, sustaining relationship. Throughout our culture, from the trashiest of soap operas to the most well written novels, we find evidence of these concerns. In our day, loneliness and the inability to establish and maintain a deep relationship are two of the most frequent complaints heard in psychiatrists' offices. Here again, the corporate economy cashes in on our desires. Manufacturers of sport cars appeal to potential male purchasers by implying that an attractive and admiring woman is part of the car's standard equipment. Makers of Dentyne suggest that we will be infinitely more kissable if we chew Dentyne rather than Beech Nut.

When appealing to our desires for status or affection, advertisers often trade on our fears and anxieties. American consumers are consistently reminded of their inadequacies and their subsequent need to be inordinately attentive to the most trivial details of everyday existence lest other people take offense at who and what we are. In a consumer society, our bodies become the final frontier. There is hardly a patch of flesh or an opening on our bodies about which we have not been told to worry by some advertiser. It is almost as if there is a conspiracy among American businesses to invade one more part of our bodies with each passing year. At the time of invasion, a product is marketed with the express purpose of repelling an offensive odor invented by an advertising copy writer. It is possible to imagine that at this very moment there are people in the process of creating MHD-masculine hygiene deodorant.

The bodies and souls of women have for years been special targets of those who live by making us feel inadequate. Most American women grow up hearing how important it is to enhance their natural appearances. This advice has not only been limited to hair care, skin care, odor control, and blemish coverups, but has actually gone so far as to promote anxiety about an American woman's genetic endowment. In many circles, the natural contours of the American female body are considered an unfortunate flaw. Women are frequently encouraged not only to get "in shape," but to get into the specific shape of a Parisian model. Beauty spas and an entire diet industry are anxious to help them achieve this goal. If a woman finds this path undesirable, the undergarment industry has developed a series of devices designed to lift, extend, fill out, or contract body parts, as the need arises.

Besides promoting anxiety about our bodies, the corporate economy trades on our fear that we—as students, teachers, friends, lovers, husbands, wives, members of a community, mothers, or fathers—may be performing some of our most important responsibilities inadequately. Our self concept partially depends on how well we perform our various responsibilities. In a consumer economy, manufacturers try to convince us that our duties only can be adequately performed by purchasing certain goods. Not to purchase these items implies inadequacy in a particular role of life.

The leaders of the corporate economy have attempted to remake the family according to their conception of the member's proper role in the consumption process. The duties and functions of motherhood inevitably are linked with a household product. The competent mother is one who can ward off the dangers lurking in the household. As early as the 1920s Lysol claimed that even the "doorknobs threaten children with disease."[8] Today, the makers of Charmin would have us believe that it is one of the principal joys of motherhood to know that your children are using the softest toilet tissue on the market.

Fathers have fared no better than mothers in the corporate economy's portrait of their responsibilities. Originally a father's role was basically confined to bringing home the money necessary to purchase the family's consumer goods. Fathers who did not consider this their primary function in life were portrayed as inadequate men. Now traits such as personal integrity, social commitment, ability to perform meaningful work and a capacity for love and compassion are occasionally evident in the consumer economy's depictions of American fathers, but they are connected in some way to purchasing behavior. A father who loves his daughter buys her a sporty Mustang or a Barbie doll, depending upon her age. In the consumer society, father serves the function of a year round Santa Claus.

The consumer economy's efforts to educate children may well be the most shameful aspect of its entire operation. Before they reach the age where they can distinguish the show from the commercials, children are exposed to advertisements in which their favorite heroes and most endearing characters are peddling products, telling them how much fun a toy will bring or how scrumptious a cereal tastes. It is possible, of course, for parents to exert a measure of control over their children's habits. But the assault is so total that it is a constant struggle for any parent to shelter the children from the corporate economy prior to the time when they can become reasonable judges of a product's worth. There may be no better indication of the corruption at the core of the consumer economy than to note that grown men and women make a handsome living by spurring children to badger their parents into buying any number of worthless products.

The continual effort to pit child against parent reinforces a theme we presented at the beginning of the chapter: the corporate economy's concern about the family is a self-interested one. The family is valued only to the extent that its network of duties and responsibilities can be employed for the benefit of those wishing to sell products and maintain the existing structure of the economy. When family values get in the

---

[8]Stuart Ewen, *Captains of Consciousness* (New York: McGraw Hill Book Company, 1976), p. 170.

way of these goals, they are conveniently shunted aside. If money can be made in encouraging children to badger their parents, if a profit can be turned by badmouthing mom's cooking, and if more thrills can be provided by ads which make children the implied object of sexual fantasies, a justification will be found to violate the integrity of the family.

All these efforts by the corporate economy to persuade us that our inadequacies and anxieties can be removed by purchasing consumer goods is extremely misleading. The remedies which are offered necessarily deal with symptoms and not with causes. In Chapter 4 we shall discuss the systematic degrading of work and the damage this does to the lives of people who must perform it. The consumer society offers more consumption as a solution to the problems it has created. It is ironic that the *source* of so much anxiety professes to be the *cure*. The very last thing that Bayer wants to do is to eliminate the causes of headaches.

Staff at the Wayne State University School of Medicine monitored all the health material presented on a single Detroit station in a week and found that 70 percent of it was either inaccurate or misleading. "Very few of the health categories actually contain health information. . . . [Most] are primarily profit oriented and contain health information only to the extent necessary to justify the particular product or service being rendered."[9] In this situation, remedies will continue to be disappointing because genuine needs will not be addressed.

This is why newness is so important to the claims of advertisers. Past disappointments evaporate in a sea of promises about the future. Today's gateway to happiness must become tomorrow's bad taste. If it did not, if today's products did bring happiness, consumption would dwindle and the economic structure would become endangered. This is why there is such a persistent emphasis upon newness. New products are constantly invented, old products become "new and improved." The American Association of Advertising Agencies report the following rather startling information:[10]

1.   Over half of manufacturers' total business today is in products developed in the last 30 years.
2.   Between 30 percent and 40 percent of current grocery sales are in products that did not exist ten years ago.
3.   In 1971, 1,150 *new items* (including health and beauty aids) were introduced into this nation's grocery stores.

There is also a built-in futility to the promises expressed throughout the corporate economy. Although satisfaction is promised if we purchase the basic kit of

[9]Paul Lowinger, et al., "Health Information During a Week of Television," *New England Journal of Medicine*, 286: 1972, p. 516.

[10]American Association of Advertising Agencies, *New Product Advertising; Managing the Risks and Costs*, 1976.

consumer society, that satisfaction will never be obtained because the make-up of the kit is altered every year. There is always a bigger home, a new scent, a jazzier car, and a more fashionable suit that we will be compelled to purchase to keep up with the times. Given this, it is not surprising that as America became more affluent after World War II, there was not an accompanying rise in personal happiness. Tibor Scitovsky reports that between 1946 and 1970 real per capita income rose by 62 percent. Yet the proportion of people who considered themsleves very happy, fairly happy, or not very happy hardly changed at all.[11]

It is fashionable these days for conservatives to argue that "problems cannot be solved by throwing money at them." But this is precisely what the consumer economy encourages, and this is harmful as well as misleading. Today, as Wendell Berry suggests, the giving of money has become our characteristic virtue.[12] We give to the United Way, the Red Cross, the political party of our choice, or the Jerry Lewis Telethon for Muscular Dystrophy. These are worthy causes and surely in need of funding. Yet we often give money or its equivalent in lieu of time, care, action, and thought. We may even seek to repair eroding human relationships with money and goods instead of time and effort. In this situation, we find it more difficult to make genuine connections with others and we begin to experience the loneliness that consumer society supposedly prevents.

The harmfulness of consumer society is by no means limited to those who are sufficiently well off to purchase its basic kit. The damage is perhaps more deeply felt by those who occupy the lowest rungs of the economic ladder. While these men and women struggle to make ends meet on a daily basis, they are immersed in a culture which informs them that they are inadequate in every way. Innumerable messages urge them to spend more than they can afford. They are compelled to raise their sons and daughters in an atmosphere where children will expect more than they can provide. And to add insult to injury, they will be informed that their economic plight is caused by their own personality deficiencies. In a consumer society, the poor live with their dignity under perpetual attack.

CONSUMPTION AND POLITICS

The values of a consumer society ultimately affect our politics. Like commercial hucksters, candidates vie to outpromise one another, proposing quick remedies to long-standing problems. In 1980, for instance, Ronald Reagan vowed that he would balance the budget, dramatically increase defense expenditures, reduce unemployment, and wipe out inflation. Jimmy Carter had to run on his record. Since Carter had failed to implement any of the extravagant promises he made four years earlier, he was no match for Mr. Reagan. As in the commercial world, promises are frequently

[11]Tibor Scitovsky, *The Joyless Economy* (New York: Oxford University Press, 1976).
[12]Wendell Berry, *The Unsettling of America* (New York: Avon Books, 1977).

made which have little relationship to real problems. Politics founders in a sea of cliches and the gulf between rhetoric and real issues widens.

The values of a consumer society sometimes influence our politics in a manner that is barely noticeable. For example, in 1978 Jimmy Carter told the American public that he believed what Abraham Lincoln believed about politics: that we should have a government "for the people." What Mr. Carter neglected to mention, however, was that Abraham Lincoln also believed that we should have government "by the people."[13] Carter's omission betrayed an outlook about politics that is becoming increasingly prevalent in our society. Citizens are increasingly considered merely the consumers of the government's goods and services. No effort is made to involve us in making the decisions that affect our lives other than the periodic public relations campaigns which we call elections.

The politics of the average citizen is also affected by the consumer society. The emphasis upon a self which recognizes being as consumption tends to draw attention away from more genuine resolutions to social problems. The citizen is not encouraged to think very much about politics, except insofar as it affects his level of consumption. Coke does *not* add life to life, but so long as we are distracted by this and countless other such babblings we are unlikely to think about what may.

We have discussed how frustration and anxiety are inherent aspects of the consumer society. These attitudes can spill into broader aspects of life and living together. Some steal because they can't afford the things which they think will bring happiness. Others buy guns to protect what they have. We build fences and install burglar alarms. Welfare cheating is detested far out of proportion to the reality of the problem. Many are resentful when "the government wishes to take our money" to spend for social purposes. Bombs are built which destroy people but leave property intact. We become a nation of individuals, divided against each other and preeminently concerned with protecting our own turf.

It is not only mainstream politics which is affected by the consumer orientation in American culture. Movements of political opposition are themselves in danger of being coopted by the corporate economy. During the early sixties, the civil rights movement posed a threat to the consumer culture. Blacks were in no way part of the American dream. In the novelist's Ralph Ellison's poignant description, they were "invisible Americans". Perhaps for this reason some blacks could point to problems in American society that escaped other people's notice. In the conservative wing of the movement, Martin Luther King and his followers spoke the language of community, sharing, and brotherhood. While they did not issue many radical economic proposals, King and his followers certainly spoke to themes neglected by corporate America.

[13]See Christopher Lasch, "Democracy and the Crisis of Confidence," *democracy*, January 1981, p. 27 See also, Sheldon Wolin, "The State of the Union," *New York Review of Books*, May 18, 1978.

The radical wing of the black movement was potentially more threatening. Leaders like Malcolm X and H. Rap Brown urged blacks to get off the bus, not to integrate it. When Stokely Carmichael put on a pair of overalls and shouted in public "Black Is Beautiful," he was striking at the heart of the consumer culture. For years, Americans had been told that beauty was the end result of a continual struggle to cover blemishes, lose weight, dress stylishly, and smell properly. Beauty was especially difficult to achieve for black Americans because the standards of beauty were established by the white culture. Blacks who wanted to be beautiful were compelled to deemphasize their natural attributes and adopt the characteristics of white Americans.

In his autobiography, the black leader Malcolm X spoke about how he straightened his hair when he was a young adult in order to be considered fashionable. Shorty, the friend who was to do the straightening for him, sent Malcolm down to the store to pick up the necessary ingredients and utensils. These included a can of lye, eggs, potatoes, vaseline, a couple of combs, a spray hose, rubber gloves, and a rubber apron. Returning to Shorty's room, Malcolm waited while Shorty mixed the potatoes, lye, and eggs together in a jar in order to make congolene. He described what happened afterwards in this way:[14]

"Feel the jar," Shorty said. I cupped my hands against the outside and snatched it away. "Damn right, its hot, that's the lye," he said. "So you know its going to burn when I comb it in—it burns *bad*. But the longer you can stand it, the straighter the hair."

He made me sit down and he tied the string of the new rubber apron tightly around my neck, and combed up a bush of hair. Then, from the big vaseline jar, he took a handful and massaged it hard all through my hair and into the scalp. He also thickly vaselined my neck, ears, and forehead. "When I get to washing out your head, be sure to tell me anywhere you feel any little stinging," Shorty warned me, washing his hands and then pulling on the rubber gloves and tying his own rubber apron. "You always got to remember that any congolene left in burns a sore in your head."

The congolene just felt warm when Shorty started combing it in. But then my head caught fire.

I gritted my teeth and tried to pull the sides of the kitchen table together. The comb felt as if it was raking my skin off.

My eyes watered, my nose was running. I couldn't stand it any longer; I bolted to the washbasin. I was cursing Shorty with every name I could think of when he got the spray going and started soap lathering my head.

Years later, Malcolm X came to believe that black Americans degraded themselves by straightening their hair. He felt that blacks had lost touch with their real identity and their inner selves to the point that they would "violate and mutilate their god-created bodies to try to look 'pretty' by white standards."[15] To assert then, as

[14]Malcolm X, *The Autobiography of Malcolm X* (New York: Ballantine Books, 1973), p. 53.
[15]Ibid., p. 54.

Stokely Carmichael did, that "Black is beautiful" was radical in two senses. In the first place, it claimed that existing white standards of beauty were not universal and that blacks possessed natural beauty themselves. Second, and here lay the real challenge to consumer America, the phrase implied that blacks did not have to buy a thing to be beautiful. They only had to be.

If thoughts like this ever caught on with a majority of the public, consumer society would be doomed. Those who operated the corporate economy thus attempted to draw blacks into it. Blacks could be allowed to be beautiful, but they could not be permitted to think that they could be so without buying anything. An array of facial creams and hair conditioners were developed to help blacks look "natural." Walk into any drugstore in an area where there is a sizable population of blacks and go to the hair care aisle. You will find entire lines of merchandise under the heading of "Dark and Lovely" and "Born Beautiful." You will find Blow Out Relaxer, Afro Soft, Afro Sheen, Afro Perm, Curl Care, Curl Activator, Curl Keeper, and Realistic Texture Curl which promises you a "whole new way to go curly." Beauty for blacks has become Americanized.

Outside of the drugstore, a similar pattern emerged. Black clothing styles appeared in department stores, adorning black mannequins. Blacks began to appear in national television commercials. New stereotypes were evident as upwardly mobile blacks were sprinkled through entertainment programs. Surly sports heroes like Jim Brown and Duane Thomas were replaced by gregarious types like O.J. Simpson and Magic Johnson. Consumer society flexed its muscles and showed its clout. Give Mean Joe Greene a Coca Cola and watch him smile. In the meantime, no one seems to note that the relative economic plight of blacks has improved very little in the past twenty years.

The women's movement is also experiencing the fate of being drawn into the consumer culture. In the late nineteenth and early twentieth centuries, the women's movement often sought alliances with radical workers' groups which offered fundamental criticisms of the social order. When the movement again gathered momentum in the late sixties, it generated a significant body of criticism of an aggressive and male dominated culture. Many argued that it was important to support women's liberation because it would improve our personal lives and the political order in a fundamental way. It was argued that the qualities of idealism and compassion which women possessed could transform America into a more humane society. It was a common saying at the time that liberating women would also help to liberate men.

Such claims have been deflected. Rather than bringing a distinctive consciousness to society in order to change it, the model of liberation is now becoming the woman who functions well in the traditional male-dominated corporate hierarchy. A spate of books and articles have been published which preach assertiveness to women. Television shows occasionally depict women performing competently in roles previously reserved for men. And commercial advertisers have had little difficulty in adapting the demands of some American women to their own profitable ends. Have American women demanded power? Business now rushes in to congratulate them on their accomplishments. "You've come a long way baby"—we have a cigarette especially for you. "You've got clout"—you can have your own Mastercard.

The fundamental critique by women of the social order which was once very common in the movement has now diminished in significance. Emphasis is currently placed on equality issues such as equal pay for equal work, equal treatment in work situations, and equal opportunity for promotion. Major women's organizations, for instance, have devoted much of their efforts to the passage of the equal rights amendment. These issues are certainly important, but they are ones which can be handled without any serious debate about the core framework of consumer society.

We have not raised these examples in order to make a wholesale criticism of either the black or the women's movement. Nor have we intended to provide a full explanation of why each movement progressed as it did. It is surely a gain that fewer blacks feel required to deny their identity and that women demand equal pay for comparable work. Within each movement, however, there was once considerable interest in transforming the social order. Blacks and women both felt that they had distinctive insights into how we might build a more humane society. The resilience of the dominant culture helped to thwart these impulses. In fact, the consumer culture worked to transform these movements. Serious and responsible debate became limited to a range of issues which did not challenge the basic premises of consumer society.

OPPOSING CONSUMER SOCIETY

In much of this chapter, we have used examples drawn from advertising to describe the workings of consumer society. When criticisms such as ours are made, it is a common response of those who defend the corporate economy to maintain that the influence of advertising is greatly overrated. They claim that advertisers exert a minimal influence on consumers and are merely striving to reach people who are often indifferent to their pleas. Defenders of the consumer society also suggest that its critics act as if ordinary Americans are the most gullible and least discerning people in the world. It is said that the critics fail to realize that Americans do not swallow the advertisers' claims whole and intact.

Arguments like these are not totally incorrect, but they are not especially enlightening either. On one hand, maintaining that Americans are not completely gullible misses the point of our analysis. On the other hand, only stating that Americans are skeptical does not tell us why they are this way. We have not been arguing that consumers find every advertisement to which they are exposed persuasive. Americans do not believe that they will be transformed into kings or queens if they spread Imperial margarine on their bread nor do they feel like white knights when they scrub their floors with Ajax. But given the pervasiveness of advertising, it is much more difficult not to be persuaded that our standard of living is dependent on the quality and quantity of our acquisitions. As we shall see in the following chapters, our schools, workplaces and mass media make it that much more difficult to battle against this notion.

The cliche often spoken by conservative politicians—"we ought to run the government like a family"—can help to illustrate our point. Conservatives often use this phrase as a rhetorical weapon in support of their moves to limit government spending and to balance the budget. When one looks at how families actually act, however, conservatives ought to be glad that they are not used as a model for the government. In 1950 the national debt was $256 billion. By 1975 that debt had increased to $532 billion. During the same period, consumer debt increased from $26 billion to $233 billion and corporate debt increased from $66 billion to $587 billion. Compared to corporations or families involved in the consumer economy, the government is a model of thrift.[16]

At its worst, the consumer economy turns human beings into pitiable clowns who act as if deep personal needs can be fulfilled by acquisitions and possessions. If advertisers had their way, human beings would never develop anything but the worst capacities which adolescents exhibit. We would be jealous of others and insecure of ourselves, but without the lively intelligence and ethical idealism that teenagers often manifest. The typical effect of the consumer economy is to play so effectively on our fears and insecurities that we feel inadequate if we are not able to purchase the basic kit of consumer society. We may not even believe that it is worthwhile to do this, yet we would have nagging doubts if we refrained.

Since World War II, American capitalism's efforts to promote the values of a consumer society have been enormously successful. These efforts have not been, however, entirely successful. While consumer values set the tone of American society, they are not uncritically accepted by the entire populace. The corporate economy's failure to convince us that its commandments should be followed at any cost can be seen in several areas of American life. This failure can be most clearly witnessed in the skepticism many of us voice about large corporate enterprise and in the resentment that is occasionally expressed when we believe that we are being treated like incompetent adolescents by those who own and manage the economy.

Many Americans, at one time or another, have been skeptical of the promises that commercial advertisers make. We do not necessarily believe that oil companies are looking after our best interests, that there exists much difference among toothpastes or that our sons and daughters ought to connect their self-worth to the possessions they have acquired. This skepticism sometimes becomes tinged with resentment. Many American workers, for instance, still resent the power which their

---

[16]These figures are taken from the 1979 *Statistical Abstract,* Tables 455, 877, and 932.

employers exert over them, even if they also believe that they are adequately compensated for the work they perform.

Opposition to the values of consumer society has occasionally proceeded further than that evidenced by skepticism or resentment. Some people have not only expressed distaste for the existing order, but have attempted to live in a manner contrary to the values of consumer society. In this respect, we might think of groups such as the Amish who have consciously declined the enticements of corporate America. But we might also consider any person whose religious values have led him or her to use material resources prudently and spend more time cultivating their inner selves than acquiring consumer goods.

During the 1960s, many young people who were critical of consumer society professed to be searching for an alternative manner of living. Most were ultimately unsuccessful. Some really never weaned themselves away from the consumer culture while others did for a while, only to return to consumer society at a later age. Although the movement of the sixties disintegrated, you can still find people who were influenced by its ideals. Much of the ecological concern that was evident throughout the seventies had its roots in the notion that prudent use of our resources should take precedence over unrestricted economic growth. Moreover, throughout America you find individuals and families still interested in discovering how to lead a more rewarding life than that offered by the consumer culture.

To lead a life opposed to the values of the consumer culture is not an easy task. People who try to do this on an individual basis learn that they almost have to immunize themselves from most of the messages we see and hear each day. Individuals also learn how many of the consumer culture's values they have themselves internalized in their previous years of living. The difficulties for social movements to oppose consumer society's values are equally formidable. As we saw above, the managers of the corporate economy seek to translate criticism of the existing order into a form which is profitable for business. Moreover, people who believe that consumer values are damaging have yet to agree on what is a more rewarding manner of living and how such a life can be made possible.

It is clear, however, upon what resources those people who wish to challenge consumer society and the corporate economy will have to call. They will have to show that our desires for dignity, good human relationships, rewarding work and personal wholeness are currently not being met and cannot be met by an order which strives to perpetuate a state of eternal adolescence. Skepticism and resentment can only form the most limited opposition. The challenge to those who wish to alter consumer society is to channel this skepticism and resentment into effective political action.

3

Schooling in America

Once the uneducated could have the humility of ignorance. Now they are given degrees and put in charge, and this delusion of learning will produce consequences more critical than the absence of it. . . . Look ahead to 1985. Those who will control a good part of the educational plant will be the products themselves of the most stringently anti-intellectual training in the country . . . to judge by the new suburbia the bulk of the middle-class parents of 1985 will know no other standards to evaluate education of their children than those of the social-adjustment type of schooling.

William H. Whyte, Jr., 1956

In 1961, Carl Bernstein graduated from Montgomery Blair High School in Silver Spring, Maryland—barely. Fifteen years later, after gaining fame for his investigative reporting of the Watergate epic, he was invited back to his high school as a commencement speaker. His speech was enthusiastically received by students and parents, although the school authorities were nonplussed. Calling his return "the ultimate revenge in this life," he wasted little time on the platitudes usually associated with such occasions. Instead, he vividly recounted the dreariness and anxiety of his high school days. He managed to graduate from high school, but only after intensive lobbying by him and his parents.

The Carl Bernsteins of this world are a perpetual embarrassment to the educational establishment because they provide evidence that people sometimes succeed despite their educational experience, not because of it. Fortunately for the establishment, he is an exception, and this led him to a mistaken assertion. Toward the end of his speech, Bernstein observed:[1]

> The real world is a lot more tolerant, a lot more interesting, a lot more fun, a lot more sensible really than the cocoon that is high school. Wherever you stand in this class, you've gotten through the worst part—high school—and you deserve to feel really good about that. Now come the opportunities, whether you're headed for university, a job, the military, marriage. Now you get to be your own person, not what your teachers want you to be, not what your parents expect you to be. At last you're not going to be compelled by others to do anything. And that really is what that piece of paper—that diploma—is all about. It's a ticket—out of this place and into life.

If Bernstein were correct, if school were simply a bad but isolated experience, there would be no reason to consider it in a book on politics. Unfortunately, this is not the case. We believe that for most people life *is* like high school, and students tend to transfer the basic things they have learned there into the adult world. More often than not, schooling anticipates and prepares us for the roles we are expected to perform as adults, and this makes it an experience of considerable political significance.

In this chapter we shall examine the process of education and its relationship to the social and political order. We believe schooling is an extremely important social process and how we think about it influences our notions of political reality. There is a conventional wisdom about schooling in America which shall be discussed and subjected to critical scrutiny. We shall examine how the everyday experience of schooling prepares us for political life.

THE SIGNIFICANCE OF SCHOOLING

We live in hard times for schools. It is not simply that schools across the nation face severe financial difficulties; the problems are much deeper than this. No one who has anything to do with schools seems happy about them. In part this is because an important function of schools is the transmission of social values. When a consensus on social values collapses, as it recently has in our society, institutions which transmit those values are bound to have difficulties.

If one were to go into classrooms across the country, whether those classes are found in elementary schools, high schools, or on university campuses, the most

---

[1] Carl Bernstein's 1976 commencement address was carried in the *Washington Post,* June 3, 1979, "Outlook", p.1.

common mood one would find in students would be boredom. Unremitting, unrelieved, suffocating boredom. The enthusiastic response of Silver Spring students to Carl Bernstein's speech could have been replicated at high school graduations throughout the land. To some, being released from school seems roughly equivalent to being released from prison. A number of students seek relief from this boredom in various forms of antisocial behavior. Others spend school days blissed out on drugs. Most, however, seem resigned to their fate. They don't make trouble, they do what is necessary to get through, but they are bored. Even at the college level, where attendance is not required by the state, evidence of boredom is substantial. Students often cut classes, and minds and notebooks close simultaneously five or ten minutes before the hour in anticipation of the class bell.

Many teachers have seen the noble vision with which they entered the profession steadily eroded. For example, the indifferent attitude of students about education is one reason why many teachers are resigned simply to get through the day with a minimum of disruption. Some think of themselves as little more than glorified babysitters. As the profession becomes more bureaucratic, teachers are overburdened with administrative paperwork. Many feel consumed by perfunctory chores such as specifying behavioral or performance objectives for students. Most of all, teachers feel unappreciated. A general lack of appreciation is clearly manifest in the erosion of the relative economic position of teachers. Salary increases are more than offset by inflation, and so the real wages of teachers decline.

School administrators are increasingly embroiled in a battle of survival. Property owners are reluctant to approve any tax increases necessitated by rising school costs; the federal government is substantially reducing its commitment to schools; and teachers' unions grow more militant. At the same time, administrators are forced to defend the schools against charges of ineptitude as reading and computational skills continue to decline.

Various citizens groups are also upset with the schools. Business leaders complain about high school job applicants who can barely read and write and who cannot perform simple mathematical functions. Others believe that schools are responsible for the moral decay of society, that they teach a secular humanism which denigrates traditional religious principles and advocates sexual promiscuity. Many parents, concerned that their children are not learning the skills necessary to survive in society, advocate a no-nonsense, back-to-basics approach to education.

Schools in America are beset by so much turmoil coming from so many different directions that it is hard to make sense out of what is going on. However, the fact of turmoil itself suggests that schooling is a significant social process. Its very pervasiveness suggests that it merits attention. Formal education is virtually universal and the total number of hours spent in a school setting between birth and adulthood is rivaled only by the hours spent with families. The increase of after-school activities, summer schools, preschools, and day-care centers may lead to more time in school settings than in family settings.

Schools also serve as an important introduction to the common culture and to social life. It is in the school where we learn to be public citizens. This has not always been the case. At the dawn of the industrial revolution, the extended family, churches, and the work place played dominant roles in introducing young people into the common culture. In this century, however, the influence of these institutions has declined and the influence of schools has increased. Prior to attending school, children develop their own collective rules, usually through playing games. These rules are the product of the immediate play situation—the various sizes and ages of the participants, the physical setting of the game, the types of play things available, and so forth. School introduces children to larger cultural norms external to their immediate relationships. Although the child may see no immediate justification for these norms, the consequences of violating them are soon learned.

Schooling occurs during critical periods of development rather than at maturity. As children enter the school setting at earlier ages, schools are given more opportunity to influence and structure lives. In short, schooling occurs when we are most impressionable. This is as it should be. Learning and development ought to occur simultaneously but this means that the stakes in schooling will be unusually high.

Surveys consistently demonstrate that the significance of schooling is deeply embedded in our collective consciousness. Although in a period of economic difficulty any public expenditure tends to be looked upon dubiously, schools remain at the top of the list of spending priorities in the public mind. In 1975, a Gallup Poll asked a national sample how any new money the government came upon should be spent. Support for public school education was exceeded only by support for health care, and it far surpassed support for such things as military defense, mass transit, welfare, and law enforcement. These results agree with other surveys conducted during the 1960s and 1970s.

The Gallup public research organization periodically conducts national education surveys. The results of these surveys generally confirm the increasing public unhappiness with education. By August 1980, confidence in public schools had eroded to a critical extent. People *are* upset with schools. However, when compared with other major institutions, the schools do comparatively well. They enjoy more confidence than state, local, or national governments, the courts, labor unions, or big business. Only the church exceeds the schools in public confidence. Clearly, the crisis in the schools is part of a broader social crisis.

That so many recent social battles have been fought on school terrain is further evidence of the significance Americans attach to schooling. In recent years such issues as internal communist subversion, civil rights, Vietnam, civil liberties, and even questions of hair style and dress have been most intensely fought in the school setting. In part, this is because of the contributions schools make to our sense of collective identity. They tell us who we are. This is one reason why the issue of prayer in public schools is so important to some segments of society. Some who see a general moral decay in society have rallied behind a constitutional amendment to allow public school prayers as a means of arresting moral decline. On the surface this seems ludicrous. It is hard to imagine that a brief prayer at the beginning of the school day would have any effect at all on our moral condition. The urgency of prayer advocates can be better understood if the school is thought of as a conveyor of social identity. Prayer in public schools would convey to us a sense of religiosity—or at least the sense that we are a people religious in a certain way. This is the force that drives school prayer advocates.

EDUCATION AND THE CONVENTIONAL WISDOM

There is a conventional wisdom about education in America—that is, a common understanding of what education does which most people share. It is not coherent enough to be called an ideology; in fact, some parts of the conventional wisdom seem to contradict others. The public seems to hold to the tenets of the conventional wisdom simultaneously and loosely, without worrying that they may be contradictory.

There are three tenets of the conventional wisdom to which we wish to call attention. The first, and perhaps most important tenet, is that schools are seen as *providing an open chance to individuals from all classes of society to compete fairly in the game of life*. It is the key to both individual and social progress.

In a society where there is constant pressure to seek competitive advantage over others, schools are widely regarded as the agents of justice. If the outside world is cold, competitive, and more easily manipulated by those who are economically and socially privileged, it is the school that supposedly brings equality to the "race of life." From the equal starting place of the schoolyard, it is commonly believed, the best will soon distinguish themselves. Americans almost universally regard education as the key to progress. Politicians may argue over such issues as local control and appropriate sources of funding for schools, but the contribution of schools to progress is rarely challenged. At the societal level, progress is equated with technological advance. Innovation in technology is assumed to lead to collective betterment. In an interesting but circular type of reasoning, progress becomes an end in itself—perhaps one that is required by our economic state—and is *defined* by increasing technological sophistication. We measure our progress by the extent of our gadgetry.

Perhaps the more important consequences of thinking of education as the key to progress occur not at the social, but at the individual level. Education is widely regarded as the means of secular salvation. Those wishing to move up the social ladder must "get a good education." Educational opportunity appears to be democratic and meritocratic. It seems open to everyone on a more or less equal basis, and it is widely believed that people rise through the educational system according to their intellectual merit and their willingness to work. Education seems to be the closest thing we have to a national religious faith.

If anything, the faith of the American people in this ideal is increasing. In a 1973 Gallup poll the question, "How important are schools in one's future success?", was asked. Seventy-six percent of the public felt that schools were "extremely important." By 1980, that proportion had climbed to 82 percent. What is interesting about this notion of schools as a means of secular salvation is that salvation, as it is in the religious realm, is an intensely personal matter. When the rules of the game are perceived to be fair, when everyone is perceived to have an equal chance of winning or losing, and when the criteria for measuring who wins and who loses are assumed to be just, the losers are left without legitimate recourse. Such are the perceptions today. One reason why the assembly line worker whose resentment toward a college educated supervisor to whom he feels intellectually superior only smolders and does not burst into flames is that the worker very likely feels he should have gotten a college education. Whatever obligations or inadequacies foreclosed that possibility are treated as simple breaks of the game.

A second tenet of the conventional wisdom holds that the purpose of education is to *promote intellectual, moral and psychic growth.* Although this tenet has an old and honorable lineage—it can be traced at least to Plato in western thought—its most influential advocate in this country remains John Dewey and his disciples. Although this tenet is not as widely held as the first one, those who support it are still substantial in number, and counted among their ranks are many who work in the education profession. This tenet implies that education has *intrinsic merit.* That it may lead to better work or to economic advancement is secondary. What is of crucial importance is that it makes us better people. With education comes increased vision, sensitivity, and appreciation of the finer things of life.

The third tenet of the conventional wisdom is that education *integrates us into society.* It teaches us how to be adults in America. Most notably of course, it prepares us for the world of work. Poll after poll reveals occupational preparation as an important function of education. Some educational tracks lead directly to occupations. In other cases, the educational process is seen as a series of steps, the main benefit of which is that they lead to certain professions. In either case, education is viewed as instrumental. It is important, not because it has inherent value, but because it is an instrument for achieving something else.

Education integrates us into society in ways other than job preparation. We become integrated as we learn common forms of communication and as we learn to depict reality in similar ways. We learn similar facts of history, and we are taught what things to value. Terms like progress, achievement, responsibility, and merit take on specific and widely shared connotations. The transmission of values is fully as important as is the preparation for jobs, although they are less frequently mentioned aspects of social integration.

Although many Americans hold simultaneously to each of these three tenets, it is doubtful that all can be pursued with equal vigor. Pushed to a certain point, the tenets are contradictory. The adult world is hierarchical and contains a substantial range of inequality. Much of the work to be done in that world is not only tedious, but unfulfilling in other ways as well. Some have much more control over how work is done than do others. People who are greatly advantaged can be expected to attempt to keep those advantages. What happens when the tenets of the conventional wisdom come into conflict? What happens when the intellectual and moral growth of persons confronts the necessity of filling jobs which are not only dreary but which in every way stifle personal development? Is competition in all cases compatible with psychic and moral growth? What happens when, in order to move up the socioeconomic ladder, people are required to repress their moral sense or act in other ways that inhibit their personal growth? And in what sense can it be maintained that students coming from widely divergent economic positions have an open chance to compete fairly? These questions require us to examine more carefully how the tenets of the conventional wisdom are played out in society.

THE CONVENTIONAL WISDOM EXAMINED

There is ample anecdotal evidence to support the first tenet of the conventional wisdom. Most of us are familiar with stories of some people who, from unpromising beginnings, worked their way to the highest parts of the socioeconomic scale. And while we cannot be sure that education had anything to do with this, it is reasonable to assume that in at least some cases it did. More common are smaller movements up (and down) the social ladder. It is not so rare for children of blue-collar parents to move into white-collar occupations. Much of this type of movement is deceptive. We argue at length in the next chapter that the character of the occupational force is changing and that many jobs which are technically white-collar ones, in that they do not involve working with one's hands, are in every other sense working-class jobs. The *appearance* of mobility is more frequent than its reality. Although the changing character of the work force can account for some mobility, it cannot account for it all. There are still cases in which people from poor families become physicians, for example. Despite these cases, broad statistical tendencies suggest that we are far from a meritocratic society.

Studies attempting to gauge the ability of schools to promote a meritocracy, greater equality of opportunity, and therefore a more just society have to be disappointing for those who believe in the first tenet of the conventional wisdom. The results of a comprehensive statistical analysis seriously undermine the idea of education as generating a meritocratic society. Figure 1 is part of this type of analysis.[2]

---

[2]See Samuel Bowles and Herbert Gintis, *Schooling in Capitalist America* (New York: Basic Books, 1971), p. 31, for an extended discussion of these implications.

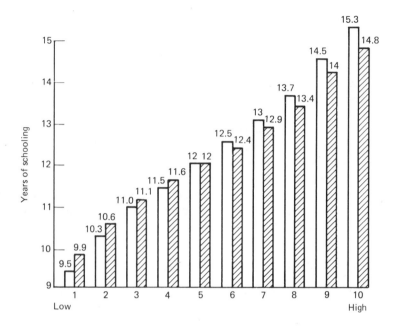

Figure 1. Educational attainments are strongly dependent on social background even for people of similar childhood IQs.

Family socioeconomic background (deciles)

NOTES: For each socioeconomic group, the left-hand bar indicates the estimated average number of years of schooling attained by all men from that group. The right-hand bar indicates the estimated average number of years of schooling attained by men with IQ scores equal to the average for the entire sample. The sample refers to "non-Negro" men of "non-farm" backgrounds, aged 35–44 years in 1962.

Source: Samuel Bowles and Valerie Nelson, "The 'Inheritance of IQ' and the Intergenerational Transmission of Economic Inequality," *The Review of Economics and Statistics,* (February 1974), Vol. LVI, No. 1.

Using U.S. census data, researchers were able to test the relationship between years of schooling, socioeconomic status (a weighted sum of income, occupation, and educational level of the parents) and also to control for childhood IQ. In Figure 1, years of schooling is represented by the length of the bars. The first pair of bars represents the lowest tenth of the population in terms of status, the second pair the second tenth, and so on. The left-hand bars indicate average years of schooling for each social group. Thus, those in the lowest decile average 9.5 years of schooling, while those in the ninth decile average 14.5 years.

It is possible to interpret such information in terms that are congenial to meritocratic ideology. One might argue, for example, that those in the ninth decile are smarter than those in the first decile, and therefore the differences in educational attainment levels are to be expected. To control for this, the researchers selected from within each decile those who had childhood IQ scores equal to the average of the entire sample. These results are displayed in the right-hand bars. It is clear that there is some relationship between IQ scores and years of education, but it is a quite modest one. The five-year discrepancy in educational attainment between the first and the ninth decile is reduced to four when IQ is controlled in this way, but this is small comfort to proponents of meritocratic education. The preponderant proportion of the discrepancy remains.

A second study of 10,000 Wisconsin students assessed the relative contributions of socioeconomic status and intelligence toward college attendance.[3] Both these factors were significant. The brighter the student and the higher the socioeconomic status, the more likely that student was to attend college. Once again, however, this result is not one the supporters of meritocracy would find comforting. For the meritocratic view to prevail, the socioeconomic factor must *not* be significant. In the Wisconsin study, however, it was slightly more significant than intelligence. It is important to note that this study did not distinguish between types of colleges attended. A community or vocational college counted as much as an Ivy League university. If the quality of the institution had been taken into account, the significance of the socioeconomic status would have increased further.

The fairest statement that can be made with respect to this issue is that schools do modestly contribute toward equalizing opportunity and promoting a meritocratic society, but far less than the conventional wisdom would lead one to believe. The dreams of working-class parents notwithstanding, dramatic social mobility is rare. There is a fair amount of upward and downward social mobility over small distances in the social scale, but it cannot be assumed that education is responsible for the major

[3]William Sewell and Vimal Shah, "Intelligence and Attainment of Higher Education," in Jerome Karabel and A.H. Halsey, eds., *Power and Ideology in Education* (New York: Oxford University Press, 1977). Sewell and Shah use multiple regression to assess the relative contribution of the variables in question.

portion of this. This should not be surprising. It would be an unusual country that would allow institutions as important as schools to operate significantly against the central tendencies of the larger society.

Education does help people get better jobs, but the avenues up the educational ladder are not equally open. The conventional wisdom faithfully espoused by so many politicians and ideologues and accepted by so much of the population remains an evanescent dream, yet as a tenet of faith it is crucially important. While this perception is widespread, it is also naive. No institutional complex as ubiquitous and significant as the schools can be unaffected by the relations of power in the society as a whole. It is more accurate to think of schools as agents of manipulation than as agents of social justice. Issues of social justice and inequality permeate all of our public relationships. To expect schools to solve these problems equitably is to engage in wishful thinking.

If education does not appear to be the key to justice for individuals, is it at least the linchpin of social progress? The answer to this question depends upon what one means both by "education" and "progress." That our society has produced a vast array of useful little items is progress of a sort, and our education system has helped to produce them. We doubt, however, that this is the type of progress for which people genuinely long, and we question the efficacy of an educational system geared to this type of progress. We believe the economic and technological structure exercise decisive influence over the education system. For education genuinely to serve social progress, influence would have to be exerted in the opposite direction.

As our educational institutions become more elaborate and specialized, they are able to serve technological advance more efficiently in two ways. First, the elaboration and specialization of education creates and dispenses the type of knowledge most useful for a technocratic society. Second, to the extent that the educational system encourages the acquisition of more and more knowledge over an ever shrinking range, it tends to disarm the student and the young worker.

Tasks that involve a high level of expertise are rarely located in a broader social context, either in the educational system or in the world of work. Technocratic education is an organic part of a technocratic society and contributes to the increasing fragmentation of social life. No one builds a nuclear weapon. Rather, people develop sophisticated forms of knowledge to be used in a very specific way so that it constitutes a fragment in the *process* of the construction of a nuclear weapon. In his study of top corporation executives, Michael Maccoby[4] reports that it was not unusual to find executives expressing concern for the quality of the environment while working for a corporation that directly contributed to pollution. They simply failed to connect their daily work life with environmental problems.

[4] Michael Maccoby, *The Gamesman* (New York: Simon and Schuster, 1976).

Let us now consider the second tenet of the conventional wisdom, the belief that an important function of education is to promote intellectual, psychic, and moral growth. If this belief were a reality, perhaps it would be possible after all for education to serve social progress—although probably not progress conceived in terms implied by the first tenet. Once again there is anecdotal support for this contention. It is possible to find instances in which personal growth has been stimulated by education. Most teachers who take seriously their obligations in the classroom can recall times when a student was provoked by a lecture, an after-class conversation, or a particular book. Such cases are exhilirating enough to sustain teachers for years, and an accumulation of such events can lead students to a deeper understanding of themselves and of the world around them.

The problem with this is betrayed by its formulation: teachers can recall such instances of increased growth. They don't happen that often and they are overwhelmed by the large numbers of students who seem to drift through school. Furthermore, the structure of schooling is such that it reduces the likelihood that personal growth experiences will occur. Large classes, rotating students, rigid schedules, and distance between faculty and students, all serve to inhibit these events.

The second tenet is further undermined by the history of public education. Public schools were not established nor were they cultivated to be means of personal growth and liberation. The idea, so prevalent today, that schooling would free people from the social bonds in which they were held, was simply not part of nineteenth-century consciousness. Indeed, freedom could not be a solution because it was considered by most education reformers to be the crux of the problem. Children, especially those of the growing lower class, were thought to have too much freedom. An ethical sense congenial to the developing industrial order needed to be implanted in these children so they might become "reliable" citizens. The cultivation of cognitive skills as ends in themselves was far less important than the implantation of dependable social attitudes. This can be seen in the public rationale offered by reformers for general education, in the social and economic groups that rallied behind the system of universal and compulsory education, and in the content of the textbooks.

Often the term industrial revolution is used casually. The change in patterns of human interaction brought about by industrial development in the nineteenth century *was* a revolution. People do not naturally arise at daybreak to spend ten to twelve hours a day doing something they do not enjoy. Nor, once such a pattern is developed, would they naturally continue it indefinitely. Workers at the outset of the industrial revolution were notoriously unreliable, often not showing up for work or quitting as soon as they had enough money to satisfy immediate needs. Such behavior made it difficult for others to get rich. The transformation of the masses into a working class was not received by workers in an outburst of spontaneous joy. Rather, it was forced upon them. In America, schools were regarded as a crucial mechanism in effecting this transformation.

Nineteenth-century school promoters believed that public education could address five major problems.[5] The first problem was urban crime and poverty, which had ceased to signify eccentric behavior and had come to be identified as a problem of social class. Crime and poverty were seen as moral problems demonstrating the failure of lower-class families. Second, cultural heterogeneity had increased significantly, making it more difficult to perpetuate a singular ethical view of society. Third, the urban work force was regarded by the elite as direly in need of training and discipline. Fourth, there was the emergent crisis of youth in the city. In pre-industrial times, life's activities had been clearly specified. This was no longer the case, and increasing numbers of young people were roaming urban streets. Finally, the middle class was anxious about its own children and how the transmission of its status could be assured. Education was regarded by the reformers as addressing each of these problems. Rhetoric about freedom and intellectual development, so commonplace in contemporary educational circles, was not articulated in the nineteenth century.

The nineteenth-century campaign for common schools was led by prominent educators such as Horace Mann, wealthy manufacturers such as Edmund Dwight, and prominent political Whigs like Daniel Webster, all of whom were concerned about the socially debilitating effects of creeping democracy.[6] It was one thing to be poor, but in the age of Andrew Jackson the poor had started to become politically active. This traumatized many "responsible" citizens. A widely held belief was that if poor people were placed in the right environment—specifically in schools—they could be molded into good citizens and dependable workers.

Workers were not enthusiastic about common schools. They did not regard them as a means of upward mobility. The immigrant Irish particularly saw them as a vehicle of cultural corruption and, indeed, the texts and curriculum were explicitly anti-Irish and anti-Catholic. The campaign for compulsory schooling in Chicago some 50 years later was similarly regarded by the ethnic groups of that city.[7] This understanding was well-grounded. The establishment view of teaching which confronted the workers is well-summarized by an article appearing in *The Massachusetts Teacher* in the 1850's:[8]

> With the old not much can be done; but with their children, the great remedy is education. The rising generation must be taught as our children are taught. We say *must be*, because in many cases this can only be accomplished by coercion. In too many instances the parents are unfit guardians of their own children. If left to their direction the young will be

[5]See Michael Katz, "The Origins of Public Education: A Reassessment," *History of Education Quarterly* 16 (1976), p. 381.

[6]David Nasaw, *Schooled to Order* (Fair Lawn: Oxford University Press, 1979).

[7]David Hogan, "Education and the Making of the Chicago Working Class, 1880–1930," *History of Education Quarterly* 18, 3, (Fall 1978).

[8]Quoted in Michael B. Katz, *School Reform: Past and Present* (Boston: Little, Brown, 1971), p. 170.

brought up in idle, dissolute, vagrant habits, which will make them worse members of society than their parents are; instead of filling our public schools, they will find their way into our prisons, houses of correction, and almshouses. Nothing can operate effectually here but stringent legislation, thoroughly carried out by an efficient police; the children must be gathered up and forced into school, and those who resist or impede this plan, whether parent, or *priests,* must be held accountable and punished.

At the turn of the century, the struggle over compulsory high schools and the centralization of school authority into "blue ribbon" boards of education was fought along lines similar to the common school struggles 50 years earlier. Child labor laws, urbanization and immigration accentuated the "youth problem" and once again schools were looked upon as a solution. Industrialists sought to establish vocational high schools for working-class children. This explicit attempt to sustain the existing social order was resisted by working-class parents—who desired upward mobility for their children—as well as by some educational reformers, most notably John Dewey and his followers. The result was the establishment of comprehensive high schools and the curricular tracking of students. This enabled the high school to do two things simultaneously which, at bottom, are contradictory. As David Nasaw reports:[9]

> . . . they had to maintain the appearance of the classless society in a new industrial order established on the separation of labor from capital; they had to maintain the pretense of unlimited upward mobility in a society where such movement was becoming much more the exception than the rule. In short, they had to preserve and present the myths of America to each new generation of Americans.

This review of the history of public schooling is not one which offers much support for the personal growth tenet of the conventional wisdom. It is possible, of course, that schools have outgrown their historical origins and that they have evolved into institutions basically concerned with personal growth. If we consider the day-to-day experience of schooling, this seems implausible. Schools tend to reward certain kinds of behavior in a manner not necessarily consistent with the personal growth tenet. In some cases, the reward structure seems geared to inhibiting personal growth.

There are interesting and significant relationships between personality traits and school grades, which would not surprise anyone who has survived an American high school. One study found that "Citizenship" and "Drive to Achieve" were positively associated with grades despite the fact that these two variables did not have a significant impact upon *actual* achievement scores.[10] Perhaps the most interesting parts of this analysis are the underlying measures for the two variables. Students who

---

[9]Nasaw, *Schooled to Order,* p. 155.

[10]Herbert Gintis, "Education, Technology and the Characteristics of Worker Productivity," *American Economic Review,* (May 1971). The Gintis work dealt mainly with a sample of merit scholars.

are ranked by their teachers as high on "Citizenship" and "Drive to Achieve" score high on such measures as perservance, control, deferred gratification, social leadership, and popularity. They ranked significantly below the sample average on such measures as cognitive flexibility, complexity of thought, originality, creativity, and independence of judgment, despite the fact that these traits are basic to personal growth.

It has been argued that the school's purpose is to thwart personal growth, not encourage it. Jules Henry,[11] for example, suggests that the school metamorphoses the child, forming the kind of self the school can manage, then ministering to the self the school has made. This is overstated. Schools encourage metamorphosis, but they cannot ensure it. There is a sense, however, in which this observation has merit. Within the school setting, educational issues are regularly defined in terms congenial to institutional authority. When a child fails to learn, is disruptive, or otherwise fails to conform to the norms of the educational institution, the institution responds by attempting to discern what the "child's" problems might be, not the school's.

There is a sense of givenness about schools which leads to the systematic distortion of such situations. In fact, the child's problem may be the institution itself, or some part of it; but even when children are alert enough to articulate such grievances, they are usually redefined in a manner that deflects criticism. For example, the professionalization of the school counseling system has led to particular clinical interpretations of nonclinical problems. A bored child may be defined as restless or hyperactive. Boredom suggests institutional problems, while hyperactivity suggests child-centered problems. A failing child is not usually asked about the attractiveness of the curriculum or the competence of the teacher. He or she is asked about the quality of home life or other personal questions. If some personal problem is discovered, as it inevitably will be, the child's failure is attributed to that. The school continues to be construed as the beacon of hope for the child. At the same time, it teaches children to control boredom—or at least not to let it appear in the form of antisocial behavior.

One of the most consistent themes to emerge in an interesting survey of the history of high-school civics textbooks is the total absence of any encouragement of a critical perspective.[12] Given the history of schooling in America and the purposes for which it was developed, this is hardly surprising. That high-school students are not encouraged to think about social matters is clearly evident. For the teacher, of course, there are some risks involved in entering into controversial discourse. Here we are not thinking simply of the risk of being considered a "subversive" in the community at large. Controversial topics can undermine the authority of the teacher in the classroom if students hold strong contrary views. Better to have students asleep than raging. It is at the college level where some critical perspective begins to emerge.

[11]Jules Henry, *Culture Against Man* (New York:Random House, 1965), Ch. 8.
[12]Frances Fitzgerald, *America Revised* (Boston: Little, Brown, 1979).

There are significant political consequences to this fact. Those whose educational careers terminate with or before high school graduation, those whose fate it is to fill the lowest levels of our job hierarchy and to be disproportionately located on welfare rolls, those who might be expected to have the clearest grievances against the social order are precisely those who are actively discouraged from independent thought and action. That this control is indirect, covert, and not explicit makes it no less insidious. On the other hand, those who are given serious intellectual encouragement tend to later hold higher-level jobs in the occupational hierarchy and, therefore, are more likely to have a concrete interest in its durability. Intellectual curiosity is encouraged in our safest children, those who have not experienced social degradation and injustice firsthand. The absence of this experience enables even well-meaning students to adopt a casualness toward public matters which is belied by social reality.

It is possible to argue that the distinction between freedom and rule imposition merely reflects maturational levels (an intensely value-laden term—obedient people are often thought of as "mature") or the difference between compulsory and noncompulsory education, but there also exists interesting differences *between* institutions of higher education. One analysis of college handbooks of over 50 schools, ranging from community colleges to elite universities, found clear distinctions according to the social class groups served by the specific institutions.[13] High-status institutions allowed more student freedom in a variety of ways, while low-status institutions were more oriented towards the imposition of rules. The concern for training working class students, so obvious in the early days of the public school movement, is still evident throughout our educational system, albeit in more subtle form.

We believe that it is the third tenet of the conventional wisdom which the schools perform most completely: they integrate us into society. They are not completely successful in this, of course, because individual experiences range far beyond the classroom. Nevertheless, it is this tenet which is most consistent with the statistical and historical evidence we used in considering the first two tenets of the conventional wisdom. We shall consider how this process works by examining the ways in which schools prepare us for work and the ways they prepare us to enter consumer society.

In 1954, the National Manpower Council made the connections between school and work explicit:[14] "The school enforces a regular schedule by setting hours of

---

[13]Jeanne Binstock, "Survival in the American College Industry," unpublished Ph.D. dissertation, Brandeis University, 1970, quoted in Bowles and Gintis, *Schooling in Capitalist America.*

[14]Quoted in Christopher Lasch, *The Culture of Narcissism* (New York: W.W. Norton, 1978), p. 138.

arrival and attendance; assigns tasks that must be completed; rewards diligence, responsibility, and ability; corrects carelessness and ineptness; encourages ambition." It is clear that many of the routines of schooling parallel those of the workplace. The school seeks to instill "workmanlike attitudes" in the student, and students who turn in assignments regularly are said to have good work habits. We call away-from-school assignments homework. But schools do not teach us to value work, or to seek personally rewarding work. They teach us only to work. When people think about work, therefore, they think primarily of the financial return the work will bring.

In an intriguing way, the very boredom of schooling, the sense of alienation it instills in so many students, prepares them for the adult world. This is the second way in which schools prepare us for work. As we shall see in the next chapter, much of the work that awaits students upon graduation from high school or college is also boring. This leads to a persistent displacement of satisfaction from life's preoccupying tasks. Students endure the boredom of schooling because they expect it to lead to more lucrative work. When they enter the work force and find it also boring, they use their money in a futile effort to find fulfillment in consumer society.

Finally, schools encourage students to think about education in terms of jobs. Universities are subjected constantly to criticisms that they need to "train people better" for the available work. They are regarded by many as little more than elaborate personnel agencies.

By the freshman year in high school students think of their educational decisions as having grave consequences for their lives. Courses are selected, grades sought, and clubs are joined in order to facilitate entry to the next level, whereupon the process is repeated. Schools answer the instrumental and mechanical questions of life—for example, telling students what to do in order to become a doctor. But for the student who is perplexed by the deeper questions that confront us all—for example, how ought one to live a life—there is likely to be only silence. That parents encourage the instrumental aspects of schooling does not justify the situation. Rather, it is an indication of the extent of the malaise.

Cicourel and Kitsuse noticed this process in their study of a Chicago area high school, and they muse about its consequences:[15]

> It is the college-going student more than his noncollege-going peer who is continually reminded by teachers, counselor, parents, and peers of the decisive importance of academic achievement to the realization of his ambitions and who becomes progressively committed to this singular standard of self-evaluation. He becomes the future-oriented student interested in a delimited occupational specialty, with little time to give thought to the present or to question the implications of his choice and the meaning of his strivings.

[15] Aaron Cicourel and John Kitsuse, *The Educational Decision-Makers* (Indianapolis: Bobbs-Merrill, 1963), p. 146.

. . . We are concerned, however, that the organizational emphasis upon talent and the pursuit of narrow specialties virtually ignores the significance of adolescence as a period during which individuals may explore the alternatives of personal style, interests and identity.

Schools are frequently criticized for the continuing decline in national achievement scores. This anxiety exists because concrete achievement is typically regarded as the gateway to success in our society. It may be, however, that schools are serving existing society all too well and that high *average* achievement levels are not only not important, but are dysfunctional. The workaday world is markedly hierarchical and unequal. Most paid workers exist in the corporate or public sectors of the economy. Both these sectors are noted for their hierarchical organizational forms. Hierarchy not only assumes inequality, but, by definition, provides only a few opportunities at the top. Moreover, the world of work is increasingly fragmented and specialized, as technology generates ever greater job elaboration.

One usually thinks of increasing technological sophistication as requiring increasing levels of education but this is true for only a narrow range of jobs. As jobs become more technologically elaborated, the skills necessary for their adequate performance become more narrowly focused, and education, in any conventional sense of that term, less relevant. Christopher Lasch believes that the general decline in computational skills and levels of literacy is indicative of their declining social significance.[16] Schools train people largely for work, but since most jobs are routine, they require only marginal levels of intellectual competence. There is much weeping, wailing, and gnashing of teeth among educational leaders about the lower levels of achievement on standard examinations. These incantations are not taken seriously, however because, if they were, achievement levels would be raised. When intellectual achievement is considered to be a serious problem, we are able, as with the space program, to produce results with astonishing speed. The fact is, most people already are overqualified for the positions available to them.

Consider the "problem" of illiteracy. It is not some mysterious and incomprehensible social problem that we are unable to solve. We know how to teach people to read. When Richard Nixon announced the establishment of the Right to Read program with much fanfare—it included the personal involvement of Mrs. Pat Nixon—he was going through a ritual. The program was totally symbolic and involved no special commitment, either in effort or in funds. If illiteracy were a serious social problem, that is, serious to those with political power, it would be eliminated.

Schools not only integrate us into society by preparing us for work, they also encourage, both directly and indirectly, the acceptance of the values of consumer society. The direct relationships between school and societal norms—the cultivation

---

[16]Lasch, *The Culture of Narcissism,* p. 126.

of competition, radical individualism, instilling self-doubt, the explicit promotion of consumerism—are fairly clear and do not need comment. The *indirect* promotion of the consumer society is less apparent however, and so we shall briefly sketch some of its dimensions. Consider this observation of Jules Henry:[17]

> . . . our children get the best education compatible with a society that requires a high level of stupidity in order to exist as it is. A moment's reflection will convince anyone that this is true. For example, if television had a truly well-educated audience and the newspapers and magazines well-educated readers, the economy would collapse because, since nobody would then be impressed by the advertising, they would not buy. Adults who had been trained by clearheaded, sharp-brained teachers . . . might . . . begin to question the need for a standard of living that has spread wall-to-wall carpeting from here to California and given millions more space and more mobility than they can intelligently use. In the light of these terrifying possibilities the thought of an education in depth and sharpness for everybody can only make a thoughtful person anxious, because an education for stupidity is the only one we can afford right now.

Professor Henry is an angry man. Perhaps he is not correct in every detail, but we support the gist of his argument. There is a deeply engrained strain of anti-intellectual values in our educational system. These values indirectly promote the consumer society because they disarm students. They diminish students' critical capacities and, therefore, increase their vulnerability. One does not expect much intellectuality in elementary school, of course, and although sometimes excused at the high school level, the dearth of intellectual activity there is less defensible. What is interesting is the predominance of anti-intellectual values in university life. Anti-intellectualism is a logical outcome of many of the characteristics of schooling we have discussed thus far. Since education is widely regarded as instrumental, why should not the point be to complete it with as little effort as possible?

Anti-intellectual sentiment is evident at the first day of class registration. Consider the values that determine course selection for so many students. The more prominent ones include selecting courses that will not disrupt the student's social schedule; selecting courses that do not require papers; selecting courses with minimal required reading; choosing professors who are supposedly easy graders; selecting classes in which exams only require memorization, not thought.

Once in class, these values continue unabated. Questions like "How long does the paper have to be?", "Does it have to be typed?", "Is the book going to be on the exam?" are rivaled in their regularity only by the rising sun. It rarely occurs to students that they may read beyond the required assignments. Occasionally a student will ask if it is all right to incorporate some things learned in another class in a response to an essay question. Simply asking the question betrays the extent to which anti-intellectualism pervades university life. Students think of classes as

[17]Jules Henry, *Essays in Education* (New York: Penguin, 1977), p. 22.

discrete little packages of "knowledge" having, evidently, no relation to each other or to anything else. The irony is that students are well advised to ask such a question because some professors would regard the inclusion of non-course material as illegitimate!

The memorable aspects of university life for most graduates consist largely of what are supposedly the diversions—for example, the time State beat Tech in the big game; the great frat party; the time Farnsworth singlehandedly consumed three sausage pizzas. It is rare to hear graduates speak of college in terms of a stimulating intellectual encounter with a professor or another student. Nor do graduates often talk about the vistas opened to them by Shakespeare, Marx, or Freud.

College teachers often complain that students lack creativity and are generally disinterested. Yet often their own lives are less than exemplary. Caught in the struggle for tenure, they spend most of their time conducting obscure research projects which are written up in the highly stylized and often impenetrable jargon professional journal editors typically confuse with erudition. Many are not really proud of this work. They may not even like to discuss it. They do it because they perceive it to be important to their careers. These publications may ensure tenure, but sometimes at the expense of good teaching. Teaching becomes an afterthought, the thing professors do after they have completed their more important obligations.

These observations are not made to poke fun either at college students or professors. Both are more victims than anything else. The attitudes we have discussed in the above paragraphs are simply adaptations that have been made to a corrupt educational system. Genuine education is liberating. It consistently questions the "givenness" of our heritage, and teaches us to think not only about what is, but also about what might be. It channels the inherent restlessness of the human spirit in personally and socially productive directions. Schooling in America does not approach this ideal. It is therefore inevitably and profoundly conservative. Lacking the critical and intellectual faculties necessary to assess consumer society, our response tends to be bewilderment. We may be dimly aware that something is wrong, but we are unable to articulate what it is. Our inability to generate an alternative vision consigns us to a reality that continues to damage us.

Any assessment of general trends in education tends to obscure significant variations, not only among schools and teachers but between children. Students are not equal in their ability to resist or to follow the school's lead. Peer groups and family are obvious and important independent sources of authority for the developing child. Most of the time they serve to reinforce the broad lessons taught by the school, but not always. In adolescence, the peer group can serve as a particularly exasperating counterweight to the school's authority. This is one reason that high school administrators work so assiduously to gain the loyalty of peer group leaders. Through a system of subtle rewards, athletes, cheerleaders, and other "student leaders" are coopted and become an important source of legitimacy for the school's authority.

Students by no means learn all that is taught, and of course they learn many things that are not taught. Because schools seek to inculcate dependence, it does not mean that all students accept their dependence. Yet it is difficult for even the brightest and most inventive students to thrive outside the school's realm of authority. Those who do will tend, like Carl Bernstein or Paul Simon, to look back upon schooling as a dismal period of their lives which is best forgotten. The important point is that schooling nurtures certain attitudes and encourages certain modes of behavior while it discourages others. Some may resist these pulls, but it is unlikely that they will do so without psychological and social costs.

CHAPTER 4

Work and the Sense of Self

Through want of enterprise and faith men are what they are, buying and selling and spending their lives like serfs.

H. D. Thoreau

In 1973 a special Department of Health, Education and Welfare task force published a major study on the nature of work in America.[1] In this study certain assumptions were made about the nature of work and these provide a useful benchmark for our discussion. The task force scholars assumed that people are inherently workers, that work is a distinguishing characteristic of the human species. As far back as we have evidence of human existence, we also have evidence of the human as worker. When anthropologists seek to determine whether a new find is a human community or that of some other form of primates, the presence of tools is a crucial type of evidence. The human species seems relentless in its intent to act upon its environment in some creative way.

Obviously, people work to sustain physical life, but work is much more than a necessity. It has been basic to establishing an identity, that is, it provides people with a sense of who they are. In colonial towns, simple symbols hung outside shops to identify the crafts. When strangers meet today, typically one of the earliest pieces of

---

[1] *Work in America: Report of a Special Task Force to the Secretary of Health, Education, and Welfare* (Cambridge: MIT Press, 1973).

information that is exchanged is the type of work each does. It is widely assumed, not always correctly, that to know the occupation is to know the person.

But what is work itself? The task force defined work as "an activity that produces something of value for other people." To this we would add that work is basic to the distributional process. A working person produces something that others are willing to acquire. The exchange makes it possible for the producer, in return, to acquire other goods or services. Work is an activity people decide to do to achieve certain ends.[2] Its directing mechanism is the power of conceptual thought. Humans are distinctive in their capacity to think in abstract and conceptual ways and to imagine the possibility of things being other than they are. In this sense, work is the special product of humankind. People can visualize the possibility of altering nature, and through the personal effort involved, enhance the value of what is produced.

If work is a special product of humankind, it is also true that humanity is affected by the relations emerging from the form of work. Society shapes work and is in turn shaped by it. Because the type of work one does indicates to others who one is, work is a principal component of personal evaluation. If work is an activity that produces something others value, then it contributes to our self-esteem. The sense of doing something for others helps one to feel good about oneself.

Work may contribute to self-esteem in other ways as well. It can impart a sense of mastery over oneself and at least a portion of one's environment. Participation in the basic decisions about what is produced, and how it is produced allows for the full play of human capacities. Control, participation, and usefulness all contribute to building self-esteem. In a broad sense they lend dignity to work. This is obviously an idealized vision of work, but ideals are essential to daily living since they provide the vision against which to assess the quality of everyday life.

It is understandable that work should be so important to us on a personal level, because it dominates adult life. Any time-consuming activity like work will inevitably affect self-evaluation. In college, the question of what to do with one's life assumes surpassing importance precisely because the issues of self-esteem and identity are tied to work. It is doubtful that any society has ever existed in which everyone had fully satisfying work. Beyond this limiting case, however, it is possible to consider whether, collectively, work has been more or less satisfying.

We believe that in modern America work is far less satisfying than it might realistically be, that work in this country damages people as much as it contributes to their self-esteem, and that this state of affairs has grave social and political consequences. For far too many people, work is a trap. Upon graduation from high school, college, or professional school, people often enter the world of work full of youthful exuberance. The argument of Carl Bernstein, which we quoted at the beginning of the last chapter, is taken seriously and people leave school thinking that, at last, they are "free." Too often this exuberance quickly fades as the reality of work

---

[2] Harry Braverman, *Labor and Monopoly Capital* (New York: Monthly Review Press, 1975).

presses down upon young workers. They find that work is not a means of self-expression. It is a grim necessity. What we wish to explore in this chapter is how and why this happens and to show the implications of the everyday world of work for political life.

We recognize that some people find work that is fully gratifying, and others may claim to be "happy in their work." We do not wish to minimize the significance of the extraordinary inventiveness of some people in bringing some dignity to unlikely work situations. Such instances exemplify the resilience of the human spirit. They are remarkable precisely because, given the conditions of work, they are unexpected.

The specific comments that are made about work in this chapter are directed toward work in corporate America, for we believe it is the corporation that largely controls the nature of work in our society. This is obvious at the core of the economy, but this core is expanding outward at a rapid pace. In the competitive sector, mom-and-pop operations are being swallowed or destroyed by conglomerates and franchises. As this happens the conditions of work characteristic of the corporate sector will increasingly be evident in the small competitive sector as well.

We do not comment directly on the nature of public employment even though numerically a significant number of people are involved in this type of work. We believe any differences existing between the work life of the public and private sectors are differences of degree, not of kind. Like the corporate sector, public work life is dominated by hierarchy and division of labor. Although public employees do enjoy more security than workers in the private sector, alienation is still deep and pervasive there.

Our position is that the state is essentially an appendage of the corporate sector.[3] Workers in the public sector are involved largely in two broad tasks. The first is to dole out money directly to corporations in the forms of contracts. All major departments at every level of government are significantly involved in this task. The second is to transfer some of the costs incurred by private corporations to the public sector and to correct for the "excesses" of capitalism. The building of roads, unemployment and workmen's compensation, job training, environmental cleanup operations, research and development, and preparing Americans to fight for corporate interests abroad are only a few of the more obvious examples of this phenomenon. Both of these broad functions are derivative. They serve to shore up the capitalist system, not to offer alternatives to it. As a consequence, we believe that genuine changes in the conditions of work must begin in the private sector.

Because work is fundamentally related to self-esteem it is a political issue—political in the sense that it involves the distribution of social values. What is remarkable in our society is that work is not on the political agenda. The control of the

[3]See James O'Connor, *The Fiscal Crisis of the State* (New York: St. Martins, 1973) and Ralph Miliband, *The State In Capitalist Society* (New York: Basic Books, 1978), for elaborations on these themes.

work process remains basically in the hands of those who reap enormous economic benefit at the expense of the degradation of the many. Although work is perhaps the arena of most extensive social interaction, the work process is considered "private." When students think about what they are going to do with their lives, they think about what is meaningful, useful, and gratifying far less than they think about what is available. A student who is thrilled and challenged by English literature may nevertheless suffer the drudgery of majoring in business because of the promise of a job upon graduation. It never occurs to that student to challenge the values implicit in that decision. The student knows that "nothing can be done" with an English major, but rarely stops to consider why.

THE REALITY OF WORK: WORK AND SATISFACTION

It is true that when most Americans are asked in surveys whether they are satisfied with their work, they respond that they are. We doubt the capacity of surveys to convey much about the real meaning of job satisfaction except possibly for comparing responses over time. Survey responses may only reflect the fact that most Americans have developed a wide tolerance for demeaning work or that their current job is not very different from any other realistic choices that they have. Workers may say they are "satisfied" with their work if they simply perceive it as steady work. One can hardly imagine, for example, people who were employed during the depression reporting that they were not satisfied with their job.

There is considerable impressionistic evidence that work in contemporary America is unsatisfying. Most people do not like to talk about their work. "Leaving the work at the office" is often regarded as a sign of mental health. However, it is increasingly clear that, in order to reduce the damage that work does to personal lives, people are segmenting their lives, giving to work the absolute minimum that is possible, then trying to forget about it during the remaining portion of the day. We believe people need to integrate experience and that segmentation contributes to psychological stress. Stand outside any factory gate or office building at 4:30 PM or 5:00 PM and notice how the people exit from work. Notice the mad scramble to get away from work. It is not an accident that bars across America have designated the 5:00 PM to 7:00 PM time period as "Happy Hours."

Evidence of deep hostility to work is abundant in the popular culture. The popular success of movies like "Nine to Five" and "Take This Job and Shove It" are obvious examples. What is most interesting about these films is the *audience reaction* to the work rebellion scenes contained in them. When the secretaries in "Nine to Five" have dreams of revenge against their bosses and when the young executive rebels against the corporate structure in "Take This Job and Shove It," the audience becomes ecstatic. The unbridled glee shows clearly that they strongly identify with the protagonists in the film.

Studs Terkel's remarkable collection of interviews with people from all walks of working life provides further impressionistic evidence that work is less than fully satisfying.[4] In interview after interview, people speak of degraded lives. Steelworker Mike LeFevre: "The first thing that happens at work; when the arms start moving the brain stops." Bob Sanders, strip miner: "There's a lot of things I don't like about my work. I've never really appreciated seeing ground tore up. Especially if that ground could be made into something." Frank Decker, trucker: "Went home for a day of sleep . . . live like a human being for a day . . . and be off again." Maggie Holmes, domestic: "When it come to housework, I can't do it now. I can't stand it, cause it do something to my mind." Larry Ross, executive: "Fear is always prevalent in the corporate structure . . . you've got to fit in the mold. You've got to be on guard."

Often even people who report that they like their jobs in the Terkel interviews display attitudes that reveal ambiguity. Anne Bogan, executive secretary: "I feel like I'm sharing somewhat of the business life of the men. [I am] an extension of a successful executive. I'm perfectly happy in my status." Johnny Bosworth, car salesman: "I like my work. I have to like it, I must like it. . . . If you're not happy, you can't sell. You have to be ready: Let's sell, sell, sell. You're all gung ho."

Reading these interviews is a moving experience and Terkel came away from the project with distinct impressions about work in America. In his introduction he writes:

> This book, being about work, is, by its very nature, about violence—to the spirit as well as to the body. It is about ulcers as well as accidents, about shouting matches as well as fistfights, about nervous breakdowns as well as kicking the dog around. It is, above all (or beneath all), about daily humiliations. To survive the day is triumph enough for the walking wounded among the great many of us.

Perhaps Terkel exaggerates his point. Work is certainly about more than violence. We have no doubt, however, that his commentary is fundamentally correct in one sense. The people interviewed by Terkel demonstrate with unmistakable clarity the connections between the daily experience of work and attitudes about the world around them. People may try to block out work from their consciousness, but they are inevitably affected. The process of blocking out itself builds resentment.

For years the U.S. Bureau of Labor Statistics has compiled information on job satisfaction based on the question, "How satisfied are you with your job?" Between 1958 and 1977 there was no change in response to this question. People generally responded that they were satisfied. In 1969, however, the Survey Research Center at the University of Michigan began asking the public a series of more specific job satisfaction questions. From these questions researchers have been able to measure job satisfaction more precisely.[5] These reports show that job satisfaction declined

---

[4]Studs Terkel, *Working* (New York: Pantheon Books, 1974).

[5]Graham L. Staines and Robert P. Quinn, "American Workers Evaluate the Quality of their Jobs," *Monthly Labor Review*, January 1979.

between 1969 and 1973, and declined further still by 1977. The decline in job satisfaction has been pervasive, with nearly all demographic and occupational groups tested showing some drop. Among the various educational groupings, those with a college degree suffered the largest drop in satisfaction.

It must be stressed that these studies were taken from a compressed time period—less than a decade. It is impossible to say that these changes in attitude resulted solely from the changing nature of work. Work was not transformed between 1969 and 1977. On the other hand attitudes have not been transformed either. They have changed in degree. But limited as these reports are, they do lend credence to the theoretical argument that the work place in this century is in the process of being transformed, and this transformation is not positive. This is an argument that will be considered shortly.

TOWARD A MIDDLE-CLASS SOCIETY?

Before this argument is taken up, however, we should consider another more widely accepted and benign assessment of the transformation of work. A commonly held view is that work is being transformed positively in response to technological innovation. As our society becomes more technologically complex, there is a need for a commensurate increase in skills. Our prime social need is for workers trained to perform various intricate and complex operations. One reason for the dramatic increase in college-trained people, this argument runs, is that they are required.

With this transformation America has become a middle-class society. The proportion of middle-class or white-collar jobs increases at the expense of working-class or blue collar jobs. Through this process, more and more people will come to realize the American Dream, which will eventually become a reality for the majority of American citizens.

A further aspect of the University of Michigan study undermines this point of view. Workers increasingly report that the skills required for their current jobs would be useless in five years and also that they have other skills that they are unable to use in their present jobs. (It is important to remember that the report compares different time periods. For example, in 1973 27 percent of the respondents claimed their skills were underutilized. In 1977 36 percent of the respondents made the same claim.) These data suggest that the American workers may be caught in a double bind: They are becoming increasingly educated for work that requires less skill.

Members of the work force do not feel the demand for increased skill. Furthermore, the evidence which is usually offered to support the growing middle-class theory is questionable. It is true that the middle-class is increasing in size, if one takes seriously the manner in which Americans identify themselves. Far more than citizens of other Western industrialized nations, Americans are apt to identify themselves as members of the middle class in response to questions on the subject. Such responses are problematic, however, because they may reflect an absence of class *consciousness,* not actual class standing. Americans habitually call themselves middle class even if they perform menial tasks. While absence of class consciousness is in itself important politically, it does not necessarily help us understand the reality of work in twentieth-century America.

It is also true that real wages have increased in this century. At the same time the proportion of white collar workers has increased dramatically, although this increase has not precipitated a decrease in the proportion of blue-collar workers. The growth in white-collar work has come mainly at the expense of agriculture. In 1900 about 38 percent of the labor force was in agriculture while in 1974 about 3 percent of the labor force was so employed.[6] Is this evidence of a growing middle class?

The answer to this question will in part depend upon what one means by the term middle class. If one means relative material affluence and not working with one's hands, then perhaps it can be argued that the middle class has increased. Historically, the term middle class has implied much more than this. The operating distinctiveness, what made the achievement of middle class so desirable, was personal autonomy and skill. The middle class has traditionally been dominated by those occupational categories, (small business owners, proprietors, and some professionals) that enjoyed relative autonomy regardless of income. An important reason for this autonomy was the capacity, through training, experience, or both, to do things few others could do. Therefore it is important to know whether the growth in white collar employees can be traced to occupations which yield such autonomy.

Information on occupational categories since the turn of the century suggest that we cannot identify the increase in white-collar workers with an increase in middle-class status in the historic sense of that term. Although the proportion of white-collar workers has almost tripled in this century, to about 48 percent of the labor force, the largest single increase is attributable to clerical workers. In 1900 this group comprised 3 percent of the labor force. Today about one in five workers is so classified, and the *Occupational Outlook Handbook* estimates that by 1990 22.5 percent of the labor force will be white-collar clerical workers.

There has also been a substantial increase in the proportion of managers (from 6 percent to 10 percent) and in the proportion of professional, technical, and kindred workers (from 5 percent to 15 percent). The latter category has been somewhat inflated because some occupational groups have actively sought professional status. In 1900 morticians were not considered professionals. Today they are. Other significant changes have occurred in sales and service occupations.

Although the white-collar middle class has been greatly inflated by the factors just discussed, there has also been some growth in traditional white-collar occupations. Yet it is important to understand that the character of the work in these

---

[6]The ensuing data are taken from two sources: George Ritzer, *Working: Conflict and Change* (Englewood Cliffs: Prentice-Hall, 1977), p. 14, and *The Occupational Outlook Handbook, 1980–1981* (Washington, D.C.: U.S. Government Printing Office), pp. 20–23.

areas has undergone dramatic transformation. Independent lawyers, doctors, and accountants still exist, but increasingly these skills are put to use within the framework of large organizations. Although they are paid better and enjoy many more perquisites than their working-class counterparts, the increment of autonomy enjoyed by these employees is marginal, if it exists at all. Similarly, the small, independent business owner comprises a diminishing proportion of the work force. To make it in business these days, young people typically acquire MBA's and then seek out positions at the lower levels of large corporations.

In Chapter 3 we discussed a major dilemma of American education. To sustain the pretense of egalitarianism, the education system must appear to be open and fair. At the same time it is clear that the system is turning out too many educated people for the challenging positions available. This may be one of the more significant causes of job dissatisfaction. One of the biggest declines in the satisfaction index discussed above was in the job challenge measure. It is certainly not true that our society is producing college graduates to meet the demands of an increasingly complex society. The Department of Health, Education and Welfare task force on work reported that, "The expansion of professional, technical and clerical jobs absorbed only 15 percent of newly educated workers; the remaining 85 percent accepted jobs previously performed by individuals with fewer credentials."[7] Ironically, this may intensify the struggle for credentials, for as the college graduate penetrates the occupations where such training is unnecessary, those without credentials are faced with greater obstacles to employment and advancement. Unemployment begets underemployment.

We do not believe that existing evidence supports the notion that America is increasingly becoming a middle-class society—at least in any meaningful sense of that term. In fact we propose a contrary hypothesis: that traditionally white-collar occupations are assuming more and more characteristics of the working class. We believe that this transformation not only can be demonstrated but that it also helps explain the increasing sense of dissatisfaction and even desperation about work in America.

THE TRANSFORMATION OF WORK: THE TRADITIONAL WORKING CLASS

Let us think of working-class characteristics as more or less the reverse of those of the traditional middle class. A working-class occupation requires little skill. The particular work involved may take some training but that training can be compressed into a relatively short period. The span of control that the individual worker has over the work process is quite narrow. Such workers are not autonomous. Their lack of distinctiveness makes them more dependent upon the capitalist for work because it is apparent that they can be easily replaced.

[7]*Work in America*, p. 135.

In working-class occupations, the ideology of F.W. Taylor reigns triumphant. Taylor, an early twentieth-century psychologist of sorts, was interested in increasing the "efficiency" of work. He believed labor owed to management "a fair day's work" which he defined as all that is physiologically possible at a pace that can be sustained throughout one's lifetime. Taylor sought to eliminate all "excess" activity of the worker and undertook a series of time-and-motion studies to achieve that end. These studies exist as monuments of detail. The work of a machinist, for example, was broken into a series of movements including such things as stooping, picking up tools of varying sizes, placing them into position, turning them, and so forth. Out of these studies, Taylor developed his specifications for a fair day's work. The idea was to make the worker as efficient as the machines he tended.

Given Taylor's insensitivity to human beings, one might well ask why he was taken seriously at all. For Taylor, turning people into robots represented scientific achievement. And yet he was taken seriously. He was a frequent counselor to management and a recognized expert in Washington, D.C. It is the reigning business ethic which bestows legitimacy upon Taylor's theory. When the work process is conceived largely as a problem of control, that is, when it is seen through the eyes of management, Taylorism seems plausible.

Taylor was never able to install his scientific management system in any major operating business organization. His white-coated operatives were greeted with the open hostility of workers. Taylorism provided a very clear picture of labor relations as seen from a management perspective, and so resistance to it tended to undermine control. It is not accidental that Taylorism and radical unionism (the type of unionism that challenged the notion of management control) occurred in the same historic period.

Although Taylorism failed as a social movement, important aspects of its ideology survive to inform management relations today. Its legacy can be seen directly in the relations of work. There has been an increasing reliance on technical expertise, efficiency experts, and task division. Job specifications, including standards of adequate performance, can be directly traced to Taylorism as well.

What is significant about the movement, however, is that it was explicitly rejected by management as formal ideology. It was too disruptive. Thus, to avoid serious disruptions, management may place limits upon the division of labor. This helps to explain the interest of some firms in job enrichment, enlargement, and rotation. This has been called by some "management with a human face," but recent articles in trade publications reveal the true motives of these efforts. Consider the titles of three articles:[8] "Combining Job Enrichment and Efficiency for More Productive Workers," "Job Enrichment for Profit," and "Job Enrichment: How to

---

[8] "Combining Job Enrichment and Efficiency for More Productive Workers," *Management Review*, August 1978; "Job Enrichment for Profit," *Human Resource Management*, Spring 1979; and "Job Enrichment: How to Get Your Employees to Work for You," *Hospital Financial Management*, November 1978.

Get Your Employees to Work for You.'' The idea that people ought to have decent work because they are human beings does not receive much attention. ''Enrichment'' programs are in fact one indication of the extent to which elements of Taylorism have penetrated the work place.

It is well known that traditionally working class occupations have been subjected to the ''deskilling'' process in this century. The rise of the assembly line is only the most obvious example of this process. In occupation after occupation it is apparent. It can be readily seen in the construction industry, in beauty salons, in mining, in automobile maintenance and repair, in the textile industry, and throughout the working-class occupations of the industrial sector of our economy. The major impetus for this movement toward deskilling is that it decreased the value of labor and thus increased profit potential.

Classical economists argue that decreasing the value of labor also serves to lessen the price of products in a competitive market, and that this process is therefore highly efficient. But with the rise of oligopolistic power, particularly at the core of the economy, theoretical arguments about price competition are not particularly relevant. Moreover, this type of reasoning requires a rather strange construing of the meaning of efficient. The question, ''Efficient at what?'' must be posed. Even granting the assumption that decreasing labor value lowers prices and is therefore efficient to that end, it must be asked whether lowered prices so obtained supercede other social goals. If, as we contend, people gain a significant portion of their self-esteem and identity through work, then lowering the value of labor also lowers the value of people. The economic efficiency model triumphs at the cost of human degradation. Efficient in in some ways perhaps, the model is very inefficient in the production of values (such as human dignity and happiness) that do not find their way onto corporate production costs sheets.

Anyone who has worked in a factory could not miss the degradation and genuine human waste that exists there. Richard Pfeffer, a political scientist who assumed a false identity to work in a factory for a year, has recently recorded and reflected upon his experiences.[9] He argues that a sense of degradation, fragmentation, and isolation is basic to the industrial process and is directly linked to the division of labor and the deskilling process.

For Pfeffer, the process of degradation began when he was looking for work, as he realized how unnecessary he was and that there were hundred of others who were competing directly with him. Once employed, he describes how quickly the job comes to dominate the worker. The fragmented and repetitious nature of work is overwhelming. Moreover, workers are so divided that they often see other workers as their enemies. Anger toward the production process itself is deflected in the daily life of the factory. Taking pride in one's work or doing a good job is ridiculous under the circumstances, so workers seek just to get by. Two rules seem paramount for survival: don't make waves and avoid all plant leaders.

[9]Richard Pfeffer, *Working for Capitalism* (New York: Columbia University Press, 1977).

THE TRANSFORMATION OF WORK: THE MIDDLE-CLASS SLIDE

One might accept the argument to this point as a lamentable but nevertheless diminishing side effect of developing capitalism. It is possible at least, that as capitalism matures and as our economy diversifies a decreasing proportion of the population will be subject to the labor process just described. In fact, the opposite seems closer to the truth. More and more of the work of the middle class appears to be falling under the sway of what we have called working-class characteristics. Harry Braverman[10] has done the most extensive analysis of this process.

Braverman argues that a fundamental, unique, and distinctive characteristic of work is that it is a conscious and purposive activity. Because humans can think conceptually, work is possible. Work involves both conception and execution, but this unity can be dissolved. For Braverman, the history of capitalist development is the story of this dissolution. Originally, manual laborers were separated from conceptual thinking. Other occupations of the traditional working class quickly followed. Now that process can be seen in middle-class occupations, as work life in this sector becomes increasingly fragmented and degraded. When work becomes "rationalized" into concrete operations, it becomes less autonomous, and the worker becomes more dependent. A growing proportion of the "middle layers" of the work force finds itself working for the interests of capital in exactly the same sense that the factory worker does, and such workers are therefore subject to the same processes. Braverman's examination of the development of various middle-class occupations in this century supports this argument. It is extensively illustrated in service, trade, and clerical occupations. We shall discuss this process in terms of developments in the computer field, supposedly one of the glamour industries of modern life.[11]

Throughout the 1960s, the computer industry was widely cited as an indication that the labor force was being upgraded. Many authorities believed this industry decisively demonstrated that technology would inevitably pull a growing portion of the working class into the middle class. Most of the new jobs in this field were classified as technical and professional and in fact required considerable skill.

The computer industry had a glamorous aura, and was commonly seen to be on the cutting edge of change. Salaries were high and, commensurate with our traditional definition of the middle class, computer technicians enjoyed considerable freedom and mobility. Originally there were three basic classes of technical workers in this field: operators, who ran the machines; programmers, who instructed the machines; and technicians, who repaired the machines. Despite this formal division, in practice the workers themselves typically overlapped in their tasks, often making their jobs larger than they appeared to be.

Managers in this industry were in a disadvantaged position, because they needed the technicians more than vice versa. Complaints were heard in management

---

[10]Braverman, *Labor and Monopoly Capital,* especially chapters 15–18.

[11]This account is taken from Joan Greenbaum, "Division of Labor in the Computer Field," *Monthly Review,* July–August 1976.

circles about "the loss of management control" in data-processing functions. Additionally, there was an increasing demand for more complex machines to process larger amounts of information. The IBM 360, introduced between 1965 and 1970, solved both these problems. From the workers perspective, the emergence of this computer made possible the division of labor. Analytical tasks were separated from those that required only translation into programming, and systems analysts were separated from programmers.

The process of sorting out the repetitious tasks from analytic ones continued for the next ten years. Programming jobs have been divided and divided again. Skill has been concentrated in as few hands as possible. Four levels of programming languages were developed, and a clear hierarchical structure emerged in the industry. This deskilling has been accompanied by a lowering of educational requirements for work, and an oversupply of workers. University graduates in computer science flooded the market and many have been forced to take work that is far below the level at which they have been trained. Except for a very few exceptional programmers in the industry, that work is now routine. Most computer programmers are not members of the middle class in any meaningful sense of that term. They may not work with their hands, but they do not work with their heads either.

Terkel's interviews with working people form all walks of life provide striking confirmation for the more abstract and theoretical arguments of Braverman. In his introduction he writes:

> The blue-collar blues is no more bitterly sung than in the white-collar moan. "I'm a machine," says the spotwelder. "I'm caged," says the bank teller, and echoes the hotel clerk. "I'm a mule," says the steelworker. "A monkey can do what I do," says the receptionist. "I'm less than a farm implement," says the migrant worker. "I'm an object," says the high fashion model. Blue-collar and white call upon the identical phrase: "I'm a robot," *"There is nothing to talk about,"* the young accountant despairingly enunciates.

The deskilling process cannot permeate the entire organization. The upper reaches of a large and complex organization are especially difficult to fragment into routine behavior because it is at this level that organizations seek to handle novelty, unanticipated events, and broken down routines. Top level management will certainly maintain a significant span of control. It would be a mistake to assume that the work life of those holding such positions automatically generates personal self-esteem, autonomy, and control, however, because recent studies of top managers suggest that frequently these are the very qualities that must be given up as the price for gaining power. It is a major organizational conundrum: People seek upward mobility to gain autonomy. As they move up, however, they must cede ever more of their personal autonomy to the corporation. Ultimately they may gain considerable power, but this gain is achieved on the organization's terms, not their own.

Because the work of top management cannot be routinized, a level of discretion, often associated with autonomy, is inherent in it. This introduces into the organization a certain amount of uncertainty, which one researcher calls *the* fundamental problem for complex organizations.[12] To reduce this uncertainty, organizational leaders seek to recruit and train predictable and trustworthy top managers. Social homogeneity serves as an important bond of trust. Organizational leaders seek to ensure that "the right sort of person" reaches the positions involving personal discretion. This pressure is put to double service, because in determining that people like themselves reach the top, organizational leaders not only yield authority more easily, they become more convinced that their kind *deserve* authority.

One way to test for trustworthiness is to build a management ethos that asks for total devotion. It is a commonplace observation that those interested in getting ahead are often consumed by their work. There is nothing wrong with this if one finds the work intrinsically interesting, but the evidence is that this is not usually the case. People typically work long hours because they think it will help them get ahead.[13]

Since there is an element of uncertainty in the *work* of top management, there is an element of uncertainty in the process of *evaluation* as well. Members of typing pools can be judged on the quantity and quality of their output, but judging managers is more subjective. This subjectivity increases the pressure toward social conformity. In Tom Wolfe's memorable phrase, aspiring managers seek to show they are made of "the right stuff." Thus personal development is affected by corporate requirements. Certain characteristics are encouraged and developed, while others are impeded.[14]

The upwardly mobile executive may begin his or her journey because of a desire for autonomy and personal control. Some may succeed in gaining power but the process exacts its toll. Often the price of power involves giving up the very things that motivated the executive originally.

What capitalists desire above all is not to jeopardize their positions as the legitimate reapers of profits from the labor of others.[15] This places limits on the extent of work degradation. Unlike the feudal system where serfs worked on the lord's land on some days and their own on other days, the worker cannot distinguish at the daily level of experience that portion of his labor value that is returned to him and that which is skimmed by the capitalist. This is the fundamental feature of capitalism and the one which, above all else, the capitalist wishes to keep obscure.

In order to maintain the basic relationship between capitalist and worker,

[12]Rosabeth Moss Kanter, *Men and Women of the Corporation* (New York: Basic Books, 1977), p. 48.

[13]Ibid., p. 64.

[14]For an extended treatment of this issue see Michael Maccoby, *The Gamesman* (New York: Simon & Schuster, 1976).

[15]For an extended critique of Braverman on this point see Michael Buraway, "Toward a Marxist Theory of the Labor Process: Braverman and Beyond," *Politics and Society* 8, 3 and 4, 1978. Also see David Stark, "Class Struggle and the Transformation of the Labor Process," *Theory and Society*, January 1980.

concessions may be granted in nonprofit related areas. The issue once again is that of control. Top management wishes to sustain both profitability and control. The deskilling process evident throughout the work force in the form of extensive division of labor helps to do this. Beyond a certain threshold, however, division of labor becomes counterproductive. If either middle- or lower-layer workers are excessively alienated, profits may be depressed by worker unrest, absenteeism, indifference, and sabotage. Furthermore, persistent unrest can lead to more strident revolt and more deep-seeded demands.

BARRIERS TO RESISTANCE

This raises the question of why there has not been more resistance to the process of work degradation. Part of the answer rests in the number of options available to the worker. One might assume, for example, that with the growing disjuncture between skill utilization and jobs, workers would manifest more freedom of movement. After all, the classic solution for those who are not happy with their work is to find new work. However, such options are decreasing, at least in the minds of workers. In 1969 workers were asked, ''About how easy would it be for you to find another job with another employer with approximately the same income and fringe benefits you now have?'' In 1969, 40 percent thought it would be very easy to find a similar job. Eight years later only 20 percent thought finding a similar job would be very easy.

Work must be considered within the context of possible options. In the past, people seemed to be in more personal control of their destinies. They could survive economically by working the land or moving to a new area and starting a business. Such options are much less available today. Increasingly the choice facing Americans is becoming either to work for someone else or not work at all. This narrowing of the quality of choice might be more tolerable if the quantity of choice were ample. Unfortunately this is not the case. There is a large and persistent reserve army of unemployed persons anxious to have work—any work.

A fairly widespread misconception in business and academic circles is that unemployment is not a serious problem in the United States. Many responsible people believe that unemployment is not the sustained and chronic problem that it was in the 1930s. Increasingly, many believe unemployment ranks are filled with people who are between jobs, homemakers who are only casually looking for work, employable middle-class people who are trying to beat the system by living off government benefits, or poor people who really do not want work. Although there is anecdotal evidence to support each of these contentions, this image is on the whole very misleading.

A recent national survey of the work force can dispel many myths about unemployment.[16] The survey clearly indicates that the overwhelming majority of people want to work, partly for reasons of self-esteem. When one's identity is

[16]Kay Lehman Schlozman and Sidney Verba, *Injury to Insult* (Cambridge: Harvard University Press, 1979).

dependent upon the work place, unemployment diminishes self-esteem. There is a marked increase in family tensions when workers become unemployed. The extra time gained by the unemployed—always a precious commodity to workers—now confronts them as a burdensome weight. The research also revealed the marked increase in psychic strain on the unemployed was attributable to loss of self-esteem and self-definition.

Beyond the issue of self-esteem, however, unemployment hurts economically, for it is invariably accompanied by loss of income. Even with unemployment compensation, it is never full compensation. Since people typically live to the limits of their income, the net loss of income resulting from unemployment compensation is quite painful. This is more true at lower-income levels, where nearly all income is spent on essentials like food, clothing, heat, and transportation.

Another recent study carried in the *Harvard Business Review*[17] shows that unemployment is far more extensive than is commonly realized. The way the goverment defines unemployment serves to shield its true dimensions from us. In June 1980, for example, about 6 million Americans were officially regarded as unemployed, but an equal number of people who were out of work were not counted because the U.S. Bureau of Labor Statistics defines as unemployed those people in the work force who are out of work during the week of the survey and *who have actively looked for work in the last month.* Discouraged workers who have given up looking for work are not considered part of the labor force and therefore are not counted as unemployed.

The researchers estimate that out of all the people who leave unemployment ranks in a given month over 45 percent drop out of the labor force and are not counted as unemployed for this reason! Yet it is the turnover in the unemployed that gives the impression that unemployment is a relatively brief experience. Actually over two-thirds of all joblessness can be traced to people who are without work more than six months of the year. Moreover, the magnitude of long-term joblessness is increasing, contrary to the conventional wisdom on the subject.

Rather than being a function of job instability and turnover, the authors argue that unemployment is in fact a function of a chronic job shortage. There simply is not enough work to go around. They cite a *Fortune* Magazine study of want ads in a mid-sized city in New York. Ads for low pay, no skill jobs were swamped with applicants within 24 hours of placing the ads. Many had more than 70 applicants per job for work that paid $3.00 per hour. It is comfortable, if somewhat self-serving, to believe that unemployment is not a serious problem. Such beliefs suggest that nothing needs to be done about unemployment and enable politicians to harangue about welfare cheaters. Moreover, since unemployment is concentrated among the least powerful and most alienated, those who are without work often cannot or do not speak for themselves.

---

[17]Kim B. Clark and Lawrence Summers, "Unemployment Reconsidered," *Harvard Business Review*, November–December, 1980.

The psychological dimensions of unemployment increase its pervasiveness as a social problem. Over an extended period—say ten years—the ranks of the unemployed will change considerably even though the proportion of unemployed remains constant. However, if a person has *ever* been unemployed, the effects of that experience will remain. Nor need unemployment be felt directly. Seeing a friend, a relative, or a neighbor lose a job or even seeing a plant closing on television increases one's sense of vulnerability, even though unemployment may not be an immediate personal threat. The memory of the depression has shaped that generation's attitudes about work throughout their entire lives.

Work in America cannot be considered outside of the context of massive and persistent unemployment. For millions of Americans, unemployment is neither an academic issue nor a cold statistic. It is a real possibility, and this reality affects attitudes about work itself. Given this, it is remarkable that Americans express as much dissatisfaction with work as they do.

When people are vulnerable, and when they are constantly reminded of their vulnerability, they become fearful. From the factory floor to the management boardroom, fear pervades the work place. Richard Pfeffer notes that fear dominates the politics within the factory. Workers who are disgruntled are nevertheless unwilling to "go out on a limb" and make their grievances known lest they be tabbed as troublemakers. This might lead to dismissal, which is an acute problem because workers are deskilled and can be easily replaced by one from the large pool of unemployed anxious to have the job. Even if the loss of work is not a real fear—a worker may be a member of a strong union—workers know that troublemakers often are passed over for promotion. Since the work place is a hierarchy, promotions are always competitive and management obviously will reward loyal rather than troublesome workers.

Maccoby's study of top management shows that fear is not limited to those at the bottom of the corporate ladder. If anything, it becomes more acute the higher one moves in the corporate hierarchy because of fewer positions and more intense competition. Moreover, management executives are bred on the notion that they should reach the top. Many nonmanagerial workers have a more realistic sense of their opportunities and so invest less of their ego in advancement. Maccoby notes that the first time an executive is passed over for a promotion often precipitates a personal crisis.

The pervasiveness of fear in the work place encourages conformity to what are perceived as the dominant values of the organization. Contrary values are repressed or at least not acted upon. This is even the case in work places supposedly not organized according to market values. The plight of nontenured faculty in most university settings starkly illustrates the role of fear in encouraging conformity. The pressures to publish are constant. In order to publish, junior faculty often resort to writing things they imagine journals will accept, regardless of their personal estimation of the value of the work itself. Thus they seek to create images of themselves that conform to the expectations of the organization.

In the interests of "efficiency" management will degrade work to the limits of toleration of the work force. Workers in part determine the level of acceptable degradation. The threshold of revolt may be relatively high or relatively low. In making such determinations the American worker is ill served by a cultural heritage of individualism and isolation, by a dominant ideology that cloaks management decisions abut the nature of work in a veil of legitimacy, by a deeply felt sense of inadequacy that is a common result of the conditions we have described and by the predominance of fear.

WORK LIFE AND POLITICAL LIFE

The natural opposition to this type of degradation would be the collective solidarity of the workers. If each worker is individually unable to control his or her fate, why is there not more effective collective action? A number of historic factors have served to depress fundamental opposition to the basic conditions of work. Mobility and individualism have been important. So has the ethnic variety and the immigrant status of our work force—especially around the turn of the century. Because our immigrant population grew rapidly then, it is easy to overlook the revolving door status of many immigrants. Between 1908 and 1910 for example, 44 East Europeans left for every 100 that came into this country. These workers were interested in making money, not in building durable opposition. Many of those who stayed were anxious to be regarded as loyal Americans and were unwilling to pursue activities that might be regarded as disloyal. Also, the work force was stratified along ethnic lines, with older immigrant groups holding the better working class jobs. This type of division discouraged working class solidarity.

Despite these obstacles, a fairly strong socialist movement existed early in this century. With the outbreak of World War I, union militance decreased as more jobs became available, and as union leaders pledged that there would be no strike "for the duration." After the war, radical unions like the Industrial Workers of the World (IWW) were repressed by the government, and moderate unions were beckoned by the consumption ethic. The 1920s were a crucial period in labor history, for it was during this time that union demands were solidified within the context of the capitalist order. Demands for control of the work place were replaced by demands for higher wages, shorter hours, better fringe benefits, safer working conditions, and the like.

Even victories at this level were by no means achieved easily. Labor disputes on such matters are often extremely rancorous and the issues themselves are important. Whatever gains are made by labor in thse areas, however, can be easily absorbed by capitalists in an oligopolistic economy. After all, higher wages mean more people buying more things, and in any case can be passed on in the form of administered price increases. Although these issues have been fundamental to today's collective bargaining process, they do not touch upon the basic control of the labor process. Here managerial prerogatives are simply assumed. In this sense, the impact of organized labor in this society has been profoundly conservative.

Left largely alone in the struggle against degrading and demeaning work, the workers respond in individual, idiosyncratic, and sometimes even heroic ways. They may seek to control their job within the narrow limits available. They may reverse or mix their routines. The workers may respond playfully by inventing counting or stacking games, or they may respond with panache by employing a theatrical flair to the motions of their work. Barbara Garson reports in *All the Livelong Day* that some women overcame the tedium of working on an assembly line in a tuna fishing cannery by having erotic fantasies about the fish. Sometimes, of course, workers try discreetly to get away with sabotage. What is most common and perhaps most pathetic is that workers seek to block out that portion of their lives from their consciousness—that is, for 40 hours a week they seek to feel nothing, and to be nothing. This has obvious implications for production quality. In the late 1970s, 27 percent of all American workers felt so ashamed of the quality of the products they were producing that they would not want to buy them themselves.[18]

The character of American work life is fraught with political implications as well, for one cannot separate work from social life in general. Even the attempt to separate life and work has disastrous moral and social consequences. One person who is abused and humiliated consistently at work institutes a reign of terror elsewhere, at home or in a social setting. Another may seek to languish in front of an insipid and escapist television screen. In the semidocumentary film *Quadrophenia*, the Mods and Rockers were employed in menial and subservient occupations such as bellhops or messenger boys. At night they emerged to terrorize those to whom they were subservient during the day. Each of these responses, while not directly political, has political consequences because they affect our perceptions of and our interactions with the human community.

The world of work has more direct political consequence however. While corporations have become less competitive in the traditional economic sense, the world of work is still extremely competitive for workers as individuals. Even meaningless work is desirable when the only realistic option is no job at all. This competition stirs resentment and fear. Consider the implications for affirmative action programs. Such programs attempt to redress historic and legitimate griev-ances, and a profound moral and intellectual case can be mounted in their defense. Nevertheless, when blacks are hired for positions that were formerly open only to whites, white workers are threatened because this decreases their own opportunity for employment and advancement. So they call these efforts reverse discrimination, and their animosity toward blacks is increased. Even the notion of affirmative action implies a society in which people are equally free to leave others behind. Citizens who should be united in their efforts to build a more just, open, and equitable social system are divided against each other, and see each other as enemies.

A further fact of work life that has equally serious political consequence is its

[18]Daniel Yankelovich, "New Rules in American Life," *Psychology Today*, April 1981, p. 78.

pervasive hierarchical organization. It is claimed that this is economically efficient, that it is essential for high productivity. Recent analysis casts doubt even upon this claim,[19] but we wish to make a broader point. Hierarchy, by its nature, demands inequality. There is a contradiction between hierarchical and democratic authority. One cannot expect to build a genuinely democratic polity in a social order that every day teaches the legitimacy of hierarchy and inequality. This is a basic contradiction and it is one which will continue to produce anxiety.

Hierarchy is sometimes justified by linking it integrally to the opportunity structure of the corporation. Hard working people are rewarded with advancement up the hierarchy. Corporations benefit by having good people in key positions, and society ultimately benefits by having good corporations. This argument is unconvincing because hierarchical organizations have been unable to resolve several dilemmas.[20]

Hierarchy as a principle of mobility is self-defeating. Those who are winning become less interested in actual job performance than in how the job can be manipulated to maximize opportunity for advancement. Those who lose are more disaffected than they otherwise would have been. And at every organizational dead end one can expect low commitment and shirking of responsibility. A form of organizational inflation inevitably sets in. Once movement is promised, people need to be kept moving. Organization structures become more finely graded. This reduces the value of jobs further, however, and people are stimulated to push for even more mobility. Finally, since a hierarchical structure is pyramidal, the result of this reward structure is one in which the losers consistently outnumber the winners.

It is equality which is the first condition of contentment. Any principle carried to its extreme is probably incorrectly applied, and it is doubtful that a reasonable social order would require absolute equality. But we must realize that we are all human beings and this fact places a powerful presumption in favor of equality. It is inequality which must be justified, and this justification must be cast in terms which are widely acceptable. Bosses by themselves cannot legitimately determine the appropriate range of economic inequality, because such inequalities have implications beyond the economic sphere itself. They reach into our personal lives and stretch through our entire social fabric.

When Martin Luther King asserted ''I am somebody,'' he was speaking for blacks, but the issue he raised by that assertion is appropriate on a more general level. We must decide as a nation of individuals whether we ''are somebody.'' If we think not, then we ought to give up pretense to democracy, for surely we do not deserve it, and we should be content with a work life where the few define the nature of work for the many. This is not idle speculation. The drift of governance in the past 20 years has

[19]Stephen Marglin, ''What Do Bosses Do? The Origins and Functions of Hierarchy in Capitalist Production,'' *Review of Radical Economics,* Summer 1974.

[20]See Kanter, *Men and Women of the Corporation,* p. 163.

been in the direction of a hierarchical elitism. Elections decrease in meaning as issues are represented as ''too complicated'' for the average citizen to understand. Political substance is superceded by the politics of style, and real decision making is carried out by ''the best and the brightest,'' a self-congratulatory euphemism for the politically powerful.

If on the other hand we believe in a basic equality that is a prerequisite to democracy, we must think seriously about how democracy can be extended to the work place. If we believe that people are important and have dignity, then a system of work consistent with these values ought to be established. We shall return to this issue in Chapter 10.

CHAPTER 5

Media Reality

As humans have moved into totally artificial environments, our direct contact with and knowledge of the planet has been snapped. Disconnected like astronauts floating in space, we cannot know up from down or truth from fiction. Conditions are appropriate for the implementation of arbitrary realities. Television is one recent example of this, a serious one, since it greatly accelerates the problem.

Jerry Mander

And that's the way it is.

Walter Cronkite

In any political order with democratic aspirations, what the people believe is taken seriously. Pollsters and scholars who investigate public opinion too frequently may ask silly or shallow questions; and from the answers to such questions implausible inferences may be drawn. The public may be regarded as feebleminded or as wisdom incarnate. The intensity of such scholarly disputes reflects the desire to understand what and how citizens think. Politicians show similar concern. They may use or abuse public opinion; or they may seek to lead the populace to a new level of insight, but politicians ignore public opinion at their peril.

This leads to an enduring difficulty, for people commonly develop opinions on public matters that are based upon mediated experience, not upon direct experience of the issues at hand. This is not always true of course. A woman who feels she has been denied a promotion because she is a woman may have opinions about the equal rights amendment that are independent of how the media present the issue. Yet, when one thinks about the entire realm of public affairs, the extent to which people are dependent upon mediation is apparent. Our knowledge of political candidates is derived through images conveyed in print and electronic media. None of us know the Ayatollah Khomeini except as he is presented to us by the media. The options considered with respect to energy policy are often a function of the options presented. Even the distinctions made between public and private matters are influenced by what the media choose to make public matters.

This would not be a matter of particular concern if the media simply conveyed reality objectively. This is what many in that industry claim. It is often argued that the media are messengers, that they do not significantly influence reality—at least when they do their job well. For years, Walter Cronkite concluded the CBS evening newscast with the bromide, ''And that's the way it is.'' Thus is illusion elevated.

If the news-gathering process were an objective one, a compelling abstract definition of the news would be easy to come by. No such definition has emerged, however. Any proposed definition is infused with subjective components. Is news a recounting of important daily events? Important to whom? Why should events be the focus, and why *daily* events? Who does the recounting? Why should events be recounted at all, rather than simply displayed? Other attempts at objective definitions meet with similar difficulties. Therefore, most analysts of the process retreat to definitions that state essentially that news is what the news gatherers say it is. If this is the case, however, what is and is not news becomes an arguable point.

The direct reporting of news events is only the most obvious way in which the media affect perceptions of public life. The media, particularly television, have achieved an unprecedented level of penetration into our daily lives. The cultural force of television conveys values, contributes to the shaping of attitudes, and encourages patterns of politically relevant behavior.

Because the media are so commonly used to interpret and therefore to provide structure for reality, they are crucial components of everyday life. Accordingly, it is useful to think about the media in terms of the theme of this book. Two aspects of the media process draw our attention. First the media *systematically* structure the perception of *public* events in ways that trivialize politics and leave fundamental issues unexamined. We describe the nature of these distortions and provide three examples of them. Second we argue that the media, and in particular television, have had a more diffuse but equally important impact upon popular culture. Television contributes significantly to the consumer culture, and the promotion of the consumer culture leads to popular attitudes that significantly impact upon the quality of public life.

MEDIA AND DISTORTION

Although the philosopher Friedrich Nietzsche did not speak about gathering news, he has identified the major difficulty for those who view quality news as a faithful reporting of reality: the number of things one might want to know is, in principle, infinite; therefore, every act of knowing requires a prior act of choosing and desiring. An infinite number of events occur in the world each day. Why should any one of these events be considered news? When the news industry is dominated by fewer than a dozen organizations and when these organizations interact extensively, the problem of news selection becomes more acute. What the typical citizen can choose to know about public affairs is sharply circumscribed. Therefore, what major news organizations decide to *make* news is crucial not only in determining what news *is*, but what our reality is as well.

This does not necessarily suggest that the media are irresponsible. Irresponsibility implies the willful distortion of facts or a story line. It is essential to recognize, however, that there are many ways to be responsible, and the media need to be assessed in this light. In the course of this analysis, the terms "bias" and "distortion" are used. Such terms usually carry pejorative connotations, but such connotations are not necessarily intended by our use of them. Total objectivity in reporting public events is an unattainable goal. In our sense of the terms, therefore, any reporting of public events would involve some bias and distortion. That total objectivity is unattainable, however, implies neither that standards are irrelevant nor that nothing can be done about fairness in reporting. Indeed, it increases the need for critical and continuing analysis of how news becomes news.

By being alert to the "distorting" influences in the news-gathering process, the limitations of that process will become more obvious. It is hoped that this awareness will enable one to perceive more clearly what the news means.

Sources of Distortion

A description of the news-gathering process might well begin with its most obvious feature: it is a profit-seeking enterprise. The media are businesses selling products. It is true that they are businesses of a distinct sort, in that the industry also has a heritage of public responsibility, but they are businesses nonetheless.

The news industry simultaneously sells its product and its audience. In purchasing a book, one pays for its entire cost, including the profit. The transaction is straightforward. A newspaper, on the other hand, sells its product to customers, but it also sells its audience to advertisers. Eighty percent of revenues of the Washington *Post*, for example, comes from advertisers. Nearly all revenues for television are derived from the sale of time to advertisers, although subscription television has made some inroads. Conversely, corporations are interested in advertising on television because of the huge audiences they can reach. Thus, the news-gathering enterprise operates in a milieu of inherent tension. On one hand, there is the popular expectation, fortified by the public pronouncements of industry leaders, that news should not be fettered by outside influences. On the other hand, news organizations must be constantly aware of profit-and-loss issues. They are businesses and businesses are expected, at least in the long run, to turn a profit.

How might news organizations be expected to respond to this tension? A rational news organization would seek to build large audiences in ways that are not offensive to advertisers. There are many ways to do this. In newspapers, audiences are routinely sought through format changes, sensationalism, expanded features, and the like. Similarly, television seeks to attract news audiences by hiring ''compelling'' anchorpersons, using roving reporters, and developing short, snappy stories. Walter Cronkite has reported, with some outrage, that ''business consultants'' to CBS News recommended all news stories be limited to 30 seconds! That nothing substantial can be reported in that time was evidently beside the point.

The profit-seeking context of the news industry also affects output indirectly. News is one of the less profitable segments of network programming, since its audiences tend to be small compared to audiences for other evening programs. Therefore, there are organizational pressures to keep news programs out of prime time, which from an industry perspective would siphon revenues from potentially more lucrative entertainment programs, and to restrict national news programs to 30 minutes (actually 22 minutes when commercial time is deleted). Although it is impossible to do justice to national news given the 30-minute format, to the corporate mind the 30-minute format makes economic sense.

From the economic perspective, both the decision to keep news programs out of prime time and to restrict them to 30 minutes is reasonable. It appears unreasonable only when one is prepared to deny the legitimacy of the market mechanism as a means for making such choices. If one assumes that a wide range of easily accessible information is essential for a democratic society, and that one of the best means to disseminate such information is through detailed television news programs, then it is profitability that must be called into question. The important point is that good television and good news reporting are not the same thing. When there is conflict the tendency is for the former to prevail.

The view that suggests news programming is simply dictated by economic interests is not convincing. The news industry has run items that are adverse to corporate interests, but such instances tend to be exceptional. What is most characteristic about the corporate structure in the yearly flow of thousands of news stories is that it enjoys ''benign neglect.'' Even though within its sphere decisions are routinely made which affect millions of lives, private enterprise is generally not considered part of the public domain. The media tend to operate on the assumption (which is self-serving given the economic imperatives earlier discussed) that ''private'' business is no one's business. This is true even of the largest corporations. One study of the values of news personnel reports that the assumption that capitalism is a benign system which misfunctions only occasionally and idiosyncratically is one of the enduring values of those who work in the news industry.[1]

A second source of distortion of the news process relates to its organizational

---

[1] Herbert Gans, *Deciding What's News* (New York: Random House, 1979), Ch. 2.

characteristics. This distortion is primarily bureaucratic, although it is related to economic distortion. With the costs for each camera crew totaling close to one million dollars per year, networks can afford to maintain only a limited number of crews. It is expensive to move these crews around, and going into remote areas for "live" stories may involve the substantial costs of telephone cable transmission. A recent study of network news[2] reveals that news is far more likely to come from areas easily accessible to camera crew location. The value of the story must be weighed against the cost of producing it. In order to provide the illusion of national coverage, producers encourage "timeless" news stories from the more remote areas—Charles Kuralt's on the road series is a good example—which can be mailed to headquarters and shown at any time.

Any form of organization implies regular ways of doing business, or standard operating procedures. These procedures in turn influence news content.[3] For example, news in this country is daily news. Each day is fresh and news becomes that which surprises. We expect news to happen every day. Not receiving a morning paper can be disorienting. One cannot imagine John Chancellor appearing some evening to announce that there will be no newscast because there was nothing worth reporting that day. This encourages an orientation toward novelty, toward a mentality that asks what has happened since yesterday. The reader or viewer tends to be jerked from story to story and from day to day without any kind of ordering context.

Daily stories increase the difficulty of understanding the news. Even long-running stories, such as when the Americans were held hostage in Iran, tend to be treated as a daily series of episodes. Knowledge that would provide an ordering context,—that is, explanatory stories related to the major story—are not congenial to the daily news format and tend to be ignored or treated superficially.

A second routine is implied by the daily news format: reporters characteristically work against deadlines in gathering the news, and this also helps define the news. One consequence of daily deadlines is that the news gatherer is not encouraged to reflect upon the developing story. Rather, deadlines encourage the uncritical promotion of a received point of view. Because news gatherers do not have time to be reflective, a press release from a government agency or from some corporation is more likely to be reported at face value. The existence of daily deadlines also is congruent with the norm of objectivity as developed by the media. Simply reporting what one in authority says not only encourages the illusion of objectivity, it also avoids the responsibility implied in judgment.

Another organizational routine that distorts the news-gathering process is the so-called news beat. Beats are areas of presumed news significance to which reporters are regularly assigned. The rationale for the beat system is twofold. Some areas, such

---

[2]Edward Epstein, *News from Nowhere* (New York: Vintage, 1974).

[3]Leon Sigal provides an extensive discussion of the routines of newsgathering in *Reporters and Officials* (Lexington: D.C. Heath, 1973).

as the White House or a police department, are considered deserving of regular coverage because of their significance. Additionally, it is believed that the news-gathering agency benefits from having a reporter serve for an extended period on a beat because of the opportunity such service provides toward gaining access to key officials and learning the complexities of pertinent issues.

The beat system also has its costs. The concentration of resources on beats means that some areas will be underreported or ignored completely. Moreover, once sources are cultivated and relationships established, there may be reluctance to criticize these sources lest they dry up. In fact, there are strong pulls in the opposite direction. If a reporter is passive and simply reports the establishment view of the particular beat, sources remain open, the reporter is spoon-fed daily stories, and the job becomes much easier. The reporter rarely receives any criticism from the news hierarchy because stories are regularly filed which are similar to the stories filed by other reporters on the same beat. Indeed, it is the reporter who *deviates* from the stories others on the beat file who finds explanations to the news hierarchy necessary. Given these pulls, it is not surprising that most reporters go along with the system.

We have seen that the economic context and the organizational process of news gathering serve to distort the final news product. The *form* through which the news is presented is a third distorting influence. Whether the news is seen on television or read in a newspaper can make a significant difference on what the news is. That there are broad similarities between print and electronic media should not mask these differences. A good daily newspaper carries far more stories than does a network news program. The entire CBS evening news, for example, would fit on about one-fourth of the front page of the New York *Times*.

Despite this, television has one major advantage over papers: it is a more believable medium. The viewer is under the illusion that television allows reality to be viewed directly. In the phrase of some defenders of TV news, "the camera's eye never blinks." This may be one reason why many people report relying on television news as their primary source of news information. Surveys now show that about two-thirds of the public report this to be the case. Thus, there may be more and more reliance upon a medium which offers less and less content.

The false sense of objectivity is one of the most dangerous deceptions of television. When one reads about an event in a paper, one is constantly aware that the event is mediated. Even if the report is accepted at face value, the reader recognizes his or her dependence upon an outside source for information. The mediating role of television is less apparent. The viewer of television news is more likely to think that the world is being viewed directly. Television falsely imparts the sense of "being there," and yet what the television "eye" decides to focus upon is beyond our control. We only see what the camera focuses on.

The sense of objectivity is dangerous because the logic of television requires distortion. A canon of TV news gathering, for example, is that action is better than inaction. Action sequences address our field of vision—our eyes pick up motion and change—and therefore they make more compelling features. But compelling television is not the same thing as a disinterested portrayal of reality. An antinuclear demonstration may last for six hours. It may include several speeches in which grievances are articulated in detail. If there are also two minutes of violence, or if arrests are made, this is what will be shown on evening news. News producers are not trying to subvert the rally but rather to make ''good'' television. However, what the audience receives is a terribly incomplete depiction of the event.

The claim of many television journalists that the camera is an ally in the quest for actuality is belied by the necessity of interpreting stories for the viewer. Events recorded by the camera are in themselves unintelligible to the viewer; they must be explained by the omnipresent reporter. The TV viewer is presented with a neat package: a highly interpretive story, with a beginning, a middle, and a summing up, with the film used to justify this interpretation. In 1969, fully four years before the American withdrawal from Vietnam, ABC Evening News executives decided to alter the focus of their Vietnam coverage from combat pieces to stories pegged to the eventual pull-out of American forces. Saigon bureau personnel were told to gather film footage and to develop stories related to this theme.[4]

A number of scholars argue that the media have been excessively critical of political leaders and political institutions. Survey and electoral data suggest increasing popular disenchantment with our political institutions and place the blame for this on mass media obsessed with reporting ''bad news.'' Thus, the decision by CBS News executives to close each evening's newscast by stating the number of days American citizens had been held hostage in Iran had an immediate effect upon the fate of Jimmy Carter, but also an indirect effect upon the presidency itself. This argument is necessarily speculative, since proofs are impossible to come by.

Our perspective differs from this analysis. We believe that the media do contribute to a national malaise, but not in the way these scholars suggest. There is a crisis of confidence in our institutions but, far from being artificially generated by the media, it is borne out of real political events. These events have been discussed in Chapter 1 and need not be reiterated here. This crisis is too deep for the media simply to ignore if they are to retain credibility. On the other hand, for many of the reasons just discussed, the media are too constrained to provide a compelling analysis of the sources of the crisis. The result is that bad news is rarely explained more than superficially. Even when in-depth analysis is provided, problems are typically defined within a rather narrow political framework. This type of analysis will soon be illustrated by examining media coverage of Watergate.

Types of Bias

Two sorts of bias can be associated with the media: one relating to the content of the message and the other to the structure of the process. *Content bias* is more easily discernible because it involves a concrete message which draws one's attention. The

[4]Epstein, *News from Nowhere*, p. 17.

use of pejorative adjectives to describe a candidate, the regular display of photographs unsympathetic to a political official, the structure of headlines, the location of stories in a telecast or a paper, the amount of time or space given competing candidates, and other similar factors have drawn the attention of political authorities and scholarly analysts. Bias of content may appear only as a question of judgment to the news gatherer. These judgments are believed to be fair as long as they accord with publicly acknowledged standards. Accordingly, standards of fairness have emerged in the news industry to which most reputable news media profess loyalty.

Many scholars use these standards to gauge objectivity. Yet, even at this level, these standards are not objective in any serious sense. They exist only as a result of consensus within the industry. For example, one standard of fairness is that major party candidates should receive an equal amount of time on network news programs. In the 1976 presidential campaign, Gerald Ford exploited this standard by using what was called his "rose garden strategy:" the staging of tightly controlled media events in and around the White House which the media willingly participated in. These staged events were dutifully recorded and President Ford was given equal time on network news programs. In this context, the fairness of the standard is at least questionable.

Another standard of objectivity in the industry is the belief that reporters should not interject their personal feelings into reporting. This is, of course, an artful contrivance, for any news story involves attention, summation, and ordering—all of which are subjective choices. Even on its own terms, this standard can subvert fairness because it forces some journalists to omit things that are believed to be true but which involve an element of personal judgment. Thus, Senator Joseph McCarthy's anticommunist witch hunting in the 1950s was extended credibility by the news industry, many of whose members personally felt Senator McCarthy was irresponsible. Credibility was extended by media complicity. Recently, Reagan administration officials Alexander Haig and Caspar Weinberger have painted a very grim picture about the state of our military power as compared with the Soviet Union's. Although controversial, statements made by major administration officials reach a large audience, a much larger audience than their critics will address. To report what Weinberger and Haig say without analysis may be a useful journalistic convention, but it is not, in any meaningful sense of the term, objective.

Finally, it is significant that standards of objectivity are never applied universally. The news consensus on standards of fairness exists only within a larger political consensus. The fairness standards rapidly erode or vanish altogether in considering minor party candidates, political dissidents, foreigners, and leftist or rightist political ideologies. The industry was not particularly concerned about being fair to 1980 presidential candidates Barry Commoner and Roger McBride, not to mention a foreign chief of state like Fidel Castro. Standards of objectivity are related only to mainstream politics.

Because citizens are aware of distortion, it is usually bias of content that draws their attention. *Structural bias* on the other hand, is more subtle because it relates to the process by which news is gathered, not the content of the final product. It is rooted deep in the news-gathering institutions themselves. To understand bias of structure, we must step back from the institutions. We need to understand the *range* and *form* of presentation—that is, what is offered and what is omitted.

EXAMPLES OF STRUCTURAL BIAS

To illustrate bias of structure we have selected three examples: press coverage of Watergate, public service advertising, and the television program "60 Minutes". These examples have been selected precisely because, for different reasons, they are favorably regarded within the industry and by the public at large. If structural bias exists, it should be visible in the areas of greatest strength within the industry.

Watergate Coverage

On June 17, 1972, five men were arrested while breaking into the Democratic party national headquarters housed in the Watergate complex in Washington, D.C. Originally billed as a "third-rate burglary" by President Nixon's press secretary, the story was nevertheless kept alive by a few courageous news gatherers on the New York *Times* and the Washington *Post*. Eventually, President Nixon was implicated in trying to suppress the investigation. The term Watergate came to symbolize a variety of unsavory administration activities that were uncovered during the course of the investigation. These included secret bombings of Cambodia, obstructing justice, illegally spying on U.S. citizens, and using federal agencies such as the Internal Revenue Service to harass political opponents. In August 1974, facing certain impeachment and conviction, President Nixon resigned his office.

The Watergate epic, a major story for two years, is commonly considered a triumph of investigative journalism. For a year before President Richard Nixon was forced to resign, Watergate was *the* major news story, and in the final months preceding the August 1974 resignation it was virtually the *only* news story. The House Judiciary Committee impeachment hearings filled daytime television hours and dominated network news. Major newspapers sometimes ran more than a dozen Watergate-related stories in a single day. The entire nation was caught up in the drama of the investigation. When Vice-President Ford finally replaced Nixon, he announced that "Our long national nightmare is over," and that the denouement of the Watergate episode demonstrated that our system works. President Ford congratulated the nation's press for their role in uncovering and pursuing the Watergate story.

The media were also self-congratulatory, liberally sprinkling awards among themselves. Much of the credit for breaking the story went to a pair of heretofore obscure city reporters on the Washington *Post*, Bob Woodward and Carl Bernstein.

Woodward and Bernstein wrote a best-selling book on the story, and then a best-selling sequel. A movie based on their first book won an academy award. What passed unnoticed in all the hoopla and self-congratulation was how little the public was able to learn about Watergate from the media. It is ironic that, while Watergate was the most covered story of the decade, some of its most important dimensions have been swept under the rug.

This was not necessarily a conscious decision on the part of the media; rather, it is attributable to structural features of the industry. As was indicated earlier, we are not used to thinking about the relations between private and public power. Furthermore, we have come to expect the news to reflect newness or latest developments, and to be objective—free of reporters' personal opinions—and, most of all, to be dramatic. All of these expectations, built upon years of habit, militate against analysis. They bias the news in the direction of concrete events and characters. Television was slow to take up Wategate, but when it finally did, the form of the story was firmly established: Watergate would be treated as a soap opera.

The media spent enormous space and time developing the cast of characters. While these characters are no longer prominent, during the Watergate investigation they were household names. The public came to know and love homespun and avuncular Senator Sam Ervin, the tough and incorruptible Judge Sirica, intellectual and idealistic Congresswoman Barbara Jordan, the fearless prosecutor Sam Dash, the perpetually befuddled Senator Howard Baker, the Nixon aide and recent convert to integrity John Dean and his faithful wife Mo. And the public learned whom to hate: the morally underdeveloped newcomers in the administration, the immorally overdeveloped old guard, the subhuman G. Gordon Liddy, and lurking ominously behind all of these, Richard Nixon. In the final days, television offered its own character, presidential nemesis Dan Rather. As with soap operas, the meaning of actions, the larger social context, was beside the point. People do not watch soaps for insight, they watch for diversion. The mass media focused on Watergate as a daily drama and did not seriously pursue its meaning or its implications. The best the people were offered was enfeebled news commentator Eric Sevareid chanting mindless homilies about what it all meant.

The national media were strongly biased in the direction of treating Watergate as an aberration, the unique result of a small clique of paranoid and insecure politicians. Once Nixon resigned, there was great stress by the media on "putting Watergate behind us" and returning to normalcy. An audience can tire of a daily show after a couple of years. But we must consider the possibility that Watergate was the *result* of normalcy. It is just possible that Watergate was not the result of a paranoid clique, but of an inept one. The series of scandals since, demonstrating that high officials have been involved in perjury, bribe-taking, and influence peddling, have shown that corruption has not subsided.

Andrew Kopkind has developed an interesting argument concerning the media treatment of Watergate.[5] He asks if any of us can identify Claude Wild, William Keeler, Everett Olson, and Orin Atkins. Like John Mitchell, John Dean, H.R. Haldeman, and John Ehrlichman, these men were also convicted and sentenced Watergate characters. There was one difference. The former were major corporate figures, the quiet donors of dirty money. There were over twenty such business executives, yet the public had almost no way of knowing about them.

We have been taught that it is more blessed to give than to receive; Kopkind shows that it is also safer. Unlike their political counterparts, over twenty of whom were sent to jail, all of the corporate corrupters received suspended sentences and were fined nominal amounts, usually $5000. Kopkind argues that the financial foundations of Watergate were never a source of concern to the media, and that the media have consistently demonstrated little interest in exploring corporate influence on public policy.

There is a further consequence of containing investigations like Watergate within a narrowly conceived political realm. It is obvious that the power coming from concentrated wealth is often used to achieve ends in the public arena. To regard politicians as the *ends* of investigations is not only to misperceive the problem in a fundamental way, but also to generate cynicism toward the only realm where genuine correction is possible. For all its imperfections, the public arena is one of the few places where questions of social justice can be addressed at all. If large numbers of people come to believe that politicians are corrupt, that the entire system is immune to change and therefore unworthy of attention and interest, the result will be that concentrated wealth will extend its power more freely.

Public Service Advertising

Bias of structure can also be seen in public service advertising on the electronic media. All radio and television stations are licensed by the federal government and are required by the FCC to conform to certain standards, including operating in the "public interest, convenience, and necessity." When stations apply for license renewal, they must demonstrate that they have satisfied these standards. In practice, stations have not lost their licenses for lack of public service, but the stakes are so high they don't want to risk it, or even get the bad publicity from a fight about it.

One way for a station to display its public spirit is to run public service announcements (PSAs). These noncommerical and noncontroversial ads encourage certain types of highly valued behavior such as wearing auto safety belts, picking up litter, voting, and giving blood. We watch them every evening without giving thought to the manner in which they structure our perception of problems.

Because local stations are usually approached with more PSAs than they care to run, and because they are concerned about remaining noncontroversial, they usually

---

[5] Andrew Kopkind, "The Unwritten Watergate Story," *More*, November 1974.

look for PSAs that have been approved by the Advertising Council, a national organization devoted to the screening, development, and promotion of public service campaigns. The Advertising Council membership is heavily laden with advertising, media, and business representatives, but also includes members from other segments of society, including labor, education, medicine, religion, and social work. One study showed that 80 percent of all PSAs appearing on network television had been screened and approved by the Advertising Council.[6] Although many of these campaigns have been for worthwhile causes, nearly all have been deceptive.

In the first place, one can ask whether innocuousness is an appropriate servant of the public interest. Both the FCC and Advertising Council apparently assume that it is. PSAs are a good way for stations to secure "brownie points" with the FCC without getting anyone upset. However, would not the public be better served by airing a variety of significant and substantive points of view which, while controversial, are nonetheless crucial if citizens are to develop reasoned opinions about political and social problems?

Perhaps the most pernicious deception of PSAs is that they direct attention away from political solutions to social problems and, in so doing encourage confusion and isolation. Beyond the specific content of PSAs there is a twofold message. The first is that social problems do not require collective action for their resolution nor are they the function of any particular power array. The second message is that the government is already acting responsibly in the problem areas identified in the PSAs.

A major study[7] analyzed 94 PSAs which were screened on two stations in separate localities in one week during 1973. It noted the diminishing sense of the political world that was implied. PSAs rarely depicted problems as insoluble; in fact only 7.4 percent of those studied offered no solution. All the remaining PSAs called upon individuals to solve social problems. None of the PSAs called upon the government. It is possible to infer from this that they encouraged political participation, but the authors note that this was not the case. The kinds of solutions offered fell into three broad categories: solicitations for support, recruitment (to such organizations as the military and Peace Corps), and personal admonitions (to modify individual behavior). The authors call this pseudoparticipation and note: "PSAs also define the methods by which solutions are to be achieved . . . [they] are not establishing meaningful two-way communication."[8]

The second implicit message flows from the first. Government is portrayed as acting on behalf of the whole society in solving problems. Citizens are told that the present system is working and that appropriate responses are to define problems the way the government does and to join the government in a particular effort.

[6]Robert Friedman, "Try American Capitalism Today," *Columbia Journalism Review* 6, 5, May 1976, p. 12.
[7]David Paletz, Roberta Pearson, and Donald Willis, *Politics in Public Service Advertising on Television* (New York: Praeger, 1977).
[8]Ibid. p. 97.

Just beneath the harmless surface of many PSA campaigns boils the troubled waters of interest group politics. It is a common practice for the Advertising Council to assign a public service campaign to an advertising agency that handles a commercial account in the same field. The Food, Nutrition and Health campaign, for example, was given to Young and Rubican, the same agency that handles the General Foods account. Given these overlapping interests, the agency is unlikely to develop a campaign warning about the nonnutritious products of General Foods.

The economic front groups develop campaigns that serve the interests of their sponsors. Consider the problem of pollution. If one were to mount a campaign against pollution, certainly industrial waste spillage into our rivers and our air and auto emission controls would be likely places to begin. The Advertising Council campaign reduced pollution to a problem of people picking up cans. The problem of pollution is not that Detroit builds inadequate cars, or that industry vigorously opposes limitations on what they emit or bury in our environment. It is that ''People start pollution. People can stop it.'' Even this oversimplification of the pollution problem carries its own deceptiveness for, although litter can be reduced by more individual self-control, it can also be reduced by limiting the use of throw-away containers. This campaign was sponsored by Keep America Beautiful, which is financed by major can and bottle manufacturers. These are precisely the interests that are active opponents of bills to ban throw-away containers.

Consider traffic safety. The National Safety Council, funded by the auto industry, has been active in generating PSAs in this area. Needless to say, traffic safety is not related to auto defects in these PSAs. Instead, citizens are told to wear seat belts and to refrain from driving while under the influence of alcohol. Even Smokey the Bear is used to serve larger economic interests. A coordinator of the forest fire prevention campaign is Gulf States Paper Corporation, surely as big a threat to national forests as are fires.

It is not that people should not wear set belts, or be careful in forests, or pick up after themselves. Of course they should. But the economic underpinnings to many PSA campaigns ensure that problems will be seen in a certain way. What appear as disinterested public service announcements are far from that. Moreover, PSAs contort a reasonable notion of the public interest. They abjure controversy when the public interest may require it. On important issues, they direct attention to inadequate and widely palatable solutions. Finally, they decrease the likelihood of political activity by eliciting individual and isolated responses to remedies the existing power structure approves.

"60 Minutes"

''60 Minutes'' enjoys the unusual distinction of being the most honored and most watched television show. The program's intrepid reporters constantly appear to be on the side of righteousness, staunchly defending the public interest and the powerless average person. Executive producer Don Hewitt recently stated, ''We have become the nation's ombudsman.'"[9] The show averages more than 1000 letters per week, more than any other television program. Moreover, "60 Minutes" *appears* to be an effective voice for the cause of justice. This perception is encouraged by the occasional screening of updates indicating progress that has been made for a cause originally promoted by the program. A recent article argues that "60 Minutes crusades" do indeed pay off and cites nine examples of action taken on an issue after exposure on the show.[10]

It is important to realize that, in a world where just causes vastly outnumber white knights, responsibility may assume a variety of forms. One may slay dragons or swat flies. In order to determine the scope and bias of the sense of responsibility conveyed on "60 Minutes," all 253 program segments shown in calendar years 1977 and 1978 were assessed.[11] One of the more interesting points to emerge from this investigation was that most of what appears on the show is *not* controversial.

Three things serve to exaggerate the extent of the controversy found on the program. First, investigative segments are singled out and promoted by critics. The titles of newspaper and magazine articles about the show are instructive: "Mike Wallace: Master of the Tough Question," "51 Minutes Where Safe and Bland Don't Rule," "Semi-Tough: The Politics Behind '60 Minutes,' " and "Do Those '60 Minutes' Crusades Pay Off?" In short, people may think "60 Minutes" is controversial because that is what reviewers and critics emphasize. Second, the long-running point/counterpoint segment of the show simulated controversy, even though it was completely theatrical and uninformative. Beginning with the 1979-1980 season, this portion of the program was discontinued. Finally, and perhaps most important, "60 Minutes" is a television program, and television is a medium wherein, on matters of public concern, objectivity in content often shades into blandness. That the program is controversial at all makes it seem heroic.

One critic[12] recently lauded the four co-hosts of the show, calling them "journalistic knights errants doing battle with our collective dragons: Wasteful bureaucrats, chiseling businessmen and corrupt politicians." She goes on to state that "The little guy tunes in to see the big boys and fat cats squirm for a change." If this is true, then the "little guy" is being misled, for big boys and fat cats rarely squirm on "60 Minutes."

When the list of actual investigations conducted by "60 Minutes" is examined, one finds that it is dominated by the small-time wheeler-dealers whom the establishment has always viewed with disdain: cigarette bootlegging, a fraudulent cancer clinic, rigged carnival games, fraudulent diamond sales, farm worker

[9]Quoted in Harry Stein, "How '60 Minutes' Makes News," New York *Times,* May 6, 1979.

[10]Don Kowet, "Do Those '60 Minutes' Crusades Pay Off?", *TV Guide,* March 10, 1979.

[11]The data for the analysis of "60 Minutes" were taken from an unpublished manuscript written by J. Harry Wray, entitled "Structural Bias in the Media: The '60 Minutes' Example."

[12]Ellen Graham, "51 Minutes Where Safe and Bland Don't Rule," Wall Street *Journal,* April 6, 1979.

exploitation in Louisiana, pitfalls of consumer credit, businesspersons conned into advertising in bogus publications and phony sales of commodity options. These are the stories that typify investigations of corruption and upon which the reputation for uncompromising analysis is built.

None of this implies that any of these investigations has been misguided. It is always pleasurable to see scalawags, no matter how small, get their comeuppance. But surely one reason why a Mike Wallace can build a reputation as a tough-minded investigator (besides the post-interview editing) is that he rarely challenges people who have significant power.

One of the most fascinating aspects of "60 Minutes" investigations is the response of the "villains" to the program. Often they seem either terrified of television or enthralled by it. These polar responses can be explained by the wider social context. Some small-time crooks are terrified by the public exposure because they possess no power to counteract the threat of a "60 Minutes" exposé. Yet others seem eager to confess.

One must remember the power of television as an independent force in our culture. An appearance on television is one way for the relatively powerless people in our society to confirm their existence. Many persons dissolve into a frenzy of excitement at a sports event when the TV camera turns their way, and many others will demean themselves without limit simply to appear on a TV game show. Because "60 Minutes" is a popular show, it offers the fleeting chance to hobnob with famous people like Mike Wallace, Harry Reasoner, or Ed Bradley. This could explain why at least some of the so-called villains on "60 Minutes" are so compliant and submissive. The chance to appear on national television seems worth the price of personal humilation.

To investigate those who wield power in today's world would involve political and economic risks. Moreover, their significance is daily conveyed by subalterns and sycophants, and they are not likely to be embarrassed or intimidated by television.

Of the 253 programs shown in 1977 and 1978, in only eight cases did major corporations come under critical scrutiny. This is 3 percent of all stories run during that period. Yet, it is a mistake to assume that even these programs were devoted to the critical consideration of the corporate power structure, for a review of the transcripts of these stories highlights the extraordinary care with which major corporate investigations are handled. In only one of the corporate stories was the balance clearly tipped against a corporation. This was a story on automobile safety. The Ford Pinto came under critical scrutiny, and at least one Ford executive was embarrassed by Mike Wallace's questions. The subsequent litigation involving the Pinto leaves the impression that a program like "60 Minutes" might have some social impact if such investigations were a systematic part of the format. Although corporate investigations are very sparse, much more balanced than other investigative segments, and rarely result in action, they add to the aura of legitimacy of the program.

None of the above is written in criticism of the "60 Minutes" program. Rather, the point is to recognize the show for what it is: a commercial television program which operates under the rules of that medium. From an economic perspective, optimal programming decisions aim for increased audiences, without disturbing any important and potential clients. By and large, "60 Minutes" succeeds in doing this extremely well. The executive producer speaks candidly of "packaging reality the way Hollywood packages fiction" and describes the program as "a show about the adventures of four reporters."[13]

In the larger milieu of television, "60 Minutes" seems positively stunning. But the show is not what it claims to be. It does not fight for the "little people." In fact, to the extent that it conveys the impression that it is fighting significant battles on their behalf, it misleads them. When the producer can assert that the show has become "America's ombudsman" and have that claim be taken seriously by reporters and analysts, it is a commentary not only about the deluding effects of the world of television, but also about the poverty of our politics.

Although "60 Minutes," public service advertising, and the press coverage of Watergate vary in terms of substance, they have the similar structural bias of deceptiveness. On the surface each case seems to exemplify media excellence. At the same time, however, structural features of the industry preclude analysis of important problems, or at least important aspects of problems addressed. In each case the public gets considerably less than is apparent. Responsibility is exercised only within the narrow limits of the industry.

THE TELEVISION CULTURE

The political impact of television is not limited to the ways in which news and public affairs programs are developed. Television also operates as an independent force in our culture, encouraging values that have political significance. The advent of television was so sudden, and its permeation through our society so total, that isolating its impact is extraordinarily difficult. It may be too close to understand completely and its consequences for our society may not be known for generations, if then. While we cannot state the precise extent of television's impact upon our culture, in general direction of its effects seems clear. First, television encourages loneliness. Second, unable to explain adequately the real world because of its own structural foundations, it offers the solace of a retreat from that world. For many people television becomes a substitute for experience in the real world, and the boundaries between the world of television and reality begin to blur. Third, the costs of this retreat into television are very high in personal terms, because television exists to sell products. It trumpets the consumer ethic and diminishes our capacity for critical thought.

---

[13] Hewitt is quoted in "Mike Wallace: Master of the Tough Question," Christopher Stein, Christian Science *Monitor*, April 10, 1979.

In 1950, 9 percent of American households owned a television set. Five years later that proportion ballooned to 65 percent. Today there are TVs in every American home. This does not tell the whole story because the number of sets per household is increasing while household size is decreasing. In 1955, the average number of sets per TV-owning household was 1.1, while today it is 1.7. At the same time, average household size has decreased from 3.5 to 2.8. If this trend continues everybody in America will soon have their own TV set.

While estimates of the hours per week spent watching television vary, there is a consensus that the number is substantial. Two factors affect the reliability of these estimates. One is that people tend to be embarrassed by how much television they watch, and, therefore, may underestimate their viewing time. The second is that, in a growing number of households, the TV is on constantly, with people dropping into and out of programs. In such circumstances the actual hours spent watching television is difficult to assess. The most common estimate is that the average adult spends 25 to 30 hours per week watching television, clearly a considerable portion of our leisure time.

In its early days, television watching was convivial activity. Since TV ownership was not widespread, groups of people would organize parties around this activity. The novelty of TV was at least a basis for conversation. Watching has increasingly become an isolated activity, however, as set ownership has become universal. Even within families, TV watching is fragmented. Time spent watching television is increasingly time spent alone.

If it is assumed that people in any given household do not have identical tastes, the time when any *one* member of the household is watching TV—and hence be unavailable for personal interaction with other household members—would be expanded. Thus the following scenario is quite plausible: A child comes home from school, flips on the TV and watches late afternoon programs. The family sits down to dinner and watches the evening news. The mother continues watching the early evening fare with the child while the father putters around the house. As the child goes to bed, the father tunes in a football game which preoccupies him for the rest of the evening. During this day no family member has spent more than four hours watching TV, yet the opportunity for personal interaction was virtually eliminated.

Because television is so integrated into our lives, its precise impact is almost impossible to measure, however evidence of its impact is experienced daily. Children mimic their favorite TV characters and implore their parents to purchase advertised products. Adults hum TV jingles and make "inside" jokes based upon the shared television experience. Television homogenizes experience. The poorest southern rural family watches the same programs and sees the same ads as does the most sophisticated New York intellectual. The entire nation holds its breath as J.R.'s assailant is revealed. Subcultures are transformed. The world of sports, for example, bends its rules to accommodate the huge revenues of television. Its noblest heroes are reduced to hucksters who make dubious claims about dubious products. We are sometimes supplied with nattering commentators who not only feel obliged to tell us what we are seeing, but who also manage to desecrate the English language in the process.

Television is a frame which shapes our perception of reality. As we become a nation of TV hermits, the real world and the world of TV shade into each other. Television characters become real people and "Real People" become television characters. Robert Young, the star of "Marcus Welby, MD," received 5000 letters per week while this program was aired from persons seeking medical and emotional advice.[14] Television characters emerge as real people to sell products. Robert Young (Marcus Welby) sells "healthful" Sanka coffee, Karl Malden (tough cop) hustles the safety of American Express. Robert Blake (Baretta) careens around the screen selling STP. John Houseman (stern law professor) promotes the "hard working" Smith Barney Corporation. One might argue that these things appeal only to the feebleminded, but on March 9, 1981, Jack Klugman (Quincy) appeared before the Congress of this nation to testify in behalf of some drugs which had been the subject of a recent "Quincy" episode. For his testimony, he read from the "Quincy" script!

Television is obviously escapist, but to what are people escaping? Todd Gitlin[15] chronicles the implications of the structural features of prime-time TV. He argues that the very "week to week-ness" of prime-time TV conveys the image of social steadiness. Programs check into the viewer mind on a regular basis and the viewer knows the same program will be shown next week, "same time, same station." This certitude is itself comforting when the social world seems to be deteriorating.

On television, regardless of whether the programs are dramatic or comedic, there is always resolution: Mork overcomes his naiveté, Barnaby nabs his man, Quincy gets his exhumation. The viewer, beset by the problems of everyday life and work, can take momentary refuge in a world where problems are solved. At the same time, there is a strong pitch made on behalf of authority. In program after program, the expert (whether the expert is a doctor, police officer, detective, newspaper reporter, lawyer, teacher, or coach) solves a problem that is too complex for the average person to handle. Authority figures are always responsible. "Realistic" programs like "Lou Grant" and "Hill Street Blues" which occasionally depict instances of wrong doing by some in authority, have these transgressions discovered and routed by others in authority. As President Ford said, "The system works."

Real and divisive social issues, if they cannot be ignored, are emptied of their serious content. Thus, the working class rebel of the 1950s is transformed into Fonzie, the white bigot becomes an amiable Archie Bunker, the black bigot is actually lovable George Jefferson, women's liberation is reduced to a ranting Maude, and young radicals are really Mod Squad kids who want to help the government. In this way, TV appears relevant without having to take seriously the issues that are muted by these stereotypes.

[14]Michael Real, *Mass-Mediated Culture* (Englewood Cliffs: Prentice-Hall, 1977), p. 121.
[15]Todd Gitlin, "Prime Time Ideology: The Hegemonic Process in Entertainment," *Social Problems,* February 1979.

It is possible to argue that the positive contributions of television have been substantial. Does not television provide cheap entertainment for all and, at the same time, make us much more conscious of the world around us? Through what other medium can 100 million people be simultaneously exposed to a program of the significance of "Roots" for example? The point we wish to make is that whatever gains might be achieved through television come at a high cost as well.

Television is an ideal medium for a consumer society. Not only does it constantly promote the consumption ethic, the act of watching is itself a quintessential act of consumption. Reading newspapers at least requires the energy to select stories, turn pages, and sustain attention. With TV, nothing is required. The viewer can watch program after program while simply sitting impassively.

Supporters of the TV industry argue that at least the consumer is sovereign, that the industry responds to what people will watch. This sovereignty is sharply circumscribed, however. It is like that of a "boss slave" on a southern plantation. Programs do come and go, but replacements are always generated within the matrix of corporate control. Consumer choice is exercised within the parameters defined by "CHiPs" and "Lou Grant."

It is a misperception that television is cheap entertainment because the true costs of television are hidden. It appears that the only costs rest in the acquisition and maintenance of a set, and that the programming itself is free. This is not so. The advertiser buys television time because it is profitable to do so. The costs of this advertising must be passed on to the consumer. Thus we pay for television in the form of higher prices for cars, gasoline, and aspirin. In 1970, for example, Bayer aspirin spent $15.6 million on advertising and had a suggested retail price of $.63 per 50 tablet bottle. St. Joseph's, producing exactly the same aspirin but spending only $.7 million on advertising, had a recommended price of $.39 for the same sized bottle. In 1977, Proctor & Gamble, the nation's leading advertiser, spent $460 million selling soaps. This was 5.7 percent of total sales for that year. Noxell Corporation, a cosmetic firm, spent 24.2 percent of its total sales on advertising.[16]

There are also indirect costs of television advertising. Programs are constantly interrupted with pleas for the purchase of this or that item. As we saw in Chapter 2, there is an implicit message in these harangues that our lives are inadequate without these products. Theoretically, advertising time is limited by the FCC, but in practice these limitations are rarely enforced. To determine the extent of advertising during a typical viewing day, four hours of television were monitored on June 16, 1980, two hours in prime time, one in the afternoon, and one after prime time.

Of the four hours, 54½ minutes were devoted to advertising and network promotion. In this period, there were 104 advertisements of all sorts. This means that in the course of a year the average TV viewer is exposed to about 38,000 ads solely through television. Consider the developing child. If we assume the same

[16]Taken from James Koch, *Industrial Organization and Prices* (Englewood Cliffs: Prentice-Hall, 1980), pp. 301 and 324.

amount of TV viewing (an estimate that many experts would regard as conservative for children), this would mean that by the time a child graduates from high school he or she will be exposed to at least half a million ads, even assuming a significant portion of the child's time has been spent watching public TV programs. The vast majority of these ads cultivate private acquisition. Buying products becomes a major means of self-expression, self-fulfillment, and self-improvement. Part of the costs of this so-called inexpensive form of entertainment is constant exposure to messages designed to induce anxiety about self-worth and to resolve that anxiety in the market place. Commerical television diminishes our critical capacity in two ways. First, its programmatic content is inevitably skewed in the direction of the lowest common denominator because of the economic necessity to build audience size. Instead of being challenged, audiences are pulled in the direction of the uncomplicated and the unsubtle. Second, TV's commercials persistently debase our language, depriving words of their meaning and hence their capacity for making distinctions. Regardless of what the message says, you do not "have it your way" at Burger King, but chances are you'll never think to ask why not. Commercials must stress the superlative, and so corrupt language. We agree with Robert Heilbroner[17] who recently described commercials as "instances of a process that empties communication of its content, that substitutes reflex for creative spontaneity, that destroys credence in the written or spoken word."

There is some truth to the argument that television makes us more aware of the world around us. It is possible to have a ringside seat at the coronation of a European monarch or to fly with the president on historic missions in remote areas. Such advantages must be weighed against the daily distortions of the world inherent in telecasting. In a curious way television reduces everything to the same plane. Wars, soap operas, movies, drama are all reduced to the same television screen, are interrupted by the same ads, and can be turned on or off with equal ease. Television is the world of the episode. Buildup, climax, and denouement occur at regular intervals. Even news stories are calibrated to this format.

It is ironic that truth is often best illuminated by exaggeration. Perhaps Chauncey Gardiner, the protagonist in the film *Being There*, best serves as a metaphor of a triumphant TV world. Confined to a life of TV watching, life becomes TV. He switches from sitcom, to cop shows, to war news, to opera, apparently at random and with a uniform sense of impassiveness. All is reduced to the same two-dimensional plane. He enters the world, guileless, thinking he can switch off uncomfortable situations with his remote control. He is incapable of personal involvement in life. "I like to watch," he says.

Television has a direct impact upon our political process because it bends that process toward the images it best portrays. Politics becomes trivialized. Instead of a

[17]Robert Heilbroner, "The Demand for the Supply Side," *New York Review of Books,* June 11, 1981.

process that resolves major issues confronting the nation, politics is reduced to a question of personal style. Candidate strategies, polls, candidate motives, and concrete events are covered in minute detail while issue analysis goes begging. Short, snappy charges and countercharges of the candidates are reported, as are candidate errors. Personalities are emphasized. Politics, in short, becomes a spectacle, and all of us are reduced to watching.[18]

A fascinating vignette concerning the significance of television was provided in 1976 in the first televised debate between Gerald Ford and Jimmy Carter. It would be comic were it not so tragic. For some minutes the audio portion of the debate was lost and so the debate was interrupted. Each candidate stood frozen at his respective podium, apparently afraid to move lest the camera reveal some human frailty. It was as if the candidates and the audio were simultaneously unplugged.

Political campaigns are ideally suited to the electronic media. They contain drama, episodes, personalities, and daily events. At the same time, the media reinforce these dimensions. The campaign process is extended at the expense of governance. Philip Crane announced his candidacy for president more than two years before the 1980 election, the earliest announcement in history, but a record destined to be short-lived. We have recently experienced a series of candidates who are good campaigners, but who have very little sense of what they want to do or how to do it once elected. Nixon, Carter, Reagan and Anderson come to mind. In 1980, the nation elected as president a media favorite son: the former actor and master of the one liner, Ronald Reagan.

The mass media do not help us understand the source of our discontent. Riots are shown, some problems are depicted, but analysis goes begging. The world seems too complex for comprehension. We do not understand why politicians cheat, laws are not enforced, and empty political rhetoric echoes through the land. The reason the mass media do not provide adequate analysis is that it would have to take the form of a confessional. They are part of the problem. It is ironic that this *increases* political frustration, but the media offer a balm for this as well.

As one looks at the media's reality, there is every reason to retreat into a more private self. Television beckons the populace to enter its world. Hours are filled watching insipid television shows which in turn encourage privatization. How can one go out in public with a "ring around the collar" or without proper feminine protection? Can one invite a neighbor into a home that has "waxy yellow buildup?" Whether we have the money to purchase TV's wares becomes an important issue, and we resent a public world that wants to take away some of our money. At least in the world of television things turn out all right. Regular people win money and cars, and the bad guys always get caught.

---

[18] Doris Graber presents a sound analysis of the impact of television on electoral campaigns in her book *Mass Media and American Politics* (Washington, D.C.: Congressional Quarterly Press, 1980), especially Ch. 6.

CHAPTER 6

Everyday Life and Public Policy

Unless all men and all classes contribute to a goal we cannot even be sure it is worth having.

Jane Addams

This book differs from most treatments of American politics, and so it may be helpful to summarize the main outline of our argument to this point. Most government textbooks whether conservative, radical, or indifferent in political tone focus upon political institutions and how they operate. While this approach can provide useful information, we believe it is inadequate to understand the political condition of contemporary America. For the reasons discussed in Chapter 1 we believe that the nation is in the midst of a deeply felt but dimly recognized political crisis. The consensus of values evident after World War II has been steadily eroded, but it has not been supplanted by a newer consensus. Those with disproportionate political and economic power have attempted to sustain that power through a variety of means, many of which are not commonly considered political. These attempts are hidden in the fabric of everyday life. In thinking about our daily interactions with such significant institutions as schools, work, and the mass media, we have urged the reader to consider the broad but significant political implications of everyday experience.

In Chapter 2 we attempted to show the impact of the consumer society upon our politics. This impact is not limited to the "selling" of candidates and the defusing of movements of political opposition. It extends to the way ordinary citizens conceive of their relationship to society. The consumerist mentality encourages people to identify their sense of well-being and the satisfaction of basic needs with the consumption of material goods. This mentality is ultimately self-defeating because it is the consumption of goods which is of paramount importance. In order to sustain consumption, dissatisfaction is perpetuated.

Although very few profess to be happy with schools these days, the educational system does serve the existing social order in several ways. It contributes to the belief in a meritocratic society, that is, an open and fair society in which advancement is based on merit. This belief is propagated despite evidence which sharply questions its validity. At the same time, questions of the *intrinsic* value of a meritocracy are not raised. We rarely consider what kind of merit we wish to reward in an ideally meritocratic society.

Education grows more narrow and technocratic. The value of education rests not in its liberating and critical potential, but in its capacity to prepare the student for existing or emergent job structures. Education is not seen as intrinsically satisfying; it becomes the means to satisfactions to be achieved further down the road. It is in the schools that students first confront important social values. They learn to compete, they are prepared for failure, and they are initiated into institutional alienation. Most important, schools teach that failure to achieve (with achievement being defined by those in authority) is a function of some individual inadequacy.

Hierarchy and inequality pervade the work place, and work life becomes less satisfying as the process of deskilling becomes more elaborate. Combined with pervasive and persistent unemployment, deskilling encourages fear—especially the fear of uselessness. Because the source of this fear is not easily identifiable, the worker either dismisses it or turns on fellow workers. Political solutions to this situation are not entertained because basic issues of work relations are not considered part of the political agenda.

The mass media, being corporate institutions, are particularly attuned to the interests of corporate America. In-depth political analysis touching upon economic issues does not typify the news, in part because support from economically powerful interests is necessary for the survival of the mass media, and in part because the mass media are interested in maximum audience size in order to increase profits. This drive for profit keeps news programs out of prime time, keeps them to a 30-minute format, and subjects them to a variety of gimmickry designed to build audiences. Politics is made trivial. Elections, potentially a means of discourse about important issues facing the nation, are transformed into horse races. Events, strategies, and personalities supplant issues as focal points of campaigns. At the cultural level, the media bind us closer to the existing social structure by their promotion of the consumption ethic. Simultaneously, television provides an easily accessible, but lonely retreat from a world which for many has become incomprehensible or unbearable.

The main point is that people do not enter the political arena fresh and unencumbered. All bring, as part of their consciousness, their histories and experiences. It is possible to think of politics as ennobling, as an enterprise in which people try to solve problems in order to benefit society as a whole. Given the context we have discussed, it is not surprising that the American concept of politics differs from this ideal. We make certain assumptions about the nature of American political life. Ample evidence for these assumptions can be found in political science research, but what is important from our perspective is that they follow logically from the conditions of everyday life we have described.

First, American citizens do not think very much about politics. They are preoccupied with other, more private, aspects of living. As a result there is not very much popular participation in the political process. Only about one-half of the eligible adult population participates in the simple and most heralded political activity: voting for president. The percentage of eligible persons voting in non-presidential elections is much lower. Participation in other forms of political activity, such as working in campaigns or letter writing, is low too. Nonparticipation is not evenly distributed throughout the population. Those who have been most damaged by the social system, especially the poor, participate at much lower rates than do people in upper-income categories.

Second, our political system tends to make important issues more complex and mysterious than necessary. At the time of greatest attention to politics—during national campaigns—issues take a back seat to candidate personalities, opinion polls, and political strategies. Between elections it is even more difficult for the citizen to get solid information on important issues. In the absence of such information, people are encouraged to leave crucial decisions in the hands of so-called experts who may develop policies which poorly serve the community as a whole.

Third, when citizens do think about politics, two sentiments are predominant. One deeply skeptical sentiment is the view that politics is essentially corrupt, that politicians are regularly bought and sold. This view holds that it is almost impossible for an honest person to survive in politics, and if one did survive, such a person would be unable to do much to abate the flood of corruption. The second view is related to the first. It is that politics is seen in terms of a narrowly defined self-interest. Politics is thought of as an arena for seizing as many goods as possible for oneself or one's group. It is the consumer vision extended to the political realm. The question of social justice is secondary.

Finally, we believe that these attitudes about political life are ultimately self-defeating. They ensure that basic control of the process remains in the hands of the few and that the interests of the many are poorly served. The political arena is far from perfect but it offers the only hope for addressing common solutions for common problems. When people drop out of that arena or when that arena merely becomes an extension of private relations of power, those with the most power will continue to win. The effects of these everyday experiences upon the political process can be illustrated by examining a vital area of public policy making.

THE IMPLICATIONS OF NATIONAL ENERGY POLICY

Energy policymaking provides an excellent opportunity to explore the dynamics of the political process. In the last decades of this century, energy will undoubtedly be among the most important domestic issues facing the nation. It is central to the lives of all of us. How we heat and cool our homes, how we move from one place to another, and at what cost, are matters that affect our lives on a daily basis. But the impact of the energy issue cannot be summarized simply by totaling the millions of individual decisions we make daily, for energy penetrates to the core of our economy as well. How the industrial sector is driven, the extent to which synthetic fibers are used in textile production, the use of pesticides and fertilizers in agriculture, and whether to use farmlands to produce ''energy crops'' are all profoundly political questions in that they involve the distribution of important social values.

By this time it is apparent that the choices made with respect to energy have important social consequences. It seems an exaggeration to suggest that the fate of the planet may hang in the balance of decisions about energy paths, yet it may. The choices we face are neither obvious nor inconsequential. Over nuclear energy hangs the spectres of Three Mile Island, continuous low-level pollution, the unsolved problem of how to store highly radioactive wastes with life spans of thousands of years, and the threat of worldwide proliferation of nuclear weapons. Increasing reliance upon U.S. coal means gearing up the most dangerous industry in the world to operate, as well as increasing the possibility of causing severe environmental damage through deglaciation and acid rain. Reliance upon oil raises not only the problem of continuing pollution, but the wisdom of committing the economic well-being of the nation to forces beyond our control. Solar energy, while useful and environmentally benign, constantly must fight the battle of credibility. The extent of solar's capacity to handle our energy needs and, therefore, the extent to which we should be committed to it, is the subject of intense debate.

These dilemmas are perplexing enough in themselves, but along with them must go the recognition that it is essential to maintain a long-range perspective—if for no other reason than the substantial capital costs of pursuing any particular energy source. A massive commitment to coal, for example, with an industrial infrastructure erected upon that assumption, might make conversion to a different energy source 20 years from now extremely costly. These are only some of the questions about our energy policy that ought to command the attention of the nation.

Overlaying these issues are questions of a different sort. U.S. consumption of energy has historically always been high, but in the past 20 years it has increased substantially. Today the United States consumes 30 percent of the world's energy, and we import about 35 percent to 40 percent of the oil we use. If we were willing to live with our energy consumption level of 1962, we would not need to import a drop of oil. Thus we might well ask whether all of our present consumption is necessary and whether, in any case, consumption can be made more efficient. A study by the

Harvard Business School estimates that through conservation we could use 30 percent to 40 percent less energy and maintain *at least* the same standard of living that we now enjoy.[1]

Given the centrality of energy to the nation, one might assume that thoughtful and dispassionate analyses of the options available would command the attention of the nation's media and political leadership. Unfortunately this has not been the case. Politicians do talk about energy, but the talk is not thoughtful. In the 1980 presidential elections, the topic of energy was not featured prominently as it should have been. Surely a stranger to this country would be astonished by this fact. Some light may be shed on this anomaly by describing how energy policy is made in this country.

What Is "Good" Energy Policy?

Before we examine the actual energy policy process, it is useful to think of a framework out of which a reasonable energy policy might emerge. Obviously an energy policy should *satisfy the needs of the nation*, but a nation's needs are often subjective choices which may be artificially manufactured. For example, it is not obvious that one needs a certain kitchen appliance or a polyester suit, even though some people may feel that they do. Needs may be structured by prior social choices as well. How much gasoline we need is in part determined by patterns of urban sprawl, the fuel efficiency of automobiles, and the quality of alternatives to the automobile. Beyond an irreducible minimum, therefore, a strategy of trade-offs must be developed. We must make difficult and subjective choices between such things as the comfort of larger automobiles and the fuel efficiency of smaller ones.

A second issue of importance to energy policy making is the *reliability of the sources*. Obviously, a nation is its own best source of energy supply, other things being equal. In the real world, however, other things rarely are equal. It is quite possible for the United States to become energy independent by the turn of the century, but the price of this independence may well be unacceptable. It would involve a series of decisions that in a conventional economic sense would be inefficient. Such alternatives need to be assessed but, rather than complete energy independence, the likely choices revolve around the extent and direction of our dependence.

A third question involves the *long term interests of the nation*. A rational energy program may involve the conscious rejection of momentarily easier and more economic paths. President Nixon's first response to the 1973 Arab oil embargo was to call for increased domestic production of oil. Project Independence was to be orchestrated by American oil corporations. Increasing domestic production, while reasonable from the perspective of the short-term market, ensures increasing

---

[1]Robert Stobaugh and Daniel Yergin, eds. *Energy Future,* (New York: Random House, 1979), especially Ch. 6.

dependence in the long run, as we sustain our commitment to an oil-based future while we drain our domestic supplies.

Energy policy must also takes into account *issues of public safety*, both at the use and at the production level. American coal mining, for example, is extremely dangerous. The ingestion of coal dust leads to various respiratory problems, and often to premature death. Long-term debilitation is not the only hazard of coal mining. Since 1907, more than 90,000 people have died in coal-mining accidents, and since 1930, more than 1.5 million people have been seriously injured.[2] At the consumption level, the problems of various fossil-fuel uses and of nuclear energy are well known. These issues must be sorted out.

We might wish to consider our *place in the family of nations* and make energy decisions based in part upon this vision. According to some of the other criteria, for example, we might decide to pursue an oil-based energy future. A substantial commitment to this type of future could have dire consequences for the developing world. It could not only inhibit the development of an industrial infrastructure, it could force the price of petroleum-based fertilizers up so high that poorer agricultural societies could not afford them.

Perhaps the most important criterion is one that is mentioned the least. We may want to consider alternative energy futures in terms of whether they *enhance or inhibit the development of a democratic society*. Thus we might ask whether an energy path will concentrate power unequally and therefore inhibit democracy, or whether it will diffuse power and thereby probably enhance democracy. A nuclear future, for example, would ensure that power would remain in the hands of the few, while some solar alternatives would spread power more democratically. We might wish to pursue such solar options, therefore, even if they were less cost effective than the nuclear option.

Obviously these kinds of issues are relatively easy to highlight, but are difficult to resolve. Listing these criteria places the subjective nature of the choices facing us in bold relief, but the essence of politics lies in making subjective choices. If matters were clear-cut, obvious, and objective, there would be no need for politics. Hard choices must be made, and in a democracy people must have the information necessary to make those choices.

In our political system there is a strong bias toward not dealing with this type of issue in any collective way at all. It has been argued, and indeed this argument is very powerful within the highest reaches of President Reagan's administration,[3] that the best energy policy is no policy at all. The best way to determine our energy future, this argument runs, is to allow the consumer, through the exercise of self-sovereignty in the marketplace, to make individual choices. The summation of these choices will

---

[2]David Howard Davis, *Energy Politics* (New York: St. Martin's Press, 1978), p. 38.

[3]See, for example, David Stockman, "The Wrong War? The Case Against a National Energy Policy," *Public Interest*, Fall 1978.

constitute energy policy. Planning encumbers the market and therefore ought to be avoided. President Reagan argues that we should unleash American businesses, that they should be allowed to do "what they have always done," that is, go about their business without significant public intrusions. It is appropriate to consider whether the "market solution" is an effective way to establish energy policy.

The Market Solution

A major advantage of the market system is in its elasticity. Anything, it seems, can be sold if the price is right. By allowing prices to be regulated by supply and demand, it is believed, the nation will solve the energy problem automatically, and in the least painful way. But market systems are not born in some neutral stratosphere from which they descend to earth. They reflect the distributions of power, the rules of the game, and the institutional settings in which they operate. Reagan administration officials used a free-market justification for making deep cuts in the solar research budget. They claimed that solar energy should succeed or fail in the marketplace without benefit of federal subsidy. However, the same officials provided for an increase in federal support for nuclear energy research. Such inconsistencies are commonplace in so-called free-market systems.

The market may help determine how much fuel would be sold in a given city assuming a certain distribution between private cars and public transportation, but it cannot help decide whether to add more public transportation or to reduce its price. One cannot simply say "Let the market decide, let each transport system pay its own way," because automobile usage has been heavily subsidized historically in a number of ways, most notably in the construction of a vast federal highway system.

The true social costs of a particular energy path are often not revealed by the market system because part of the costs may be borne by society as a whole, not by the parties to a specific transaction. Costs that have been externalized, that is, transferred to the social level, are not part of the market transaction and are difficult to measure. The more power an industry has, the greater the opportunity to externalize costs. Let us once again consider automobile usage in comparison to public transportation, this time assuming there are no institutional biases against the latter. Comparative costs of the two systems still may not be reflected in the market system because of the extent to which the auto industry has been able to externalize its costs. Road maintenance, for example, is not reflected in the price of cars, nor are the costs of inflation which is stimulated by our continuing dependence upon foreign oil. Such matters deserve attention. Good energy policy may require the expansion of subsidized public transport systems, even if such systems are inefficient in the narrowly construed economic sense of the term.

There are also two notable inequities when the market solution is applied to energy problems. An inherent tension exists between market forces and assumptions of conservation usually associated with energy policy. In a free competitive market, prices are driven down to their lowest natural level. For energy policy this is a catastrophe because lower prices encourage the consumption we are trying to limit. (Thus, following the logic of the economist, large consumers of energy get cut-rate prices!) Simultaneously, supplies tend to be erratic because, in a pure competitive situation, suppliers are regularly entering and being forced out of the market. The early history of both the coal and oil industries in this country was typified by erratic supplies before clear thinking men such as John D. Rockefeller emerged to impose order. Industry magnates soon came to recognize the wisdom of planning. If planning is necessary, however, the rationale for leaving it to private persons who stand to gain or lose fortunes is murky at best. The dilemma in such situations is that private and public interest intersect only by accident.

The second major inequity of the market solution to energy policy is the disproportionate burden such a solution places upon the poor. Even if the market solution is economically wise, it is morally outrageous. The demand for fuel is relatively inelastic under current conditions. Poor people can do such things as turn down thermostats and eliminate pleasure driving, but beyond such measures there exists a fairly fixed need for energy. Increasing fuel costs must, therefore, cut deeply into household budgets. The Energy Department's Fuel Oil Marketing and Advisory Committee estimates that in 1980, 20 percent of a middle-income household's budget was devoted toward energy payment. This is a substantial figure, but low-income families must spend double that proportion on their energy needs.[4]

This inequity is compounded by the greater difficulty the poor have in conserving energy. Housing of the poor is characteristically more dilapidated and less insulated, therefore more expensive to keep heated. The poor are generally unable to afford any fuel-efficient repairs. Detroit has only recently and reluctantly begun to build relatively fuel efficient cars. Poor people who live in rural areas where public transportation is nonexistent must drive, but, of course, they cannot afford to buy the new fuel-efficient cars. Instead, they use older, inefficient cars which if not maintained, increase inefficiency. Free-market advocates can claim that although this is too bad, it is still important to cling to market principles, but they must realize that while inefficient use of energy is catastrophic for the poor, it is also contrary to the interests of each of us, except those who profit directly from the sale of energy. If conservation is a legitimate and valued collective goal, any waste hurts us all.

Perhaps the most significant argument against a market solution is that, with respect to energy, a market does not exist at all in the classic sense of the term. In the first place the Organization of Petroleum Exporting Countries (OPEC), an international cartel, is unusually resistant to free-market doctrine. It is unwise, therefore, to rely upon the market to bring demand down and thus to reduce prices. In

[4]"Billions to the Poor for Fuel Bills, but not a Penny for Transportation," Susan Thero, *National Journal,* May 17, 1980.

1974 Milton Friedman predicted the OPEC cartel would collapse well before the price of crude reached $10 a barrel. By 1981 the price had reached about $35 before it temporarily levelled off. The reason for this is that many of the most important OPEC nations are not compelled by their need for revenue to keep their oil output to a maximum. Oil is an exhaustible resource with an exceptionally bullish future. Leaving it in the ground *increases* its value. This reality is subversive of the free-market doctrine.[5]

Concentration and control typifies the energy industry on the domestic side as well. There is no price competition. Corporations of staggering size control the flow of oil into our economy. With the decontrol of oil prices, American oil corporations have in effect joined OPEC. Some would argue that they never left. Each time OPEC raises the price of oil, Exxon, Mobil, and Texaco reap a proportionate benefit. Moreover, ownership of this nation's energy resources is becoming increasingly concentrated in the hands of the nation's major oil corporations. Seven of the 12 largest oil companies have an interest in every fuel resource that is, or might become, competitive with oil. Increasingly, they have the power to control the pace of development in all major energy fields for their own economic advantage. Based upon reports filed by oil corporations with the Securities and Exchange Commission, two Pulitzer Prize-winning reporters pinpoint some dimensions of their wealth. It is of the sort the average mind cannot readily comprehend. Therefore, we will quote the report at length:[6]

> Look at the potential value of the energy reserves of the oil industry. Calculated on the world price of oil, the oil, natural gas, and coal holdings of only two companies—Occidental Petroleum Co. and Shell Oil Co.—are worth $831 billion.
>
> That exceeds the combined assets of the more than 400 non-oil-producing companies on *Fortune* magazine's directory of the nation's 500 largest industrial corporations—such as Ford Motor Co. and General Electric Co. and Goodyear Tire & Rubber Co. and Eastman Kodak Co. and General Foods Co.
>
> It exceeds the individual savings of all Americans 10 times over. It surpasses expenditures for all health care services—private and government—in this country in the last five years.
>
> Using the same energy reserve valuation formula, the oil, natural gas, and coal holdings of just one oil company—Exxon, the world's largest—are worth more than $1.3 trillion.
>
> What does it mean for one corporation to have financial resources of that magnitude? How much is $1.3 trillion?
>
> It is the equivalent of 12 BankAmericas, the nation's largest bank. Or 23 Prudential Insurance companies, the country's largest life insurer. Or 79 Sears, Roebuck companies, the nation's largest retailer.

[5] For an interesting commentary on this point see John K. Galbraith, "Oil: A Solution" *New York Review of Books*, September 27, 1979, p. 3.

[6] Donald L. Bartlett and James B. Steele, "Oil Firms Have Tentacles in Every Energy Field," Chicago *Tribune*, December 17, 1980, p. 1.

It exceeds the combined gross national products, the total value of a nation's goods and services, of 17 countries—Britain, West Germany, Greece, Norway, Thailand, Israel, Egypt, Nigeria, Saudi Arabia, Iraq, Yugoslavia, New Zealand, Ecuador, Bolivia, Chile, Venezuela, and Nicaragua.

Furthermore, the $1.3 trillion figure takes into account only Exxon's holding of crude oil, natural gas, and coal reserves in the U.S.

Reliable estimates of the company's oil shale reserves have not been made public. Nor does the figure include Exxon's vast uranium reserves. Or the company's growing interest in solar energy. Or its energy reserves in foreign countries, where oil and gas deposits exceed its U.S. supplies three times over.

And Exxon is not the nation's largest holder of energy reserves.

That distinction goes to Conoco, Inc., formerly Continental Oil Co. Because of the company's massive coal holdings, the value of Conoco's reserves—calculated at the world oil price—stands at $1.9 trillion.

To speak of market solutions in such circumstances is little more than a bad joke. There is an enormous gap between the cost of producing energy and the value of that energy. Energy is valuable because of inelastic demand but it need not be expensive because of this. Water, after all, is similarly valuable. What makes energy so expensive is that concentrated power has been able to force prices up to the value of energy instead of having it stay somewhere close to the cost of producing it. This is not necessarily unfortunate because, except for solar energy, our energy supplies are exhaustible. The judicious use of energy is a prudent course to follow. At the same time, tilting the price of energy towards its value rather than its production costs means there are enormous profits involved in its production.

The most significant policy question with respect to energy is the uses of the enormous profits. Will they be used for private gain or for public benefit? We can be certain that energy policy will be made for the United States. Except for purposes of propaganda, the "market solution" will not be used, and for reasons earlier stated we believe it should not be used. The major question about energy policy is whether it will be made in duly constituted public institutions or in the boardrooms of major oil companies. A look at Carter and Reagan administration efforts may help us find the answer.

The Political Setting of Policymaking

When political scientists call attention to political settings they usually focus upon such institutional phenomena as the separation of powers, the structure of Congress, and federalism. We wish to call attention to the setting that is the legacy of economic inequality. Particularly when operating defensively, entrenched interests enjoy a distinct advantage in our political setting. Inequality perpetuates itself. Let us look at the political world from the perspective of a national political candidate who wishes to be elected or re-elected. Due to the growing professionalism of political campaigns, the growing use of such things as pollsters and consulting firms, and, more important, due to increasing use of radio and television, campaign costs are skyrocketing. While such things as personal dynamism, tactical mistakes, and the nature of the times affect the outcomes of campaigns, increasingly the effective campaign is the well-financed one.

Furthermore, since no one is certain what will work in a political campaign, the natural inclination of a politician is to do as much as possible, which means the pressure for money is always there. If a candidate is unable or unwilling to finance the campaign personally, it is necessary to find sources of support. All candidates have mental lists of "good guys" and "bad guys." Liberals may accept funds from organized labor, the Friends of the Earth, or the ACLU with a clear conscience just as conservatives may be anxious recipients of funds from the National Association of Manufacturers, the Moral Majority, or the American Medical Association. It is also not surprising that candidates receive money from and speak vigorously for interests that are important to their constituencies. For example, Senator Henry Jackson, a liberal on many domestic issues, is known in Washington D.C. as the Senator from Boeing because of his vigorous support for a corporation that is vital to the economic health of the Seattle area. One expects North Carolina senators from either party to speak for, and be supported by, tobacco interests. All of this is part of the normal warp and woof of American politics.

What is interesting is why candidates would accept money in exchange for political favors that are inimical to the interests of their constituents. Does this not place them in political danger? Democratic assumptions imply that it would, but such assumptions do not take into account the distorting influence of money in the political process. A candidate may accept money to serve interests contrary to those in his or her district if it is calculated that the votes to be purchased with the money at least offset the votes that would be lost by the unpopular action.

To understand how this can work, we must begin by recognizing that people are basically inattentive to politics. It is highly unlikely that the average citizen will know many of the specific actions taken by his or her representative, even if those actions are publicized by the representative's opponents. Even in a worst case scenario, a representative's vote loss may be in the hundreds. Second, a representative can easily mask support for the unpopular interest. Support may be buried in obscure but vital committee proceedings, and the representative may *oppose* the interest when the vote is not vital. Organized interests are sensitive to the representative's problems and do not expect total loyalty. Third, the money that is gained will not be used to advertise the representative's position on the unpopular issue. It will be used for *general* purposes. The representative may use the money to develop an attractive commercial, to establish a phone bank, to make extra visits to the district, or for any number of other things that will help gain votes.

We do not wish to imply that all politicians work in this fashion. Undoubtedly there are many who do not. These temptations, however, are real. They are an integral part of American politics and will remain so as long as money remains vital to continuing in office. Public life is not a secure one, nor in a democracy should it be. So long as security can be increased by attracting wealthy supporters, we can expect many politicians to attempt to do so.

The significance of money in the political process places the corporate sector in a position of great advantage. Political action committees (PACs)—essentially political fund-raising committees formed by various organizations—have a strong corporate flavor. In 1974, shortly after the passage of the first campaign finance law sanctioning PACs, there were 201 labor PACs and 407 corporate and trade PACs. Four years later the number of labor PACs had increased only to 217 while corporate and trade PACs had more than tripled to 1269. With over 2 million corporations in America, the potential for PAC growth in this sector has barely been tapped. A study prepared for the *Congressional Quarterly* in 1979[7] revealed that there were 133 PACs in the energy field alone, and this number has increased since then.

PAC and individual contributions to political campaigns are not the only bases of political power for American corporations. There are numerous other fringe benefits. These range from relatively insignificant items like picking up a restaurant tab to free rides in corporate jets to large speaker's fees for banquet appearances. Representatives loyal to powerful interests may rest in the knowledge that they will be well taken care of whether or not they win an election or if they retire. Finally, there is no way to estimate the amount of illegal money that changes hands, although the recent FBI Abscam investigations demonstrates that kickbacks do occur.

A most important fact is that corporations enjoy a legitimacy which augments their political power. As we saw in Chapter 5, the media tend to treat the corporate sector with benign neglect. Furthermore any major corporate executive, no matter how mediocre, can command the respectful attention of the media if desired. Corporations are considered to be repositories of expertise and right thinking. Any blue-ribbon commission seeking to assess some social problem is heavily sprinkled with representatives from the corporate sector, and we regularly speak of making our schools or our various governments as efficient as a business. All of this augments the substantial political power of business. The political setting is far from neutral. It is one in which economic interests enjoy major advantages. This factor must be kept in mind when considering energy politics.

THE WONDERLAND WORLD OF ENERGY POLITICS

Any efforts to establish a significant energy policy must confront entrenched economic interests in that area. This helps explain why, despite widespread recognition of an energy crisis, very little has been done to develop a reasonable plan for our energy future. Clarion calls for action by political leaders have been followed

[7] Alan Berlow and Laura Weiss, "Energy PACs: Potential Power in Elections," *Congressional Quarterly,* November 3, 1979, p. 2455.

by specific plans which were quite timid. Even these timid plans met with major opposition from industry, which waged intense public and private campaigns in support of the status quo. Programs proposed by President Carter were substantially watered down in Congress. When the emasculated bills finally passed, President Carter had little recourse other than claiming victory. Little had changed, however, and the positive changes which did occur are threatened by President Reagan who seems interested in getting government "off the backs" of energy corporations.

Prior to the Carter administration there were no serious attempts to establish an energy policy in the United States. The Arab oil embargo caught President Nixon by surprise. He instituted limited price controls on oil, and solemnly announced the birth of Project Independence, but after gasoline lines subsided the nation returned to normalcy. This meant that no serious attention would be given to the need for a public energy policy. Rapidly increasing energy costs and widespread predictions of impending catastrophe convinced President Carter to make energy policy the domestic centerpiece of his administration.

The long gasoline lines in 1973 had angered the public. There was talk in Washington about oil corporations having too much power and when the first post-Watergate election returned an unusually young and liberal class of Congressional leaders to Washington, a few politicians began to speak of the necessity of stemming the horizontal and vertical integration of the industries. These politicians wanted to restore competition within the oil industry and between various energy sources.

In reaction to this, the big oil companies launched a massive public relations campaign to create the appropriate climate for a debate on energy policy. The intent was to convince the public of the essential good will, responsibility, and expertise of the industry. At the most diffuse level, oil corporations sponsored a number of public service ads unrelated to oil issues. Parents were encouraged to make sure their children had dental checkups, and businesses were asked to hire veterans, compliments of a concerned oil corporation. Extensive grants were made to public television with the only requirement being a simple statement indicating the source of the funds.

The tone of oil ads began to change dramatically. Since demand for gasoline was largely inelastic anyway, people were encouraged to drive safely, and to conserve energy. Shell "answer men" emerged to tell the public how better gas mileage could be achieved. Bob Hope was hired to convince people that Texaco was "working to keep your trust," and that the owners of Texaco were a school teacher here, a grandmother there, just "people like you and me." Ads piled on top of ads seeking to prove that oil corporations were working tirelessly and selflessly to solve our "energy crisis." In newspapers, oil corporations ran ads that displayed their vision for a better America. Social goals included plenty of jobs, adequate education, equal opportunity, and a national energy policy.

There was also propaganda on gut oil issues, although these were targeted to more elite audiences. In 1975 Mobil began a campaign in which they ran paid editorials periodically in over 100 of the nation's most prominent newspapers. Academics were invited to expense-paid information seminars. The American Petroleum Institute (API), the major industry representative in Washington D.C., developed films to show to school children and distributed *Petroleum Today*, an expensive publication, free of charge to thousands of "opinion leaders" in government and industry. Over 500 newspapers, radio, and television stations regularly receive API press releases, which are often run *verbatim* as news stories.

What is significant about this campaign is the absence of any substantial power to present an alternative point of view. Opponents have neither the resources nor the revenue to offset this type of propaganda offensive. Given their dependence upon corporate power, the media, particularly public and commercial television, are not anxious to generate analyses which might reflect adversely upon big oil companies. The main effects of this campaign were to generate confusion in the minds of citizens and to sharply limit the range of policy debate. Politicans soon ceased to speak of breaking up the oil companies, let alone to question the ultimate legitimacy of private exploitation of energy. Instead the debate focused on how much *more* should be given to the oil industry—how much more drilling on public lands, how much more off shore drilling, how much to relax environmental standards, how small the windfall profits tax.

President Carter called the energy crisis "the moral equivalent of war" in a major national address and urged us to reduce our energy dependence by conservation methods and by increasing coal's proportion of energy consumption. In the days that followed, he spelled out his battle plans. These plans did not match the Carter rhetoric, for the National Energy Plan released on April 29, 1977, called not for a reduction in energy consumption, but only for a decrease in the projected rate of *increase* in energy use.[8] Conservation meant that we would expand our consumption more slowly. Half of the *new* demand would be met by increased coal production, while one-quarter would come from an increased use of nuclear power. Only 2 percent of the increment would come from solar energy sources.

The plan submitted by President Carter to Congress indicated that he would fight his "war" with BB guns. The ten key proposals were quite modest and incapable of significantly altering the nation's subservience to domestic and international energy cartels. Even those modest proposals were decimated by Congress in the next year. Although the President hailed what emerged from Congress as a significant victory, this was more the rhetoric of a politician who had staked his credibility on energy policy than it was a reflection of political reality.

Of the ten original provisions,[9] two survived intact: citizens would be given

---

[8]Barry Commoner, *The Politics of Energy* (New York: Alfred A. Knopf, 1979), Ch. 1.
[9]For a summary of the fate of the Carter program see "Energy Boxscore," *Congressional Quarterly*, October 21, 1978, p. 3040.

some modest tax credit for home insulation, and mandatory efficiency standards for home appliances were set. (These standards were repealed by the Reagan administration in February 1981.) Five provisions were rejected outright. There would be no boost in gasoline taxes, no rebates for people buying fuel-efficient cars, no tax on crude oil, no tax on industrial use of gas and oil, and instead of *extending* natural gas price controls, Congress agreed to end these controls by 1985. Three remaining provisions were substantially watered down. Industrial conversion to coal was relaxed, state utility commissions were only required to *consider* the use of energy saving methods, and the standards for a tax on "gas guzzling" cars were substantially reduced.

Such a program would not fundamentally alter our energy relations. It is also clear who the winners and losers were. The first cautious steps taken by the president against concentrated power in the energy industry simply collapsed in Congress. In 1979 when gasoline lines formed again at service stations across the country, the President again decided to try to establish an energy policy. In early July, he went into seclusion at Camp David. His aides let it be known that he was preparing the most important national address of his administration. Officials and citizens from all walks of life were summoned to Camp David for consultation. This time it seemed the American people were to share the blame with OPEC for the energy crisis. To quote President Carter: "We're coming to understand that the reasons for our energy crisis go beyond gas lines and wasteful habits, to a loss of confidence that divides us and threatens us." To be sure many Americans have lost confidence in our political institutions but this is in part a result of our energy crisis, not the cause of it. President Carter was attempting to cast blame on the victim. He argued passionately that "we must face the truth" and then proceeded to mask it. The legitimacy of what energy corporations were trying to achieve did not receive sustained attention.

The proposed energy program included a massive commitment to the development of synthetic fuels, the development of a solar bank to help ensure that by the year 2000, 20 percent of our energy would come from solar power, utilities cutting their use of oil in half by 1990, increased conservation incentives, increased development of rapid transit, the creation of an Energy Mobilization Board to cut "bureaucratic red tape" for priority projects, and subsidies to the poor to help them pay for rising fuel costs.

Obviously such an effort would be costly. In order to pay for such a program the President proposed the decontrol of oil prices which would mean a massive increase in profits for oil corporations. No one was exactly sure how much the profits would increase but most estimates were that the oil industry would reap at least one trillion dollars in *new* profits in the next decade simply as a result of decontrol. This is roughly $4450 for every living person in America. President Carter proposed that these "windfall profits" be subject to a tax with the resulting revenues to be used to finance the new energy program.

On July 15, 1979, the White House issued a fact sheet earmarking how the new funds would be spent.[10] Over 60 percent of the revenues would be pumped into a synthetic fuels program. To a large extent this involved giving the taxes back to energy corporations for the purpose of producing new types of fuel. Seventeen percent of the tax would go to the poor to offset the rising costs of energy brought on by decontrol. About 12 percent was earmarked for various transportation projects, 3 percent would go to promote utilities' conversion to coal, 2 percent was for solar conversion with the rest to be used for residential and commercial conservation.

It was clear at the outset that some tax would be passed. The money involved was simply too substantial to ignore. Even Russell Long, the chairman of the Senate Finance Committee and the major advocate for Big Oil in Washington recognized that the tax was "the price we have to pay for decontrol." Indeed the most obvious question, given that oil corporations were already making record profits—why should oil companies get any of the estimated one trillion?—was never asked in Washington. The industry proclaimed that the new profits were necessary as incentives to promote new exploration and development, even though existing profits were being used to diversify, not to develop energy sources.

On June 28, 1979, the House passed an amendment to the windfall profits tax bill offered by Congressman James Jones of Oklahoma, a rising star of Big Oil. This amendment had two important provisions. First, it reduced the tax rate from 70 percent to 60 percent, a move which, it was estimated, would cost the government $20 billion. Second, and more important, the amendment proposed that the tax be terminated by 1990. The significance of this was not simply that the industry would begin to reap even more phenomenal profits after 1990. It was also that the amendment provided a very strong inducement to leave oil in the ground until that time. There is no reason to increase production now if greater profits are guaranteed further down the road.

According to the most common estimates, even the emasculated bill that passed the House was going to produce revenues of $273 billion over the next ten years, assuming the trillion dollar new profits figure. The Senate Finance Committee, which considers all revenue-related matters in the Senate, has very strong oil industry connections and it cut $135 billion from the House version of the bill. Eventually the two houses compromised and a bill was reported and signed by the president that would yield an estimated $227 billion. This cutting and slicing of the bill occurred precisely at the time that the oil industry was reporting quarterly profit gains of up to 300 percent!

It is useful at this point to consider the significance of corporate power in Washington D.C. A *Congressional Quarterly* survey[11] revealed that in 1978 and

---

[10]"There's not Much Left for Production from the $227 Billion Windfall Profits Tax," Richard Corrigan, *National Journal*, February 22, 1980. Because the amount of estimated profits have varied, we have converted original dollar figures to proportions to better indicate direction of interest.

[11]Berlow and Weiss, "Energy PACs: Potential Power in Elections."

1979 alone, 12 of the 20 Senate Finance Committee members, not all of whom were involved in campaigns, received $433,000 from energy PACs. This is merely the tip of the iceberg because it does not include individual contributions from energy executives. A Tulsa *Tribune* investigation revealed, for example, that Oklahoma Senator David Boren, who made a policy of refusing PAC contributions for his 1978 campaign and thereby enhanced his public image, nevertheless received 37 percent of his campaign funds from individuals with oil connections.[12]

A good example of how oil money works in Washington can be found in the 1979 House vote on the Jones Amendment. Obviously critically high stakes were involved for the industry and for the nation. A study conducted by the Public Citizen's Congress Watch, a consumer advocacy group, examined the relationship between oil PAC contributions and voting.[13] Only the 26 top oil PACs were examined and only PAC contributions in 1977-1979 were tabulated. Individual contributions were too difficult to trace. Limited as these findings are, they corroborate the general significance of money in policy decisions. Three-quarters of the Congressional representatives who received oil PAC money in 1978 voted for the amendment. The greater the contribution, the more likely the pro-amendment vote. Fifty-five of 58 Congressmen who received at least $2500 voted for the amendment. Twelve of the 18 members who received $5000 or more were freshmen. Freshmen are typically in the most precarious electoral position and, therefore, are likely to be most appreciative of contributions. Of the twelve freshmen, ten came from oil *consuming* states.

Would that this were the end of this sad story, but alas there is more. It is possible that the windfall profits tax may yield as much as $100 billion *less* than the commonly quoted $227 billion estimate.[14] This is in part because of an underestimation of tax deductible items allowed by the law, and in part because estimates of U.S. production of oil are too high. (Given the time limitation on the windfall profits tax, one would expect depressed domestic production.)

There remains a final irony to this story. The original White House fact sheet explaining how the new revenues would be used has no legal status. The revenues which are raised simply go into the general fund. The President and Congress must develop a statutory basis for allocating the funds in the manner proposed by the White House. As it turns out, most of the funds will be used to trim the federal deficit or to cut corporate or personal income taxes. The bulk of the remainder will go into synthetic fuels "demonstration" projects which are little more than multibillion dollar welfare programs for the oil industry. Our dependence upon foreign oil will not be reduced by these projects because the industry continues to

[12]Robert Sam Anson, "American Petroleum Institute" *Common Cause* (October 1980), p. 27.
[13]Congress Watch Press Release, 6:00 PM, Monday, July 23, 1979, "Nader Study Links Oil Contributions to Pro-Oil House Vote."
[14]"The $100 Billion Mistake—Is the 'Windfall' Revenue Estimate Too High?" Robert J. Samuelson, *National Journal*, April 26, 1980.

profit from OPEC price setting and from the existence of huge oil reserves worldwide. As long as these conditions exist, the industry is perfectly willing to sit on their coal reserves. In the meantime they will profit from massive government contributions for synthetic fuels projects. In the 1950s, before oil corporations owned coal reserves, they lobbied vigorously and successfully against government subsidization of synthetic fuel plants. Today, now that they own coal reserves, the oil corporations insist upon subsidies.

In the meantime the energy status quo will remain. Little will be spent upon residential and commercial conservation efforts, there will be no significant federal support for alternative transportation systems, and the plight of the poor will become more desperate. In early 1981 there was some chance that the poor might get 1 billion dollars for energy relief. Even this was not guaranteed but if it happens, it would not even account for 10 percent of their energy needs.[15]

Any realistic assessment of the nation's energy program would have to conclude that it has been a dismal failure. The terms of that program have been dictated by industry, not by national interests. We are not significantly less dependent upon foreign oil. There has been some conservation but that has been brought on by a pricing system that has no relation to a classic market. The extraordinary profits reaped by the rigged market will not be used to develop alternatives—such as mass transit systems and solar energy—that would break the stranglehold of the energy corporations. On the contrary the profits are being used to bind the nation more closely to these private interests.

Despite the timidity of the Carter administration and an even more timid Congress, those who voted in 1980 elected a leader who believes the government has been too harsh on the oil industry! In the eyes of President Reagan, the government has been picking on Big Oil and this is a point of view that is also predominant in the new, more conservative, Congress. During the campaign, President Reagan suggested that the windfall profits tax should never have been imposed, although he stopped short of calling for its repeal. He argued that the Energy Department, which occasionally takes exception to the more outlandish claims of the energy industry, should be abolished. And one of his first acts as President was to decontrol the price of gasoline immediately rather than waiting until the Carter target date of September 1981.

CONCLUSION

If we think about the criteria for establishing a good energy policy which were offered earlier in this chapter, it is clear that none of them was particularly important in establishing that policy. Some of the criteria found their way into politicians' speeches but they seemed to serve mainly rhetorical purposes. Rather than applying

---

[15]See Susan Thero, "Billions to the Poor for Fuel Bills."

tests of reasonableness to the formulation of energy policy, we can gain a clearer picture simply by understanding the distribution of power in our society.

Let us, therefore, reconsider the assumptions we made about political life in America with the energy policy case study in mind. Even though energy policy is probably the most significant domestic issue facing this country in the latter decades of this century, people tend not to think about it unless they are suddenly forced to spend hours waiting in gasoline lines. This situation endures for several reasons. Both the mass media and politicians treat the issue poorly, since they are tied into a social system in which inequality abounds. It is dangerous for politicians to speak of social justice except in the broadest terms. Specific distributional issues are better ignored.

It is not simply that those in power refuse to speak honestly about our energy future. The consumer society turns people from social problems as well, because it emphasizes the self. The extraordinary emphasis upon self-concern in our society works against the public spiritedness necessary for a just resolution of the energy crisis. At least two consequences flow from this orientation. First, self-concern encourages retreat to privacy and away from the arena where common solutions are sought to common problems. Second, a politics of selfishness is encouraged, wherein people are reluctant to give anything up or to make personal sacrifices in the common interest.

Resolutions to serious political problems flounder in the ethos in which they have been nurtured. Brought up as consumers, we seem incapable of thinking in other categories. We lack the vocabulary of community. The corporate nature of things appear to us as natural law itself, and politics emerges as an extension of consumption. We are reluctant to make the personal sacrifices necessary to ensure the integrity of a genuinely democratic society. President Carter's timid energy program was doomed to failure. By its own terms, it was incapable of assuring a reasonable energy future. Lacking vision and imagination, it was not worth struggling for. Defeated, President Carter decided to call failure "success." Without a compelling vision of his own, he was helpless before Reagan's attacks. In 1980, President Reagan's most frequent promise was "to get government off our backs" and to reduce our tax burdens. This seemed attractive, first because it is very difficult to think of government in terms other than it being on our backs, and second, because since we compete as consumers, no one ever seems to have enough money to spend.

The everyday world is one in which human dignity is regularly assaulted. The political consequence of this cannot be ignored. People may not seek just resolution to social problems because they do not feel they deserve it, or because they feel incapable of achieving it. When compelling social issues are thrust upon the political agenda they appear unintelligible to the average citizen. Lacking any background, the citizen is told in many small ways that "experts" will handle the problem. Often these experts are self-interested. The public, dimly sensing this but unable to respond coherently, grows more cynical about political life. This is especially true for the poor whose hopes are consistently dashed in the political arena.

The denigration of political life is very serviceable to those with great power. For all its imperfections, and despite the ill uses to which it has been put, it is the public arena that offers the only hope for redressing grievances and establishing a more just and a more humane society. To abjure politics is to accept the agenda of corporate America—and its continued domination of our lives. At the same time it shoud be recognized that changing what is commonly perceived as our political structure—voting registration requirements, the primary system, and the like—all will not lead to significant reform so long as the underlying concentration of power remains undiluted.

7

The Conservative Illusion

For a century the dominant conservatism has uncritically worshipped the most transforming force, the dynamism of the American economy. No coherent conservatism can be based solely on commercialism. . . . [Commercialism] takes a severe toll against small towns, small enterprises, family farms, local governments, craftsmanship, environmental values, a sense of community and other aspects of humane living.

George Will

Jayne Reynolds is a conservative and a member of the Republican party. Jayne was born in New York City to relatively well off parents, attended Barnard College as an undergraduate, and completed law school at New York University. She met and married her husband Alan while she was a law student. They purchased a suburban home in New Jersey and have raised three children, two of whom are away attending college. If you ask Jayne Reynolds why she is a conservative, she will respond with a justification that is philosophical and economic as well as personal. She will tell you that the Republican party believes in limiting government interference in the marketplace and that this guarantees economic efficiency and safeguards individual freedom. Jayne also remarks that she has personally achieved a good standard of living and doubts whether she would have been able to do this in a highly regulated economic system. America has worked for her and, she believes, it can work for anyone who has a modest amount of brainpower, a commitment to hard work, and a bit of luck.

Joe McCann is also a conservative, although he is not a member of the Republican party, or any party for that matter. He works as a bus driver in St. Louis, and makes approximately $19,000 per year. His wife Suzanne is a clerical worker and together they support two children and a modest home in a working-class section of the city. If you ask Joe why he considers himself a conservative, he will not offer a detailed philosophical justification. He will, however, tell you that things are falling apart and much of it is the liberals' fault. Liberals are in favor of busing to achieve racial integration and he is not. Joe will tell you that liberals in Missouri favor abortion on demand and he does not. Finally, he will tell you that things have simply changed too quickly: there are drugs in junior high school; teenagers smoke marijuana on his bus; kids have sex too early; and sometimes boys do not act like boys or girls like girls.

The explanations which Jayne Reynolds and Joe McCann give for their conservative political dispositions surely do not exhaust the possible reasons for being conservative. Their reasoning does, however, point to a couple of themes which regularly appear in conservative political discussion. The first theme, one expressed most clearly by Jayne, is that an unregulated—or at least a much less regulated—economy would be more desirable than its present organization. The second theme is one that pervades all Joe McCann's comments. It suggests that we are currently experiencing a cultural crisis in which the traditional values of American society have been progressively eroded by the practices of liberals and radicals.

This chapter interprets and criticizes two principal variants of conservative politics in contemporary America which stresses these two themes. We first examine the free-market brand of conservatism which has been most deftly explained by Milton Friedman and most visibly practiced by Ronald Reagan and the rightwing of the Republican party. Both Friedman and Reagan have consistently deplored the effects of government intervention in the economy on individual liberty and economic efficiency. Both suggest that most social problems could be effectively solved by permitting the market to function with a minimum of regulation.

The second variety of conservatism that we examine is currently known as neoconservatism. Neoconservatism is a catch-all term used to describe a number of political and intellectual dispositions which share the attitude that liberal policies have been politically unwise and culturally disastrous. Neoconservatives typically believe that some welfare state measures are appropriate and they acknowledge the propriety of some government interference with the free market. Yet they claim that liberals have gone too far with these measures. They contend that liberals have made us into a society of hospital patients in the sense that we have come to expect the government to provide for our well-being. They also suggest that liberal policies have effectively weakened our resolve to pursue our best interests and act vigorously on the world stage.

The second half of the chapter assesses the significance of American conservatism for the themes concerning everyday life that have been raised in the previous chapters. We ask whether conservative reform is likely to improve the quality of everyday life in America. Our argument, in general terms, is that the most prominent strains in American conservatism either aggravate or leave unattended the critical problems with American society that we have outlined. We defend this assertion by noting the inadequacy of the conservative response to problems at the work place, by showing the unduly narrow conservative position in a controversy over sex education and, finally, by noting how conservative political stances neither maintain individual liberty nor preserve communal integrity. In almost every instance, conservatives slight the contribution which the capitalist ethos makes to the critical problems of everyday existence.

One final word has to be said before we begin our analysis. By examining two varieties of conservatism, we are not implying that no overlap exists between the two. Nor do we mean to imply that every conservative has to be either a complete free-market advocate or a neoconservative. Many people who consider themselves conservative will tend to agree with many of the specific claims of both positions, even when these are mutually contradictory. This is especially true of persons who try to reconcile traditional community or religious values with the ethics of the marketplace.

The issue of pornography is a case in point. In her book, *The Power of the Positive Woman,* the conservative Phyllis Schlafly maintains that the ''real liberator of women in America is the free enterprise system.''[1] By the end of the book, however, Schlafly is calling on the government ''to prevent the display of printed or pictorial materials that degrade women in a pornographic, perverted or sadistic manner.''[2] What Schlafly never acknowledges is that it is the free enterprise system, the supposed liberator of women, that invents, produces, distributes and sells the very material she finds degrading. If Schlafly were a consistent defender of economic liberty, she could not support government control of pornography because it is able to survive and flourish in the free market.

Remember, however, that not everyone is perfectly consistent. Do not be surprised if you find people arguing one moment that economic liberty is absolute and equally fervently the next that the community has the right to restrict the liberty of businesses that it finds repugnant. You can often learn more about people from their contradictions than from their expressed logic. Such persons are not necessarily fools, but only people who, like most of us, have yet to succeed in the difficult task of reconciling political principles.

FREE MARKET CONSERVATISM

Milton Friedman is perhaps the most renowned advocate of free-market conservatism in contemporary America. A Nobel Prize winning economist, Friedman has recently

[1] Phyllis Schlafly, *The Power of the Positive Woman* (New Rochelle: Arlington House, 1977), p. 30.
[2] Ibid., p. 175.

become a celebrity intellectual. Having established a substantial reputation in academic circles for works such as *A Program for Monetary Stability* and *A Monetary History of the United States*, he has presented his ideas in less technical fashion and more popular forums during the last decade. Lately, Friedman has written columns for *Newsweek*, has been interviewed on "60 Minutes," and has conducted his own series on public television. Instead of the academic tomes he authored in the 1950s and 1960s, he now titles his books with such catchy phrases as *Free to Choose* and *There Is No Such Thing as a Free Lunch*. Despite this change in his marketing practices, Friedman's basic outlook has remained the same. He is still the most representative as well as the best known free-market conservative.

Before we examine the particulars of Friedman's view and how this perspective has been applied by conservative Republicans, we have to clear up one matter which might be confusing to a person who reads this chapter and then decides to pick up one of Friedman's books. A potential for confusion exists because while we label Friedman a freemarket conservative, he insists on calling himself a liberal. The confusion can be easily dispelled by noting how the accepted meaning of liberalism has changed over the past two centuries and how Friedman sticks to the eighteenth-century version. Put simply, a liberal in 1982 typically endorses a relatively extensive business-government partnership. A liberal in 1882 typically advocated a much more limited role in the management of the economy by government. Friedman believes that nineteenth-century liberals were not only "true liberals" when compared to their namesakes today, but wiser ones also.[3]

Individual liberty is the political value that free-enterprise conservatives cherish most highly. They believe that social, political, and economic arrangements that maintain and expand liberty should be preserved. Arrangements that restrict and circumscribe individual liberty should be discarded. Although Friedman and his followers never tell us precisely what they mean by liberty, it is clear that they think it is maximized in a capitalist system where the government establishes only a basic framework of law and does not bother to restrict the workings of the market.

To defend this position, Friedman has to argue that capitalism actually generates and maintains liberty and that a government which does not interfere in the marketplace is preferable to one that does in most instances. Central to Friedman's analysis is this distinction between coercive government and the noncoercive marketplace. Since we intend to question the validity of this distinction below, we wish to describe clearly the three major arguments by which Friedman attempts to uphold it.

1. Friedman believes that families, if they so desire, are not required to enter the market and only enter it at their own discretion and choice. He maintains that families always possess the option of producing for themselves. Given this opportunity, no family can ever be coerced into entering the marketplace.

[3] Milton Friedman, *Capitalism and Freedom* (Chicago: University of Chicago Press, 1962), p. 6.

2. Friedman argues that people in the work force are essentially free. He claims that so long as there ''are many employers, all employees who have particular kinds of wants will be able to satisfy them by finding employment with corresponding employers.''[4] Thus anyone who is dissatisfied with a job retains his or her liberty in a free market system because he or she can always switch jobs and find employment under more satisfying conditions.

3. Friedman contends that consumers who enter the marketplace retain their freedom when they purchase various items. In his mind, consumers are protected so long as there are other sellers from whom they can purchase goods.

Friedman believes that the role of government in a free society should be limited to establishing the legal framework ratifying the operations of the market, setting up the procedures by which the legal framework can be modified, and defining penalties for those who break the rules of the marketplace. The metaphors commonly used to describe the government Friedman envisions are nightwatchman and umpire. After agreement is reached on the rules of the game, the government ensures that all the players follow them.

The government ought not, in Friedman's mind, to take an active role on behalf of certain favored participants. Friedman thus opposes much current government activity. In a ''far from comprehensive'' list, Friedman suggests that social security programs, rent control, public housing, national parks, detailed regulation of industry, price supports on agriculture, tariffs on imports, military conscription, and publicly owned toll roads are practices which violate his basic principles.[5]

Given these leanings, Friedman is obviously no friend of contemporary liberal reformers. He believes that liberal reforms are normally unjust infringements on our liberty and inefficient infringements at that. These basic arguments are clearly reflected in Friedman's position on minimum wage laws. Friedman notes that these were initiated because liberals believed that it was inhumane to pay people at the rate for which some people agreed to work. He maintains that laws establishing a minimum wage violate the freedom of employer and employee alike. He claims that employers should not be prevented by government edict from paying whatever they consider a fair rate. Likewise, he thinks that potential employees should be free to work for whatever wage they find acceptable.

Furthermore, Friedman maintains that minimum wage laws—and innumerable other liberal reforms—often work directly contrary to their original intentions. Instead of actually helping the poor, Friedman contends that minimum wage laws further disadvantage them since the unskilled are normally the first to be fired whenever minimum wage hikes tax financially strapped employers. Ultimately, Friedman thinks that with friends like the liberals, the poor have no need for enemies.

[4]Ibid., p. 116.
[5]Ibid., pp. 35–36.

Ronald Reagan is probably the most prominent representative of Friedman's point of view in contemporary American politics. This is not to say that Reagan necessarily adopts a free-market perspective on social issues, but that he frequently endorses such solutions as the best remedies for our current economic troubles. Reagan is an especially interesting figure for our purposes because he is careful to connect his rhetoric to the day-to-day concerns of average Americans. He consistently argues that adopting his positions will improve the quality of our everyday lives. Anyone who has heard Reagan speak to an audience on the campaign trail cannot fail to be impressed by his rhetoric, even if one violently disagrees with the content of his arguments.

Prior to winning the election, Reagan gave a standard speech on American domestic politics. He began by telling the audience that he was interested in work, family, neighborhood, and peace. He then proceeded to sketch out a picture of contemporary society as one in which the liberals and their bureaucratic friends have systematically denied us the fruits of our labors, invaded our homes, undermined parental control of the family, and destroyed neighborhoods. As the audience warmed to him, Reagan suggested that the answer to our anxiety and fears consists of pushing the government out of our lives and permitting the market to operate without restrictions. By doing so, Reagan claimed that we would not only operate our affairs more efficiently, but that we might be able to restore the traditional values of American life. With respect to schooling for example, Reagan maintained that if we got the government ''out of education, we could then put God back in.'' All in all, it was a persuasive message and one which ultimately led to the White House.

We do not doubt the intelligence of Professor Friedman or the sincerity of President Reagan. Yet their entire framework of politics is constructed on the flimsiest of foundations. It is simply incorrect, plainly indefensible and it would be comical if it were not so tragic, to propose in 1981 that the marketplace and the government can be neatly cordoned off into realms of freedom and realms of coercion.

How many families can, in reality, opt out of the market and begin producing for themselves? How many workers would believe that they are as free as Professor Friedman claims they are? As we have shown in the previous chapters, much of the coercion which takes place in America on a minute-by-minute, hour-by-hour basis occurs at the work place. Anyone who has much experience with the nonmanagerial side of work knows this, as does almost every country and western songwriter in America.

Nor is it self-evident that consumers possess as much freedom as free enterprise conservatives seem to think. While we have no intention of arguing that each and every one of us is controlled by advertising, we think that it would be equally foolish to ignore the effects which both advertising and unethical business practices have exerted on the notion of consumer sovereignty. Besides questioning the amount of sovereignty consumers actually possess, it is also important to question the very notion that our freedom is best evidenced by our ability to purchase a wide array of consumer goods.

It is not our purpose in this book to celebrate liberal reformism. In fact, the next chapter argues that liberals have often compounded the basic problems of a democratic-capitalist order. Yet it is no endorsement of conventional liberalism to ask President Reagan and Professor Friedman to explain how some of the most pressing dilemmas of a capitalist order would be remedied by allowing the key institution of that order—the market—to be even less controlled than it is today. Ought we to sacrifice worker safety in order to reduce governmental bureaucracy? Are efforts to ensure that coal mine accidents are less frequent and less lethal when these do occur wrong? Is it really more desirable to pay workers subsistence wages, compel them to rent houses from the company, and even force them to buy their groceries from the company store? Surely, some of this would be the result when the logic (or better put, the illogic) of the free market played itself out.

NEOCONSERVATISM

Perhaps the most notable trend in American politics during the 1970s was the growing influence of what came to be known as neoconservatism. This political outlook, originally associated with ideas expressed in two journals of intellectual opinion, *Commentary* and the *Public Interest,* is now said to be shared by much of the general public. Yet the rise of neoconservatism is a curious phenomenon. While any politically attentive person will tell you that it has become a significant force in American politics, you will not find a neoconservative party or any one document setting forth the basic premises of a neoconservative political philosophy.

The problems in pinpointing the meaning of neoconservatism are basically reflections of the fact that at its core is not a set of clearly defined policies, but a set of attitudes about recent American political history, our present conditon and desirable avenues to follow in the future. This broad set of attitudes can best be described in the following way. Neoconservatives believe that America is experiencing a cultural crisis in which many good, traditional values have been discarded. This crisis is largely a consequence of radicalism's success in changing our values in the 1960s. Specifically, we have lost respect for duly constituted authority, we have made too many demands on government and we have lost our verve as a nation on the world stage.

Given the broad set of attitudes at the core of neoconservatism, it is easy to see why it might be attractive to a wide variety of people. It appeals to intellectuals who were upset by the protests and politics of the 1960s. It appeals to some politicians, academics, and religious leaders—authority figures themselves—who are concerned with the decline in respect for authority. Finally, it appeals to ordinary people like Joe McCann who simply believe that events have changed too rapidly for anyone's good.

Neoconservatism seems to be a political outlook in which people are soldered together as much by temperament as by political party, class status, or level of educational attainment. This is not to say that implementing the recommendations of leading neoconservatives would benefit all classes of people equally. The corporate sector and the economically privileged would certainly fare even better than they currently do if this were to happen. It is to say that the neoconservative recommendations draw on a mood which is not limited to people in the upper strata of American society.

For the sake of clarity, we shall examine neoconservative political notions as defined by its leading publicists and by works published in its leading journals. The neoconservatives' proposed deradicalization of America has two major components. The first argues that social welfare measures endorsed by liberals have gone too far. Unlike Friedman, neoconservatives typically approve of some social welfare measures. Many believe that the government should provide a minimum floor for everybody's income. They support health-care plans whereby the government would protect individuals against catastrophic costs and they believe that the government should support some of the minority group claims for equal rights. Despite these inclinations, neoconservatives spend most of their time complaining about existing social welfare programs. They argue that liberals have gotten out of hand with their demands and become overly radical. They claim that liberals have become egalitarians, committed to leveling American society to its lowest common denominator.

Neoconservatives defend their reasoning with a mix of moral and practical arguments. Like Friedman, neoconservatives believe that many welfare state measures—especially the expansion of the government's regulatory apparatus—threaten the liberty of businesses, particularly those of small entrepreneurs. Moreover, they suggest that the expansion of the welfare state tends to foster an attitude of dependency in the citizenry. Having seen the government take such an active role in our affairs, neoconservatives argue that the public now expects the government to relieve us of all our anxieties. According to the neoconservatives, liberals have raised public expectations to a much higher level than the government could meet. The unfortunate consequence has been a general decline in respect for government because our public standards have been too high. Peter Steinfels has described this neoconservative position as one in which the government is said to be the victim of "overload." By "attempting too much," the government has "naturally failed and undermined its authority.[6]"

Neoconservatives frequently maintain that the same Americans who have become too demanding of government in respect to domestic programs have exhibited a failure of nerve in international relations. In their minds, Americans have become so guilt-ridden about our nation's actions that we have become reluctant to

<hr/>

[6]Peter Steinfels, *The Neo-Conservatives: The Men Who Are Changing America's Politics* (New York: Simon & Schuster, 1979), p. 58.

protect our own interests on the world stage. We have become overly hesitant about using our power and overly friendly toward our natural enemies.

These foreign policy mistakes were said to be most glaringly evident in our relations with the Soviet Union. Neoconservatives maintain that we acted as if the Soviet Union was not intent on expanding its sphere of influence, but was instead a nation with the more reasonable goals or aspirations of the Western democracies. While we dramatically reduced the percentage of our gross national product devoted to defense, the Soviets engaged in a military buildup designed to strengthen their position on the world stage. The consequence of our blindness has been an increase of Soviet power relative to America's and also an increase in Soviet adventurism throughout the world.

If we are to solve the twin problems of excessive demand in domestic politics and lack of will in foreign affairs, neoconservatives contend that we have to revise our policy orientation and also change our general attitude. Domestically, neoconservatives maintain that the public's expectations must be tamed and the authority of government restored. Neoconservatives advocate a greater reliance on the market and less government intervention in the economy. As Peter Steinfels has noted, their argument for greater reliance on the market has a curious justification. Where conservatives like Friedman argue for the market on "grounds of liberty and efficiency, neoconservatives added what might be called an argument from inefficiency: when nothing works the market has the advantage of not providing the citizenry with anyone to blame."[7] The presumed benefit is that once government acknowledges its inadequacy in solving social problems, people may respect it for the modicum of security, liberty, and peace that it does provide.

Foreign policy recommendations offer a similar mix of government action and attitude modifications. The particular initiatives endorsed by neoconservatives include a larger defense budget, greater support for those leaders who are friends of America, and the adoption of a tougher posture toward the Soviet Union and Cuba. Concretely, this appears to mean that arms buildup be accorded a higher priority than arms limitation and that America actively oppose left-wing revolutionary movements in Central and Latin America.

Neoconservative prescriptions for foreign policy reform invariably place heavy emphasis on the presumed need for Americans to expunge the sense of guilt they have about past activities. The political scientist Jeane Kirkpatrick who is now our ambassador to the United Nations has been a forceful advocate of this position and her remarks are a good example of the exhortations put forward by neoconservatives. "A posture of continuous self-abasement and apology vis-à-vis the Third World is neither morally necessary nor politically appropriate. No more is it necessary or appropriate for our leaders to forswear unilaterally the use of military force to counter military force. Liberal idealism need not be identical with masochism and need not be

---

[7]Ibid., p. 64.

incompatible with defense of freedom and the national interest."[8] Echoing the advice of those self-help manuals that are popular best-sellers, neoconservatives tell us to be assertive and not to feel guilty about using power.

The neoconservative political stance is an attempt to restore order, authority, and respect in American society. It tries to make sense out of our disorientation. It tells us to lower our expectations about government on the home front and not to feel guilty about our actions abroad. While we agree with the neoconservative assessment that we are a troubled people, we believe that their diagnosis of our problems is inaccurate and their prescriptions misguided.

Neoconservatives frequently lump together liberals and radicals and then proceed to blame them for almost every problem. The principal (but not the only) mistake in this line of reasoning is that it attributes too much influence to liberals and radicals. For example, very few people in American society have succeeded in gaining a serious hearing while proposing such standard radical political fare as the redistribution of wealth or worker control of industry. It is much more accurate to say that radicalism in America has never been really tried than to suggest that it has been tried and found wanting.

The idea that many domestic problems have been caused by excessive citizen demand on government and by the subsequent efforts of government officials to accomplish too much is also overdrawn. Our problems were not caused by an excess of demand on the part of the poor and their liberal friends. The problems had much more to do with our attempt to remedy some of the worst outcomes of our economic system without changing the basic structure of the system. The problem is not that people wanted to eliminate ghettoes, but that we pretended this could be done without challenging the privileges of wealth.

It is certainly true, as the neoconservatives claim, that the government cannot do everything. Yet this should not be interpreted to mean that we should forget about existing inequalities and simply ratify the status quo. Indeed, if respect for authority and trust in our fellows is to be restored in American society, there is a need for that very equality that the neoconservatives abhor. The bitterness that we presently witness among the powerless and the poor cannot be excised merely by telling them to be respectful. It requires the creation of a more responsive government.

The neoconservative analysis of American foreign policy contains many of the same shortcomings that flaw its discussion of domestic affairs. We agree that it is desirable that the citizenry respect the actions of its government. Yet that government has to be worthy of respect. Moreover, government should gain that respect not simply by pointing to actions of others who are purportedly worse than us and proclaiming that we are the "party of liberty," but by implementing policies consistent with the ideals it professes to be upholding. Insofar as U.S. policy in

[8]Jeane Kirkpatrick, "Dictatorships and Double Standards," *Commentary,* November, 1979. p. 42.

Southeast Asia and Latin America has not been consistent with these ideals, it certainly seems rational for citizens to be skeptical of the government's foreign policy adventuring.

In general, neoconservatives fail to distinguish the legitimate demands of the disadvantaged from the self-seeking of the indulgent. Moreover, they normally fail to see that the hedonism of contemporary America is a desperate effort to find satisfaction in a society which is largely unsatisfying and in which enduring personal relationships are difficult to establish. Many values which neoconservatives endorse—hard work, thrift, and respect for authority—are presently irrelevant in today's economic system. Many values which the neoconservatives detest—self-seeking, lack of commitment, and prodigality—are promoted by the economic system which they are dedicated to upholding. In a society whose citizens are constantly informed to "live life with gusto," and to give themselves "a break today," it is small wonder that devotion to the common good and respect for authority figures is obsolete.

CONSERVATIVES AND WORK

In Chapter 4 we spoke at length about our contemporary work experiences. We argued that our lives were diminished because the meaning of work in America has been reduced to merely "making a living." We also noted that several important social costs were generated by the organization of our work lives. Because many of us are compelled to resign ourselves to feeling patently useless for nearly half our waking hours, we probably have more alcoholism, family abuse and sheer violence in America that we would if work were organized differently.

What recognition are these problems accorded in conservative thought and what place do these problems occupy in conservative politics? What recommendations have conservatives made to improve the quality of work in American society? If we first turn to Milton Friedman and the free-market outlook, we find that these concerns receive curiously little attention. Indeed, if you had read all of Friedman's books, scanned the articles he has written for *Newsweek* and watched his series on public broadcasting, you would never know that our lives were affected (and often in a negative way) by the labor we perform and the conditions under which we perform it. While Friedman and his followers never tire of professing how they want to bring more freedom to our daily lives, what we do for eight hours every day for fifty weeks a year is not a topic about which they are prompted to speak.

Friedman's silence has its origins in his assumptions that workers are free to choose their place of employment, that workers are not physically coerced into remaining on the job and that workers can search for alternative employment any time they desire. What Friedman assumes may be worthy goals for a political movement to pursue; by no means, however, do they represent an accurate portrait of contemporary America. While most workers are theoretically free to pick up and leave any time they want, their actual life situations deny them this opportunity. Most workers need every paycheck they can get. As we saw in Chapter 4, many workers have families to support and do not believe that alternate employment will be much more rewarding, either in terms of intrinsic job satisfaction or in the amount of control that they will have over the conditions of employment. Given a choice between unrewarding work with a regular paycheck and no job whatsoever, most of us will accept the former and content ourselves with singing ''Take This Job and Shove It'' on the way home.

Neoconservatism exhibits a similar reticence regarding the quality of work in America. If one looked at the pages of its most influential magazines—*Public Interest* and *Commentary*—over the past seven years, you would not find any articles about the conditions of work in America. Nor for that matter will you find our politicians with a conservative or moderate disposition talking about the quality of work on the campaign trails or in the halls of Congress. Although there is certainly not a conspiracy forbidding discussion of certain issues, it is as if the most time consuming element of our lives has been subjected to a rigorous censorship. Most neoconservative intellectuals are more likely to speak about the sexual mores of Americans than they are about developments in the factory, the secretarial pool, and on the bureaucratic ladder. Our work life is conservatism's dirty little secret.

Since American conservatives are so reluctant to speak about this matter, we are placed in the position of having to impute motives for their silence. One reason why some conservatives might pass over work experiences in their discussion of American life may stem from their belief in the idea that we should ''work to live and not live to work.'' From this vantage point a job is a necessary evil which allows us to provide for ourselves and for our families those luxuries which make life worthwhile.

For example, Charles Williams works as a New York City transit worker dispensing tokens. In order to ride the subway, a person must purchase a token and then place it in a slot which will allow the turnstile to move, thus permitting entrance onto the platform. Charles dispenses these tokens from behind a metal cage which is enclosed by bulletproof glass. He works by himself, all day long he takes in money and gives out tokens and change. An interviewer once asked Charles if he found his job worthless and if he would rather be doing something else, something which would allow him to exert more of his capacities. Charles responded that he actually enjoyed his job and would probably be unwilling to change it. He said that his job was neither physically nor mentally strenuous. He claimed that he took pleasure in fantasizing while at work and he mentioned that the time he spent with his family was enhanced by his lack of fatigue.

In short, Charles Williams told the interviewer that intrinsically satisfying work was not high on his list of priorities. He ''worked to live'' and not the other way around. What can we say about people like Charles Williams? Should he be ridiculed as a fool who does not know his own good? Or should he be used as a justification for the conservative silence on the grounds that the quality of work is really unimportant to us and only the concern of a few unduly critical intellectuals?

The most sensible reaction is to adopt neither of these positions. Certainly, some people will find tolerable what others consider a thoroughly deadening and degrading routine. People can be content in a variety of work situations depending on their personality and intrinsic needs. Yet the example of Charles Williams and others like him should not be taken to mean that *everyone* would rather perform routine work. It certainly should not be taken as a celebration of the present organization of work in America. The argument we presented in Chapter 4 about the quality of work and the extent of dissatisfaction refutes any interpretation in this vein.

Perhaps the strongest counterargument would be that we could not make significant changes even if we wanted to go ahead and try. It is argued that high technology necessarily reduces most work to boring routines and that only by regressing to a more primitive form of economic organization could we recapture a sense of meaning in our work lives. Boring work is thus considered a cost of modernity and not an outcome of a particular form of social organization.

This is a complicated argument and to deal with it completely would require a book in itself. We can, however, raise a few objections here to show why it is not a compelling argument. First, technological advances were not always the consequence of a naive and innocent development, but were, in part, developed with the intent of cheapening the work force. The craft skill of many workers was rendered useless in order to create a management monopoly in particular industries. Second, technological advances which might have been used to reduce the actual labor time in deadening tasks was instead placed in service of the consumption ethic. Rather than reduce deadening work to a minimum, we produce more consumer goods for the population. Finally, most workers these days are not directly employed tending machinery. Yet their work is often unrewarding because lines of command, power relationships, and organizational rules reduce their discretion and autonomy to a bare minimum.

CONSERVATISM, THE FAMILY AND SEX EDUCATION

Conservatives have traditionally believed that the integrity of the family is central to the stability of society and have thus vigorously opposed some practices which undermine family autonomy. Some of the conservative opposition to the growth of governmental bureaucracy has its source in the belief that liberalism is contributing to the decline of the family.

Criticism has developed over the controversy of teaching sex education in public schools. The most common justification given for this bureaucratic usurpation of parental functions has three principal components: (1) it is claimed that many parents neglect their duties in this area, forcing the schools to offer sex education so that misinformation is not provided; (2) it is claimed that teenagers are becoming sexually active at an earlier age, so they must learn to exercise their sexuality wisely; and (3) it is claimed that we are experiencing an epidemic of teenage pregnancies, so schools are serving an important social function in providing sex education. A number of conservatives have recently begun to argue against the proposition that government-sponsored sex-education programs should be on the curriculum in the public shcools. They cite deficiencies in the liberal analysis of the ''pregnancy epidemic'' and, most significantly, maintain that sex-education courses advocate tolerance of actions about which some people ought to have the right to be intolerant.

In the conservative analysis, sex-education courses propagate values about sexuality to which many parents and religious leaders might legitimately take offense. One report about the lessons being taught in a California school district noted that children in kindergarten were given a mixed group tour of the bathroom, that explicit support was given for strict limitations on childbearing, that toleration was advocated for homosexuality and gay families, and that children were shown movies about masturbation. Such lessons, the conservatives maintain, are not limited to providing the basic information which a person needs to act in a sexually responsible manner, but are intended to teach children according to the ''enlightened'' sexual attitudes of some ''progressive'' administrators.[9]

Conservatives argue that the educational system is being employed in a manner that would be thoroughly decried if its implicit values were made public. Imagine how parents would feel if a government agency began to tell them that their sexual values were unacceptable and that the schools were to be used to introduce the children to alternative norms. Would not everyone—regardless of political affiliation—denounce this action? Would not everyone argue that the state has no right to design a uniform standard of sexual practice, even if the standard seems to be as harmless as accepting your own sexuality? Conservatives believe that there are some matters about which we have the right to remain unenlightened. Indeed, there are some matters about which we have the right to remain downright backward.

The conservative argument about sex education is perceptive in its description of how a specific liberal reform can actually undermine the very institution that liberals profess to be strengthening. While any number of liberal reformers have recently claimed to be concerned with aiding the family, the liberal position in the sex education controversy comes close to implying that families are incapable of performing the most minimal tasks, such as responsible sexual education, without a strong dose of state intervention.

Yet before we begin to condemn sex-education programs as the cause for the decline of the family, we need first to recognize that the problems raised by the controversy require a deeper analysis than is contained in another polemic against state regulation. If we wish to learn how a society can promote both family autonomy and sexual responsibility, we need to examine and criticize all forces which tend to work against these goals. It is at this point that the conservative analysis fails. It fails,

[9]Jacqueline Kasun, ''Turning Children into Sex Experts,'' *Public Interest,* Spring 1979.

once again, because it is not sufficiently attentive to the actual forces which shape the contours of everyday existence.

In reality, liberal sex-education courses are a last-ditch effort to cope with the explosion and exploitation of sexuality on a nationwide scale. The government has by no means been the principal culprit in the subversion of the family's authority with respect to sexual values. Compared to the influence of the mass media and other profit-making institutions, the influence of the educational system pales. Hardly anyone interested in turning a profit has not employed and exploited our fascination with sex to their benefit. In America, we learn at a young age that a beautiful partner accompanies a particular kind of automobile, that it is good to chew Dentyne because we can attract a good looking mate, and that cigarettes can actually increase our sex appeal.

Schools are responding, in part, to this larger cultural trend and cannot be isolated as either the source of the problem or the locus of reform. Family control of sexuality can only be restored by a much more severe criticism of the institutions that helped to undermine it. As with many other issues, the conservative response overemphasizes the role of government and slights the influence of American business. A more compelling analysis would pay serious attention to the manner in which so-called respectable enterprise has developed its own brand of "soft porn" which connects the promise of heightened sexual experience to the purchase of innumerable products.

CONSERVATISM, THE SELF AND THE COMMUNITY

Conservatives are frequently divided according to whether they value the individual or the community more highly. People such as Friedman who hold personal liberty to be the highest good are labeled individualist conservatives. The vision which underlies this position is a society composed of autonomous individuals, beholden to nobody, who speak their minds and act as they freely choose. It is the conservative version of a "do your own thing" utopia.

Other conservatives, however, believe that the rights and good of the community should take precedence over individual liberty. They find our society excessively individualistic and not sufficiently attentive to the need to preserve traditional community relationships. The vision at the core of this perspective is that of a society in which close personal relations, shared experiences, and respect for common traditions unify the populace. In such a society, unrestricted personal liberty is, at best, a nuisance and, at worst, a threat to the continuation of the traditions which the community cherishes.

We mentioned in the introduction to this chapter that most people who consider themselves conservative are neither completely individualistic nor communitarian in practice. This is because few people hold fast to one position; each has an underside which, on occasion, makes it a less attractive strategy for living. We can certainly imagine a person who is, in Professor Friedman's term, ''free to choose,'' but is terribly unhappy because he or she is so uncommitted and so unattached that most of his or her choices seem trivial. All of us have probably experienced moments of loneliness when we are hauntingly and terrifyingly free, so free that no one seemed to care for us at all.

On the other hand, many of us have had experiences with small communities and close knit groups that can make us yearn for the anonymity of being free to choose. We know of townships and villages where classic literature is removed from the library shelves because narrow-minded people consider it indecent. We know of some religious groups who are so certain of having God's truth that they seek to impose their beliefs on everyone else. We know that people in some communities can intimidate us into acting against our best interests and can ceaselessly pry into our personal lives. Here we might think of soap opera America where everyone lives under the strict regimen of gossip. Just thinking about these places is enough to prompt a few of us into blurting out ''leave me alone.''

Ideally, of course, we would want to experience the best of both worlds. We would live in a community that enhanced rather than diminished our sense of self. Thus one criticism that could be made of contemporary conservatism is that it does not adequately combine personal liberty with the creation of supportive communities. While people such as Friedman tell us that the good of the community is automatically realized by permitting everybody to be economically free, we can recognize how foolish this is. We know that the result of this system is an overly possessive society, wherein one's gain comes at the expense of another's loss. We also know that constantly acting in a possessive manner may well not provide us with the self-respect we need, despite whatever material success is obtained.

Yet conservatives who believe that individual autonomy ought to be sacrificed to the good of the community are equally mistaken also. While those who claim that individual liberty should always be our highest value are dead wrong about what brings joy and hope to human life, those who claim that personal liberty should be sacrificed to the good of the community diminish us also. This strategy, taken without qualification, serves to stifle our need for self-expression and personal growth. We need to be more concerned with the quality of the community than with its mere preservation. In our minds, the communities most worth preserving are those which permit and encourage its members to grow and develop.

We can certainly understand, however, that a conservative might respond to us by saying that it is impossible to combine individual freedom with the preservation of a community. A conservative might tell us that we have to pick and choose among these, knowing full well that something valuable may be lost in the process. While we are not convinced that this point is necessarily correct, we shall not argue it to any great extent here. The brunt of our criticism in this chapter has been that present-day conservatism does not adequately defend the very values it professes to support. It neither defends the liberty of the individual from the forces which are attacking it, nor preserves the fabric of communities in the face of the strains and the tensions which are pulling them apart.

When conservatives endeavor to protect individual liberty, their typical strategy has been to oppose further governmental regulations and to support reductions in existing regulations. In President Reagan's words, "the first lesson of economic wisdom is to realize that your paycheck belongs to you and not to the government." The two shortcomings of this approach are: (1) it rarely makes a fair evaluation of those conditions giving rise to government regulation and (2) it is frequently insensitive to nongovernmental policies influencing our manner of living.

Conservatives are right to argue that individuals in America are often not free to choose their own needs. But they are blind to some of the forces which exert enormous energy trying to contour our needs. In the conservative interpretation of life, we are interested in establishing a sound love relationship, maintaining a good family, retaining political freedom and freedom from economic want. While we have some misgivings about the conservative goals of everyday life, especially the neglect of growth and innovation, we can understand their worthiness. We have fervent disagreements, however, with their analysis and recommendations. Conservatives profess to defend the quality of everyday life while asking more freedom for the institution (the market) that has diminished the quality of life.[10]

Pretend for a minute that life is, in some important ways, a treasure hunt. In this hunt we are all seeking some important goods, perhaps love, friendship, personal liberty, and economic security. We know what these goods look like and think that we could recognize them if we happened upon them. We are, however, hampered in our quest by the glasses that we are all compelled to wear—the glasses of profit and loss—because these glasses distort the objects in our view. Indeed, they remake the environment in the image of profit and loss so that everything takes the form of an accounting sheet.

In this distorted vision friendship becomes a relationship where we try to obtain the most satisfaction at the least cost. Work becomes the arena in which we try to acquire as much money as possible without regard for others' feelings. And politics becomes the activity by which we try to promote our own economic interests rather than to consider the potential common good. If we really wanted to find the treasure, we know that we would either have to take off the glasses or, at a minimum, regrind the lenses so that we only see profit and loss where these attributes have their proper place. Conservatives have put their finger on many of our fears and anxieties: that is why they have a following today. Yet by not recognizing the problems fostered by the market ethos, they only weld the distorting lenses to our eyes ever more tightly.

---

[10]Jerry Falwell, for example, does not see the contradiction between his religious beliefs and his support of the corporate economy. The same is true of some right-to-life advocates who are "pro-birth", but opposed to social welfare programs because they interfere with the market.

8

The Inadequacy of Liberalism

When their fit of feverish energy has spent itself and there is nothing to show for it except disillusionment, they cry that reform is impracticable and blame human nature, when what they ought to blame is themselves.

R.H. Tawney on Liberals

Barbara Kelly is a liberal who grew up hearing her parents talk politics at the dinner table. They spoke highly of Franklin Roosevelt and frequently claimed he was a saint who rescued a disintegrating America from total catastrophe by instituting the New Deal. While Barbara is reluctant to call any politician a saint, she shares her parents enthusiasm for the late president and, more importantly, believes in the capacity of the government to solve many of the problems that still exist within American society. Barbara works as a program analyst in the newly formed Department of Education. She is especially interested in the schools because she believes that a good educational background prepares people to accomplish their goals in life. She thinks that sound federal educational policies may eventually help to reduce the inequalities in American society and give almost everyone the opportunity to compete fairly in the economic arena. Strongly opposed to the current fashion of disparaging Washington and the federal bureaucracy, Barbara contends that the federal government has done a "great deal of good in the past and can continue to do good in the future."

Michael Donatello, a lawyer who works for a consumer protection advocacy group and a member of the Democratic party, is a liberal also. Michael is not especially positive about government or about the direction of American life in general. He has become increasingly critical about American society and attributes his disenchantment to the "knowledge I have gained." Michael is particularly incensed with what he considers to be the fraudulent and dangerous practices of American business. He thinks that the American consumer is constantly victimized by the practices of many American businesses. Michael maintains that chemical adulterants in our foods, defective and unsafe merchandise, and impure water poison our lives. Moreover, he thinks that nuclear power is a lethal technology and that we are apt to commit collective suicide through the peaceful use of atomic energy if the "power companies have their way." You will rarely hear Michael talk in laudatory terms about the government. He believes that it normally accedes to the wishes of the corporate sector. Yet Michael thinks it is imperative for the government to make greater use of the regulatory power it does possess if the public is to be protected. In today's complex world he feels there is no other choice.

The attitudes expressed by Barbara Kelly and Michael Donatello reflect commonly held reasons for adopting liberal political views on contemporary social affairs. The first reason stems from the belief that government is fundamentally good, that it has been the source of much of our prosperity, and that well-intentioned government policy can positively contribute to the quality of most people's lives. The second reason for liberalism reflects a more paradoxical judgment of government action. Government is thought to be a villain because of its leniency in regard to dishonest corporate activity; yet it is a peculiar sort of villain, because we can only be saved if it forsakes its evil ways, takes off its black mask, and puts on a white hat.

This chapter examines, interprets, and criticizes two recent variants of liberalism associated with these attitudes. We first turn our attention to the Great Society liberalism embodied in Lyndon Johnson's War on Poverty and promoted today by some liberals within the Democratic party such as Ted Kennedy. Convinced of government's potential for eliminating poverty and sustaining abundance without fundamentally altering our social and economic system, Johnson and other liberals have advocated creating numerous federal programs, funded by tax revenues, to bring relief to the disadvantaged. In Johnson's words, liberals could "open the doors of learning, the doors of fruitful labor and rewarding leisure, of open opportunity and close community—not just to the privileged few, but to everyone."[1] The second variety of liberalism we examine is the "defensive liberalism" of Ralph Nader and the contemporary public interest movement. Nader, who believes average Americans are continual victims of corporate selfishness, has advocated the creation of a more responsible government bureaucracy and a more concerned, more active citizenry.

We argue that neither the Great Society version of liberalism nor Ralph Nader's are fully adequate responses to the problems of consumer society described earlier.

---

[1] Quoted in Sar A. Levitan and Robert Taggart, *The Promise of Greatness,* Cambridge: Harvard University Press, 1976, p. 3.

Insofar as each version of liberalism has assumed that widespread reforms can be adopted without undermining the framework of the capitalist economy, reformist programs are destined to fail at critical junctures. By assuming that reforms should take place within the capitalist economy, liberals rarely question whether the present economic class structure is justified, they rarely consider changing the actual condition of our work lives, and they hardly ever question the value of many leisure time pursuits fostered by corporate America. We try to demonstrate these assertions by reference to the liberal War on Poverty in the 1960s and to Ralph Nader's consumer protection campaigns. The second half of this chapter notes the inadequacies in the liberal treatment of workplace issues, by showing the problems in the liberal position on health care, by examining from another angle the conservative-liberal sex education controversy, and by showing the difficulty that liberals have in thinking about people in other than consumerist terms. We suggest that liberals may thus unwittingly complicate the core problems of American society.

GREAT SOCIETY LIBERALISM

The liberal policies that were associated with the Democratic party in the 1960s were basically extensions of those proposed and implemented during the New Deal of Franklin Roosevelt in the 1930s. Faced with a depressed business sector and a population riddled by high levels of unemployment, Roosevelt decided the nation's revival depended on government interaction in the economy's management. The government's supposed role in economic management contained two major components that were, in our minds, ultimately contradictory. On one hand, government was to intervene in the economy to aid business. By controlling the supply of money, altering the tax rate, and manipulating subsidies to help businesses in trouble, government policy attempted to create an atmosphere conducive to business prosperity. On the other hand, the New Deal attempted to harmonize its encouragement of business prosperity with aid to the disadvantaged. Thus most New Deal liberals supported minimum wage laws, government social security benefits, and guarantees of the rights of labor to organize without fear of reprisals.

Since the New Deal, American politicians committed to liberal policies have basically followed this course. They express sympathy with the plight of the disadvantaged, are outraged with those who do not recognize the problems, and attempt to remedy these problems without recommending a wholesale restructuring of the social and economic system. They maintain that the lot of the disadvantaged is best served through a cooperative rather than an antagonistic relationship with the corporate sector of the economy.

Such a strategy was evident in Lyndon Johnson's efforts to expand the scope of New Deal aid to the disadvantaged. Given the economic prosperity of the post-World War II era, it was assumed that our social programs should be more extensive. To liberals in the 1960s, the continued existence of "public squalor" alongside "private affluence'' and the nasty reminders of this voiced in urban disorders demanded a clear governmental response. Liberals thus advocated greater health care for the poor, more extensive job training programs for educational dropouts, more federal aid to education in poor areas, ''headstart'' programs for low-income children, and an increase in subsidies for inner city housing construction.

Liberals thought these programs could be successful without restructuring the existing social and economic system; indeed, they believed capitalist economic growth actually made social justice possible. President Johnson maintained that America was the ''wealthiest nation in the world. And I cannot see why, if we have the will to do it, we can't provide for our own happiness, education, health and environment.''[2] Johnson did, of course, ask the corporate sector to be receptive to his goals and to be socially responsible itself. Yet he never felt it necessary to suggest that attaining his goals might be dependent on restructuring the corporate economy.

The cooperative relationship with private enterprise advocated by the liberals ultimately affected their reformist intentions adversely. By trying to compensate for the failures that the economy inevitably generates rather than altering its basic framework, liberals failed to see that the causes of poverty and inequality are often built in to its operation. Those who promised reform because we were the ''wealthiest nation in the world,'' did not consider how our commitment to social justice would dissipate when economic growth declined in the 1970s. By not criticizing the consumer ethos, liberals became accomplices to the modern corporate methods of social control. And by accepting the notion that our standard of living should be defined by the quantity of goods we consume, it could be said that liberals helped to pave the way for Ronald Reagan's appeals in 1980.

While it would take a book in itself to detail all these charges adequately, we can outline and illustrate why we believe that such an indictment of American liberalism is accurate. Take, for example, our charge about the problem with the liberal commitment to social justice and helping the disadvantaged. Such a commitment is relatively easy to make when it is not thought that any group of people will be heavily penalized. As long as it does not cost anybody anything, all of us would be foolish not to be in favor social justice. But it is a rare society that can balance a commitment to social justice with infinite possessiveness for a long time. Eventually, difficult choices have to be made. Americans have been discovering this for the past ten years and are likely to continue doing so for the rest of the century. The liberals, having accepted the corporate perspective in many ways, have never clearly articulated why a commitment to social justice would remain when times are difficult. While many liberals deplore what they label the ''new selfishness,'' they have never really told us why we ought not to ''look out for number one.''

A related problem is that by emphasizing American wealth, liberals lost sight of

---

[2] Quoted in Doris Kearns, *Lyndon Johnson and the American Dream*, New York: New American Library, 1976, p. 223.

the conditions under which a consumer-oriented society was constructed. We have shown in previous chapters that the generation of the consumer ethos owes its impulse to the efforts of American business to ensure a contented work force, to provide markets for the goods it overproduces, and to develop an entire lifestyle dependent on its continued existence. By not challenging the use to which American wealth was put in our individual lives, liberals consented to the very business practices they were supposedly intent on reforming. In this sense, liberal reform has been much more a concession to things as they are than a genuine vision of how things might be, no matter how extravagant the rhetoric which predictably accompanies the call for change.

As we begin the 1980s, Great Society liberals try to protect the victories of the 1960s from the more conservative leanings of the Reagan administration. Given the loss of confidence in the government's ability to solve social problems and the general anxiety about the economy, there are few calls for extension and expansion of the Great Society. In fact, there are now divisions among the liberals regarding the worth of these programs. A number of politicians who had always been considered liberal now talk about the need to reduce federal spending. Those who do believe, in Ted Kennedy's words, that the liberal goal of social justice for all "shall endure and the dream shall never die" have been compelled to adopt rearguard strategies, opposing the assaults of the Reagan administration on some cherished programs.

But if the liberal commitment to social justice is to have enduring meaning, liberals will need to do more than to oppose Ronald Reagan and the actions which his supporters endorse. Liberals will have to undertake the difficult tasks of self-examination and self-criticism. They will especially have to note how their compromises with corporate America tarnished their professed commitment to social justice. They will have to swallow the unpleasant medicine that Reagan's promises to restore our consumer paradise are entirely consistent with one component of conventional liberal politics. In the end, Great Society liberals will have to decide whether they are committed to social justice or the corporate economy. Currently, even the most committed liberals appeal to the *compassion* of the middle class. They ask the middle class to help the poor because the disadvantaged need help. Ronald Reagan appeals to the self-interest of the middle class. While there is nothing wrong with compassion and we probably do need more of it, the liberal appeals will likely go for naught until American liberals can explain to the middle class why the existing structure of a consumer society damages all of us in a very significant way.

DEFENSIVE LIBERALISM

A variety of liberal reform that developed in the 1960s was the public interest movement begun by Ralph Nader. Nader, a well-known activist gained his reputation as a critic of safety design in American automobiles, especially that of the Chevrolet Corvair. Claiming that automobiles were "unsafe at any speed," Nader maintained that the lack of attention which auto companies paid to safety was manifested in thousands of unnecessary deaths. He argued that most deaths were not the result of the first collision—that of the occupants with another car or vehicle—but of the "second" collision—that of the occupants with part of their own vehicle.[3] Nader suggested that there was no compelling reason why people should die because dashboards were unpadded, because they impaled themselves on the steering rod when the steering wheel came free, or because they collided with unnecessary protrusions inside the automobile. He felt the auto industry's greed and neglect victimized consumers and therefore required strict governmental regulation.

Nader's exposé of the auto industry and the efforts undertaken by industry representatives to damage his reputation gained him widespread public recognition. Thereafter, he contended that the auto industry should not be perceived as an island of deception in a sea of fundamentally honest businesses. In the next few years, Nader accused American businesses of selling flammable clothes which set children afire, he denounced the meat industry for using adulterants to transform diseased meat into apparently healthy and salable food, and he indicted the textile industry for gross neglect of worker health and safety. Ultimately, Nader tied his discussion of particular industries to the notion of business crime, claiming that the harm done to "human health and safety by business crime should dispel the distinguishing characteristic of white-collar crime as being the absence of physical threat. Food and drug violations, lavish use of pesticides, defective automobiles, professional malpractice, and building code violations are a much larger threat to life and limb than crimes of violence on the street."[4]

Nader was originally perceived as one man fighting city hall or as a Lone Ranger bringing truth and justice to the corporate frontier. He soon realized, however, that a sustained movement for political reform required more extensive work than that which his own personal endeavors could produce. He reminded his interviewers that he was not interested in the Lone Ranger image and he continually exhorted the citizenry to take positive action against those who victimized it. More specifically, Nader began to develop strategies and hire associates for his public interest movement. According to Nader, public interest politics encompasses a broad range of political activities. The principal elements of it are (1) public interest work in Washington, D.C., to oppose the influence of corporate America in Congress and the agencies of the federal government, (2) attempts to encourage people who work for corporate enterprises to disclose illegal and unethical practices when these occur, and (3) the development of a local and community-oriented politics to defend vigorously the public against unfair corporate practices.

---

[3]See Robert D. Holsworth, *Public Interest Liberalism and the Crisis of Affluence*, Cambridge: Schenkman Publishing Company, 1980, for an extended discussion of Nader's reformism. Much of what follows in the next few pages draws on the discussion of Nader found there.

[4]Ralph Nader, "Business Crime," *The New Republic*, September 9, 1967, p. 7.

To implement this, Nader has established a permanent presence in Washington. He has his own "bureaucracy," which is really a number of semipermanent, task-oriented projects to influence congressional legislation and administrative decisions. For instance, Nader has founded a Health Research Group to promote legislation designed to decrease occupational injuries and illnesses. A variety of groups under Nader's aegis or loosely affiliated with him lobby in Congress and try to present representatives and senators with information to combat what they believe is the deceptive information presented by the lobbyists of the major corporate enterprises.

Although Nader has gained a considerable reputation for his activity in Washington, he has also vigorously promoted "on-the-job citizenship" and greater consumer participation in policymaking on the local level. For instance, he has claimed that "tattling" is really a courageous action when we notify the proper authorities of the safety violations and other irresponsible activities of our employers. In fact, Nader has worked quite extensively to develop legal safeguards for employees who exercise this option. Moreover, Nader has recently stressed the need for widespread political participation on the local level. He has argued that "contrary to most popular impressions, the greatest tyranny in this country is not from Washington, it is not from New York, it is the local tyranny. It is the most effective and the most insistent tyranny as far as people living in localities are concerned; and so, contrary to those bogeys of federalism, it is the local community where the action has to be if we are going to have a more vital community responsible to state and federal governments."[5]

Since the inception of his activism, the broad range of Nader's activities has been given continuity and cohesion by the persistence of two central themes. First, our victimizations occur because large industry is irresponsible in its treatment of employees and consumers. Second, these victimizations persist because corporate control of the Congress, the administrative agencies, and the channels of political communication legitimates the victimization. We have called Nader's liberalism defensive because the primary function of his activity is to defend consumers. Nader and his followers rarely speak of eliminating poverty or of providing equal opportunity for everyone, but instead talk in more subdued terms of limiting the amount of deception to which consumers are subjected.

Nader has been criticized on a number of grounds and it is not our purpose to examine all the objections to his activities. We shall confine ourselves to how his politics relates to our discussion of everyday life. We suggest that by adopting a consumerist perspective on politics, Nader undermines his self-definition as a public interest advocate. By choosing the consumer as the unit of political judgment, Nader recognizes only the most explicit instances of victimization in America. He fails to

---

[5] Ralph Nader, "Corporate Violence Against the Consumer," in William Osborne ed., *The Rape of the Powerless*, New York: Gordon and Breach, 1971, p. 31.

notice the deeper and more insidious victimizations that a consumer society routinely engenders.

We can illustrate this with a simple example. Consumer advocates have been concerned for some time with the safety of sleeping pills. They discovered many brands to be insufficiently pretested and potential dangers to be frequently mislabeled and sometimes even unlabeled. To remedy these defects, consumerists have labored to persuade government officials and federal agencies to exert stricter control over the manufacture and distribution of sleeping pills. These are legitimate concerns and it would take an unusually mean-spirited person to argue that such safety efforts should not be undertaken. None of these efforts, however, addresses the question of why we need to spend billions of dollars to go to sleep in the evening.

By limiting his criticism of business decisions to those moments when our safety is demonstrably threatened, Nader remains insensitive to the process by which capitalist enterprise attempts to shape our conception of happiness and freedom according to the dictates of corporate profits. While Nader opposes blatantly deceptive advertising, he has rarely publicly criticized the psychological strategies business employs to sell its products. He has not been heard to criticize Mastercard's claim that we can relax if we get one. Nor has he criticized the same company's advertisement which equates women's liberation with giving female consumers greater purchasing clout. Yet if the analysis of American society that we have been presenting is reasonable, the discussion of consumer victimization ought to be more probing than Nader's. We get victimized not only by the defective tires that a rubber company may market, but by the assumption that deep-seated psychological needs can be met by purchasing an automobile.

Nader's defensive liberalism has been important because it has increased our sensitivity to the various deceptions perpetrated by corporate enterprise on unsuspecting consumers. Although he has not succeeded in establishing a Federal Consumer Protection Agency, Nader has made government and industry more receptive to consumer issues. Yet despite the assertion of some conservatives that Nader is a radical, he is not especially threatening to the existing system. By not challenging the consumer ethos, Nader has not questioned the psychological bedrock of contemporary business power. Nader's highly publicized confrontations with corporate America thus obscure his underlying acceptance of its beliefs. This failure to challenge corporate America on some very fundamental issues has been a constant problem with liberal reformism. We can see this reluctance in evidence once again by turning to the items we examined in the previous chapter on American conservatism and by looking at the liberal position on health care.

LIBERALS AND WORK

American liberals, it is commonly thought, are in favor of the little person. When this cliché is translated into an actual political program, it usually means that liberals are more sensitive to the needs of the working class and the jobless than conservatives. It is also taken to mean that liberals are willing to regulate the private sector for the presumed good of laborers and consumers. To a certain extent, this characterization is true. In general terms, people of liberal sympathies have normally supported labor's right to organize trade unions, minimum wage laws, laws which provide a floor for the income of the lowest paid workers and stricter regulation of many business practices.

Liberals have also supported the demands of labor with respect to many particular issues. The typical liberal position on unemployment is a case in point. Liberals have frequently argued that employment—or at least the employment of most people—should be given a high priority. They contend that Republicans are too willing to sacrifice the jobs which are the source of both income and pride to the monetary needs of the financial establishment. Jimmy Carter used this charge successfully in his presidential campaign against Gerald Ford in 1976. Ironically, when the unemployment rate began to rise in 1980, Ted Kennedy used this tactic in his unsuccessful effort to wrest the Democratic nomination away from Carter. Kennedy charged that Carter was not a "true Democrat," that he was a "clone of Ronald Reagan," and that he appeared to be directing a Republican administration. Although Kennedy did not secure the nomination, he did manage to obtain a substantial number of delegates and substantial support from industrial workers and labor union leaders disenchanted with Carter's policies.

Liberals have also been traditionally concerned with health and safety matters at the work place. During the course of the past 50 years, the liberals' concern with the hazardous nature of some modes of work have led to a number of laws designed to limit fatalities and injuries at the work place. The Occupational Safety and Health Administration (OSHA) was established to govern safety at the workplace and to attempt to secure compliance. Such action, as we noted, has been an integral part of Ralph Nader's defensive liberalism. Nader has continually claimed that life at the work place is dangerous, especially for the nonprofessional. He has maintained that these dangers could be limited if corporate America were compelled to respect the physical dignity of its employees to a greater degree than is presently the case.

To punctuate his claims, Nader has reported incidents in which scientists who worked for certain companies were threatened with dismissal if they published research findings that indicated some work environments, assumed to be relatively safe were, in fact, quite hazardous. He has also attempted, as mentioned above, to persuade people to report violations of safety procedures that endanger employees and the surrounding community. Conservatives have often maintained that since workers are free to leave their jobs anytime they so desire, occupational safety and health rules are an unjust infringement on the rights of employers. Liberals such as Nader, in our mind, have at least been aware that the real life options of American workers are not nearly as wide ranging as the conservatives pretend. They have well understood that the formal capacity to quit a job is not a real option for most people in the work force.

The liberal concern for the work place environment, however, has normally been limited to those practices which make it more dangerous or unsafe than the average person assumes it should be. A liberal analysis of the work place environment rarely includes any reference to the standard relationships between worker and management. Nor does it refer to the nature of the actual work experience. The basic form in which power is distributed and the basic definition of work tasks is taken for granted. These are not questions said to be open for debate and possible modification. For example, in all the proposals that Nader made in *Taming the Giant Corporation,* he never recommended a serious campaign to challenge management on these basic considerations. His fiery rhetoric is rarely followed up by recommendations to alter the actual organization of work.

The liberal reluctance to tackle this issue is not the consequence of having entered into an explicit conspiracy with the owners and managers of large businesses. This reluctance has its origins, once again, in the liberal acceptance of the notion that our freedoms are evident primarily in our lives as consumers. The liberal position is not that different from the viewpoint of Charles Williams mentioned in the previous chapter: work is unpleasant and unrewarding everywhere and it should only be seen as a means to a high standard of material living. What makes the liberal position different is not its basic assumptions, but only its emphasis on the notion that the work ought not to be physically dangerous as well as unpleasant.

The consequence of the liberal reluctance to politicize work place issues are not only visible on the existing political agenda, but they may well affect the agenda of the future also. A sizable body of recent scholarship maintains that economic and ecological problems will require many Americans to reduce future consumption habits. Indeed, many already are currently experiencing this imperative. Perhaps the most critical political question to face is how collectively to reduce our attachment to consumer goods without unfairly penalizing those who now occupy the lower rungs of the socioeconomic ladder. The most optimistic possibility is that we will recognize that the consumer economy was not humanly enriching and discover new forms of work and leisure that enhance our capacities. The pessimistic scenario is that our attachment to consumer goods is so deep that we can only successfully confront our challenges by establishing an authoritarian government that severely limits our freedoms. By accepting the corporate vision of consumer paradise, liberals may have helped push us down the road to political hell.

LIBERALISM AND HEALTH

Liberals have been interested in using government policy to improve the health of Americans for about 70 years. Shortly after the turn of the century, reformers argued that some form of health insurance was necessary if the poor and the middle class were to live without being ravaged by disease. Since that time, liberals have periodically recommended changes in how we deliver and pay for health care. They have proposed legislation guaranteeing health insurance for all Americans on a number of occasions. While they have never succeeded in passing these recommendations, they have secured legislation guaranteeing access to health care for the elderly and the poor.

Senator Edward Kennedy has been the most outspoken advocate of the liberal health-care position in recent years. In speeches, congressional hearings, campaign proposals, and even in a book, Kennedy has tried to call attention to the human wreckage that floats in the wake of our medical care system. For instance, in one of his congressional hearings, Kennedy called the father of the Riegel family in Cleveland to Washington as a witness. Mr. Riegel testified how his wife had lost her premature child and almost her own life when she suffered heart failure while giving birth. The bills from the hospital stay amounted to almost $20,000 and since the Riegels were uninsured, they could not pay the amount due. The hospital handed the bill to a collection agency and the agency proceeded to take away the family's car, stove, refrigerator and any other household item that had been purchased on credit.[6]

Kennedy has drawn the following conclusions about health care from the story of Mr. Riegel and other similar tragedies:

1. Health care is a basic right which all Americans should have. It is not a right which should be dependent on income or on an employer's kindness.
2. People should not be forced to empty their entire savings, exhaust their personal income, and go into bankruptcy because of their medical bills.
3. The economic rights of doctors and hospitals in a free-enterprise system may have to be somewhat curtailed in order to ensure that the right to health care is guaranteed.

Kennedy's efforts to implement these principles have centered on his proposals to guarantee health insurance for the entire American population. During the course of the past 15 years, Kennedy has sponsored a number of bills designed with this end in mind. His latest proposal, the Health Care for All Americans Act, would require every working American to be covered by private insurance plans. Employers would pay for health-care premiums, although employees could be made to contribute up to 25 percent of the premiums. The actual amount that employees paid would depend on the agreements they and their unions reached with the employers. The federal government would finance the health-care coverage for the poor, the aged, and the unemployed. Under such a plan, Kennedy maintains that no one could fall through the health insurance net.

Kennedy also maintains that the Health Care for All Americans Act would be in the long run less costly than to allow the current inflationary spiral in health-care costs to continue. At the beginning of each year, health officials and consumer representatives would meet throughout America to determine how much each state

[6]See Edward M. Kennedy, *In Critical Condition: The Crisis in American Health Care*, New York: Simon and Schuster, 1972, p. 14.

and the federal government could afford to pay for health-care costs. After this amount was determined, doctors and hospitals could not be reimbursed more for their services than was included in the original plan. While Kennedy admits that his plan initially would be more expensive because it grants everyone access to health care, it would be less expensive in the long run because of the built-in limitations on costs.[7]

Debate about whether a national health insurance plan should be implemented usually focuses on the cost of the proposal and its potential effect on the quality of medical care. Conservatives often argue that plans like Kennedy's are too expensive to implement because these merely encourage people to run to the doctor whenever they experience the slightest discomfort. A number of conservatives, doctors, and insurance industry executives have also expressed reservations about the quality of care in liberal plans. They believe that the traditional doctor-patient relationship ought not to be altered and that liberal plans might make doctors into government employees.

The liberal position on health care is praiseworthy in a number of respects. First, the right to health care should be a basic component of a society that is as technologically advanced as ours. Second, maintaining one's health or the health of a family member ought not, if at all possible, to be a catastrophic economic burden. Finally, an adequate health-care policy ought to limit the role that profiteering and financial incentives play in the treatment of the sick. Yet, however praiseworthy it is, the liberal position is by no means faultless. In fact, the problems with the liberal position are similar to those we noted with regard to other matters. Once again, the liberals do not go far enough in their criticism of the role that profit plays in providing health care. Moreover, the liberals' very definition of health is unduly narrow because health is typically seen only as a consumer good that experts provide.

We have noted how Senator Kennedy has tried to counter the conservative argument that national health-care insurance would be too expensive by putting cost limitations into his proposal. Kennedy has taken a step in the right direction. But it is only a step. A better proposal would attempt more explicitly to contour the medical care system to the actual health needs of the American public rather than be concerned with profit making.

American medicine today provides excellent post-illness treatment for those who can afford it. It is much less effective, however, in other areas of health care. We have yet to solve the fundamental problem of maldistribution in health care whereby certain areas of the nation simply do not have sufficient health-care facilities or personnel. Our improved infant mortality rates could be still better if we introduced effective programs of prenatal care where needed. Unnecessary sickness and death can be attributed to inadequate infant immunization practices. And many adult Americans would be better off if we targeted more money for

---

[7] Elizabeth Wehr, "Kennedy, Labor Launch Drive for National Health Insurance," *Congressional Quarterly Weekly*, October 14, 1978, pp. 2955–57.

prevention of the chronic, degenerative diseases that are a more frequent cause of death today than acute, infectious diseases. To deal with all of these problems, however, would require reversing some priorities that have developed in the system which has profit as such an important factor.

The problem with the liberals' position is that they seem to think that good health is nothing more than the consequence of receiving the care which doctors provide. As Wendell Berry has noted, health really implies something more than what doctors do. Since Berry has stated this idea so well, we would like to quote him at length.

> The difficulty probably lies in our narrowed understanding of the word health. That there is some connection between how we feel and what we eat, between our bodies and the earth is acknowledged when we say that we must "eat right to keep fit" or that we should "eat a balanced diet." But by health we mean little more than how we feel. We are healthy, we think, if we do not feel any pain or too much pain, and if we are strong enough to do our work. If we become unhealthy, then we go to a doctor who we hope will "cure" us and restore us to health. By health, in other words, we mean merely the absence of disease. Our health professionals are interested almost exclusively in preventing disease (mainly by destroying germs) and in curing disease (mainly by surgery and destroying germs).
>
> But the concept of health is rooted in the concept of wholeness. To be healthy is to be whole. The word *health* belongs to a family of words, a listing of which will suggest how far the consideration of health must carry us: *heal, whole, wholesome, hale, hallow, holy.* And so it is possible to give a definition of health that is positive and far more elaborate than that given to it by most medical doctors and the officers of public health.[8]

If this wider conception of health care were taken seriously, liberals would have to reevaluate their way of framing the issue. Health care would not only be one more consumer good and one item on a legislative agenda, but would be a matter that provoked discussion about how we organize our work, plan our communities, and spend our leisure time. Good health is, in many ways, a social and political accomplishment. It is the consequence of organizing a society so that people can be sustained in their daily work, can trust one another in their daily encounters, and can confidently form deep attachments to others. In a consumer society such as ours, these goals are constantly imperiled. To admit this and to work for its impovement, liberals would have to be more critical of existing affairs than they have yet to be.

LIBERALS AND SEX

Our examination in the previous chapter of the conservative position on the controversy over sex education argued that the principal weakness of the conservative viewpoint was its inattention to the social and economic forces in America which promote and encourage sexually irresponsible practices. We want to suggest here that

[8]Wendell Berry, *The Unsettling of America*, Sierra Club, 1977, pp. 102–3.

liberal reformers are guilty of a similar neglect by attempting to make sexual reform a matter of educational policy rather than addressing the social functions of sex in American society.

Liberals have typically claimed that teenage pregnancies and the irresponsibility of some parents in educating their children about the ''facts of life'' make it necessary for the schools to give what the New York *Times* has called ''sensible counsel'' about sexual matters.[9] Whether the counsel provided by the schools is always sensible will not be examined here. We want to emphasize how the entire sex education controversy in the American schools leaves unconsidered the role of sexual liberation in present-day American society.

The liberal advocacy of sex-education programs is also indicative of the problems at the core of the liberal approach to reform. Disturbed by the problems of teenage pregnancies and other irresponsible sexual activity, liberals often support sex education because they believe it is, in the words of the New York *Times*, ''surely a wiser solution than to ignore the problem.''[10] In order to reach a ''wiser solution,'' liberals would have to examine the roots of this social and cultural problem in contemporary American culture. As in many other areas, the liberal reluctance to ask fundamental questions practically ensures that their solution ''won't work.'' It is almost as if liberals are masochists who willingly give the conservatives the ammunition which is to be fired back at them.

Ironically, one can learn much more about the role of sex in American life from some rock and roll singers than one can from many sex-education reformers. As a form of popular entertainment that originated in rhythm and blues music, rock and roll's preoccupation with sex and romance has, at times, functioned as a sensitive barometer of the desires, ambitions, and fears of at least some segments of American youth. In recent years, the music and lyrics of Bruce Springsteen provide one of the most explicit statements that we can find of the connection which can be seen between sexual practices and the general tone of life in a particular society. Even if one finds Springsteen's music unappealing, he is probably worth listening to as a political and sociological resource.

Springsteen's album, ''Darkness at the Edge of Town,'' is one of rock's most vivid evocations of the context in which sex functions as a release from social anxiety and as an activity by which a person can ''prove himself'' in contemporary American society. The album's opening song, ''Badlands,'' establishes the tone of the entire work as Springsteen sings about the conditions of everyday life in a New Jersey town, calling it a place where a young person is ''caught in a crossfire that he doesn't understand,'' where you work all day, ''till you get your back burned,'' and where ultimately you have ''to let a broken heart stand as the price you gotta pay.'' The goal of Springsteen's life is also established in the opening song as he vows ''to spit in the face'' of the Badlands and thus be at least momentarily raised above them.

---

[9]*The New York Times*, Editorial, February 27, 1981, p. 21.
[10]*Ibid.*

The rest of the album basically consists of a detailed accounting of why Springsteen wants to be raised above the Badlands and a description of the actions by which he can reach the "Promised Land." In Springsteen's portrait, it is clear that his work life is one of the most influential determinants of his needs. Work, in Springsteen's depiction, is a continual insult. The men pass through the factory gate with "death in their eyes" and time on the job makes them so weak that they just "want to explode." The music on the album enhances the effect of the lyrics (or is it the other way around?) because it too literally simmers. Springsteen maintains a hard rock beat that is always at the point of going out of control, but yet remains constrained and contained. What makes work such a horrible problem is that although it influences so much of our life, the conditions cannot, in Springsteen's mind, be directly confronted. They are only compensated for after work when, in Springsteen's words, "you better believe that someone is gonna get it tonight."

You will not hear in Springsteen's lyrics of efforts to improve the conditions which cause so much tension and bring so much anxiety to his life. That work is, at best, boring and, at worst, deathlike is a matter taken for granted and not the object of attention. His efforts to relieve the tension are all directed to activities which take place after work. Thus race cars and romance—Friday night at the strip and petting afterward—become the moments for which Springsteen yearns and the triumphs which his lyrics celebrate.

While Springsteen may sing of these moments of speedway triumph and sexual conquest as times of ecstatic liberation, the world view of the desperate lies behind his bravado. This desperation is expressed in two ways. On one hand, he is simply desperate for a triumph on Friday night because of the tendency to explode after a week's work. (College students and others may frequent a bar instead of the racetrack.) On the other hand, even if he is able to relieve the tension on Friday night, he can be certain that it will have mounted to the same level by the following weekend. In the desperate world of rock and roll, happiness is a momentarily relief always to be diminished on Monday morning by the real conditions of everyday life.

Against conditions of life which make, at least for male adolescents, sex into a domineering imperative even beyond that provoked by puberty, sex education will not be an especially formidable adversary. While sex education courses may reduce the incidence of some of the worst consequences of irresponsible sexual activity, it does not and cannot make any effort to alter the conditions that give rise to the irresponsibility. It does not look critically at a society's loss of respect for the past and loss of hope in the future which gives rise to a celebration of the present, for which the perpetual orgasm is the quintessential symbol. To think in a genuinely critical manner about sex in American society would require reformers to look at adults in society and not only at the activities of the young.

The trends in sexual behavior that sex-education courses attempt to counter are not inventions of the young, but rather manifestations of changes that have, in large part, overtaken the adult world. Sexual irresponsibility among the young is a predictable outcome of the current world view in which relations are "noncommittal'' and ''open.'' Yet to believe in soap opera America where fidelity is a trap and casual affairs a liberation betrays an outlook which ignores the past and despairs of the future. The history of care, of love and struggle, and of future dreams is ignored whenever a better opportunity arises. The catalog of best sellers which speaks of interpersonal relations reflects these trends. In the last 15 years, any number of authors have told us how to maintain an open marriage, how to be assertive throughout it and how to obtain, when the marriage disintegrates, a "creative" divorce.

The culmination of this trend, we hope, was reached in 1980 with the publication of Gay Talese's book, *Thy Neighbor's Wife*. Having come to believe that our current sexual practices are revolutionary, Talese writes a 500-page book honoring such notable revolutionaries as Alex Comfort, author of *The Joy of Sex*, and Hugh Hefner of *Playboy* fame. He also describes in elaborate detail the practices of some middle-class folk who have signed up with the sexual revolution. Talese even confesses that he himself has earned his revolutionary stripes by indulging in a number of extramarital affairs. Yet Talese is really not that far apart from Bruce Springsteen. He just hangs out with a different crowd.

In fact, Springsteen is really more insightful than Talese because his lyrics weld an explicit connection between his sexual needs and the conditions of his everyday life. Make no mistake, although Talese does chronicle important facets in some middle-class lives, it is not a revolution. What Talese describes is the latest fashion in the perennial attempt to fill middle-class life with meaning. In the words of social critic Christopher Lasch, it is one more effort to "beat sluggish flesh to life."

Talese's revolution cannot even fulfill the promises it offers the recruits. The middle-class sexual emancipation is a pseudo-liberation. It never questions the conditions which make this kind of liberation necessary. Talese only manages to overburden our sex life because he supposes it can provide by itself what only a full and complete life can provide. It is not always easy to be faithful and it is not always proper to be faithful when a relationship has disintegrated. These difficulties ought not, however, cause us to glorify our inability to maintain decent and sustaining relationships by dressing up our incompetence in the garb of liberation. While there may be some who admire Hugh Hefner, it would be a dreary world if men were only studs and women were only bunnies.

Thus while it may be considered liberal to talk openly about sex these days and educate our children about it in the schools, it is not clear that those of a liberal persuasion have come to grips with the full ramifications of our openness regarding sexual practices. Most particularly, it is not clear that liberals have noticed the manner in which sexual freedom is itself being promoted as a consumer good which can compensate for the inadequacy of other elements in our lives. But given the liberal reluctance to question the bedrock assumptions of the existing order, we should not be astonished that the discussion of sex and controversies about it take place on a level at which Bruce Springsteen exhibits more insight than many reformers.

LIBERALISM, THE SELF AND THE COMMUNITY

Liberals frequently claim that they are the true defenders of the individual in contemporary America. They cite the New Deal and the Great Society programs begun under their auspices which guarantee income, food, and medical care for many Americans unable to provide for themselves. And they point to their traditional support for the civil liberties guaranteed in the Constitution and recent support for consumer protection legislation aimed at reducing the number of dishonest business practices. Because they support the right of so many individuals and so many groups of individuals, liberals claim that they are the true defenders of the common good in American society. In Ralph Nader's words, many liberals believe that their reforms are "in the public interest."

The claims which liberals make are not altogether untrue. Yet both their rhetoric and their practices are a bit too convenient and self-serving, and many conservatives realize this. Conservatives often suggest that it is not at all clear that the well-intentioned plans of the liberals serve either the public's interest or the interests of most individuals. Conservatives like Milton Friedman criticize liberals for interfering too frequently with the working of the market. Friedman, as we have seen, argues that liberals actually take choices out of our hands and try to make these for us. We agree that liberal politics do not necessarily serve the best interests of either individuals or the community, but for reasons quite different from those expressed by Milton Friedman.

We have tried to show in this chapter that the liberal criticism of American life is too accepting of the capitalist definitions of individual needs as consumption needs and of public interests as the sum of individual consumer needs. In the terms of this book, liberals take for granted many conditions of life in America which potentially could be altered. Thus we have suggested that a number of significant personal and political needs have yet to be addressed by even the most liberal of our political reformers.

As a final example, let us return for a moment to the fate of safety belts in automobiles. Although more people buckle up now than prior to Ralph Nader's activism, a significant portion of the American population still refuses to use seat belts. Undoubtedly, there are many reasons for this refusal. Some people find them uncomfortable; others contend that they will stand a better chance in an accident if their body is not restricted in any way; and other people feel that they will not make a difference either one way or the other.

Yet there are more than a few people who refuse to buckle their seat belts because they secretly relish the risk of riding without it. The automobile in American society has been a symbol of freedom for many decades now. Many of us have driven our cars hard to compensate for the sense of confinement we felt in other aspects of our lives. We step on the gas pedal and the car responds. There are not too many other parts of our everyday life where such a process occurs. Given the sense of freedom and control over our lives (however trivial an experience of freedom this really is) that driving an automobile might provide, it is small wonder that many people refuse to dilute the experience by wrapping themselves in a safety restraint.

Considerations like this are simply not acknowledged by liberal reformers. They were content to argue in the 1960s that because wearing seat belts protects individuals, car manufacturers ought to be compelled to install them. The inclusion of seat belts in cars has not put an end to the carnage that occurs every year on American roadways. Today, many liberals want car manufacturers to install air-bag systems on new cars, hoping that an expensive passive restraint system may make our daily version of demolition derby safer.

We have nothing against seat belts or air bags. The carnage that takes place every day on our highways does border on collective insanity. If the leaders of any nation randomly killed from 35,000 to 60,000 citizens a year and maimed numerous others, we would accuse them of the vilest crimes and might perhaps even go to war in order to liberate the populace from such oppression. In America today, however, we simply assume that approximately 50,000 deaths annually are the costs we must pay to travel by car. Any proposal to reduce these costs ought to be given serious consideration, including air bags and other passive restraint systems.

What the liberals have not examined is the role of automobiles in American society. They do not bother to comment on whether our personal need for a measure of power and control in our lives is best met on the road. Until recently, they did not bother to comment on whether our collective needs were best met by housing and transportation systems that made two cars almost mandatory. Both individuals and the public might have been better served if our transportation and housing patterns had been brought on the political agenda instead of only attempting to lower the number of deaths that the transportation system invariably generates.

Many liberals would probably respond to the criticisms we have made by saying that you have to be more pragmatic in political affairs than we appear to be. They might tell us that we have asked them to do the politically impossible, especially given the present tone of the country, or that they are having enough trouble defending accomplishments of 20 and 30 years ago from conservative attack. In our minds, however, it was the liberal strategies of political change that were entirely unrealistic. We would agree that many liberal measures ought to be part of a civilized society's politics: for example, minimum income, adequate health care, and guaranteed employment. Yet we do not think that the liberal methods for achieving their goals have been realistic. In the Great Society days, it was assumed that we would abolish poverty by letting the poor into the house of American affluence through the back door. Lyndon Johnson believed that we would eliminate the ghettos without restructuring the American economy and that we could even wage an expensive war in Vietnam while eliminating the ghettos. It is not our criticism that is utopian, but the liberal belief that we could have effective reforms without making some hard choices about the basic structure of American society.

In their arguments with American liberals during the past 30 years, conservatives have expressed their disdain for the reformist point of view by inventing a figure known as the suburban liberal. The distinguishing characteristic of suburban liberals is the inconsistancy between professed beliefs and actual mode of living. Suburban liberals, according to the conservative portrait, strenuously argue in favor of busing, then send their own children to private schools. Suburban liberals profess to be environmentalists in favor of mass transportation, but then drive their cars anywhere they go. Suburban liberals claim consumers lead bankrupt lives, but they themselves might be heavily in debt to Mastercard, Visa, and a variety of department stores. Conservatives point out that liberals do not live as they want the rest of the population to live.

Like any good caricature, the portrait of the suburban liberal is powerful because it contains more than a measure of truth. Almost everyone knows somebody who seems to fit this portrait. Looked at from another angle, however, the suburban liberal might be viewed as a troubled and perhaps even pathetic figure. Very few of us, either conservative or liberal, have not experienced the difficulty of trying to ''practice what we preach.'' In fact, many of us experience difficulties similar to those of the suburban liberal: we cannot bring ourselves to live the way that we deeply believe decent people ought to live. For instance, we profess to be socially responsible, but then act in ways that are socially irresponsible; or we know that life as a consumer is unrewarding, but manage to fall into a life of plastic money and perpetual debt.

Actually, it should not be surprising that many of us experience this split between how we act and what we believe. In many respects, this split is the result of the way that American social and political institutions operate. We are told that we should operate in the public interest, but then are constantly encouraged to pursue our self-interest as consumers. How capable we are of repairing this split may well determine how capable we are of discovering a humane response to our current troubles.

CHAPTER 9

The End of Consumer Society?

The difficulty of managing a socially acceptable distribution of income in the capitalist nations is that it will have to contend with the prospect of a decline in the per capita output of material goods. The problem is therefore not merely a question of calling a halt to the increasing production of cars, dishwashers or homes . . . , but of distributing a shrinking production of cars, appliances and homes.

Robert Heilbroner

In 1960 a journalist asked the head of Chrysler Motor Company's product-planning division to predict what automobiles would look like in 1980. He replied that cars in 1980 would look much like they did in 1960, with the exception that they would be longer, wider, and more powerful.[1] Given this forecast, we might say today it is no wonder that Chrysler has experienced difficulty in recent years. While Chrysler produced its longer, wider and more powerful Newports and Cordobas, Americans increasingly purchased Datsuns, Toyotas, Hondas and Subarus in order to minimize the effects of rising gas prices.

The response by Chrysler's head of product planning was not, however, only an illustration of the American automakers' lack of foresight. It also represented the prevalent outlook about life in general as we entered the 1960s. We had created the affluent society in America and it was assumed that our economy would continue to

[1]Godfrey Hodgson, *America in Our Time* (New York: Vintage, 1976), p. 7.

158

improve. It was not only automobiles, but refrigerators, washing machines, homes, and shopping malls that would get bigger and better. Young Americans were taught to expect that advances in technology would raise the material standard of living to unforeseen heights.

Much of this optimism has dissipated by 1982 as people appear to be concerned with retaining what they have acquired. A number of American bookstores have sections or aisles labeled "Survival" as if to indicate that one's very existence is jeopardized daily. Thousands of Americans have become so worried about social conditions that they are currently arming themselves to the teeth. Even Nancy Reagan feels unsafe, so that when she sleeps alone she keeps a "teenie weenie" gun at bedside. And food entrepreneurs urge us to stock up with a year's supply of survival food so that we will be prepared for any emergency.

People who talk to Americans hear them express concern about their economic condition. A writer for the New York *Times* interviewed a number of young couples across the nation in which at least one partner was a college graduate. All expressed worries about their economic future with statements such as "trying to buy a house seems to control our lives" and "I feel like we're all in a race and if you make the wrong move, you can fall hopelessly behind."[2] Many people are not so pessimistic and do believe that their personal lives will improve. But they see this improvement as a consequence of their own success in combating larger social trends. Ronald Reagan's promise to arrest these trends and restore the American consumer paradise was surely a significant factor in his election to the presidency.

This chapter begins by outlining a few problems that currently threaten to turn the American consumer paradise into a memory. We first speak about how domestic economic difficulties are reflected in rising home prices and automobile purchases. Next we show how changing international conditions may well continue to cause problems for the domestic economy. Then we examine the arguments of politicians such as Ronald Reagan and writers of self-help manuals who maintain that the American dream can be restored. The chapter concludes by showing how some major social and political problems are not adequately addressed by those who wish to refurbish consumer paradise.

To try to restore the American dream is not the best approach for coping with our present difficulties. On a personal level, this strategy will only aggravate the anxiety and rootlessness that already exist in America. The strategy is politically unwise because it is likely to bring greater inequality to our nation and make America yet more vulnerable to the vagaries of international politics. We think Americans might be better served by moving toward a more equitable distribution of wealth and by searching for more rewarding ways of living than are provided in a consumer society.

---

[2] Howard Husock, "The High Cost of Starting Out," New York *Times Sunday Magazine,* June 7, 1981, p. 48.

THE TARNISHED AMERICAN DREAM

Hardly any American is unaware of the inflationary spiral that characterized the U.S. economy in the late 1970s and early 1980s. Inflation is everywhere: at the gas station, the supermarket, the movie theater and the clothing rack in department stores. Yet high inflation does not necessarily cause material standards of living to decline. If earnings keep pace with inflation, especially inflation in key categories such as food, fuel, and housing, our economic standard of living can be maintained and possibly improved. During the 1970s, many Americans did manage to battle inflation on even terms. Nonetheless, the periodic gas lines and the price rise in some important consumer durables brought into question the assumption that our material life will continue to get better.

A home is usually the most costly and important purchase an American will make. Almost every college graduate expects to purchase a house someday and the majority of skilled workers share this expectation. In a culture that values privacy and personal space, renting is not only often perceived as an inconvenience, but also as a waste of money. Renters are typically at the mercy of their landlord regarding the price of their apartment. For all the money they invest in housing, renters do not receive any equity nor do they receive the tax breaks that homeowners do. It is a rare American adult who would have no interest in being a homeowner. Yet in the last ten years, it has become increasingly difficult to purchase a home. Choice neighborhoods are becoming unaffordable to everyone but the wealthy and a number of people who presently own homes claim that they could never afford to purchase one today.

A good illustration of this can be seen in the Patterson Avenue neighborhood in Richmond, Virginia, where one of the authors of this book resides. It is a very pleasant neighborhood in which most people would enjoy living. Almost all the single-family homes are solidly constructed, three bedroom, brick houses. The yards are not large, but there is sufficient room for children to play. The street is not heavily traveled except during rush hours, so that it is usually safe for anyone but a toddler. A casual passerby will note that the residents at least appear to be good neighbors, for they frequently stop to chat for a moment or two as they walk up and down the streets. The neighborhood is mixed in terms of the occupations which the homeowners and renters pursue. Some perform blue collar and clerical work, others are stepping up the corporate ladder, and a few college professors are also residents.

Very few people are anxious to move out of the neighborhood because it is convenient as well as pleasant. A resident is five minutes away from the down-town business district, yet not that distant from some of Richmond's major recreational and cultural facilities. If you ask the people in the neighborhood about the price which they paid for their home and the price for which they could sell it today, they will inform you that the current selling price is much higher than their own purchasing price. If you question the homeowners a bit more, a number of them will tell you that on today's market they could never afford to purchase the home in which they live. The average home in the neighborhood would require a downpayment in excess of $10,000 and a mortgage payment of more than $600 per month. In fact, some people in the neighborhood could not—based on their salary—purchase a home in any modest Richmond neighborhood.

The situation in this Richmond neighborhood can be matched in city after city across America. From 1970 to 1976, the costs of buying a new home increased from one to two times as much as the median increase in income. By 1979 the median price of buying a new home was well over $70,000 and this increased to $84,000 by 1981. In some of our major cities it is not uncommon to see homes that at one time had been considered little more than modest to middle-income homes selling for more than $100,000. This situation was only aggravated by the skyrocketing interest rates of the last few years.

The problems of buying a home these days have been underscored by various academic studies and government reports. A study of housing conditions produced by the Harvard and MIT Joint Center for Urban Studies estimated that while 46 percent of American families could afford to purchase a median priced home in 1970, only 27 percent could afford to do so in 1976.[3] Further corroboration of this trend came when the government released the 1981 figure on the $84,000 average new home. The National Association of Home Builders said that a buyer who made a 10 percent downpayment would have a monthly mortgage payment of $943 per month. The association also estimated that only about 3 percent of American families could afford to make the payments.[4]

Low-income Americans cannot even think about purchasing a home. Even people who can afford high mortgage payments often find it difficult to save for the downpayment. In fact, many realtors now maintain that people get penalized for thriftiness. Since savings can rarely match the increase in the price of a home, realtors suggest that it is economically wiser to borrow money from friends or relatives than to save for a downpayment.

People will continue, of course, to purchase homes simply because they find renting unattractive. People in high-paying occupations may still find home buying relatively painless. Others among us are very resourceful about getting what we want and will find a way to crack the market. Persons extraordinarily thrifty, industrious, and frugal may save enough to make a downpayment. Some young couples will defer having children so they can purchase a home while others will borrow money for a downpayment from their parents. The point, however, is not that everyone will be unable to purchase a home, but that nobody but the affluent

[3] Paul Blumberg, *Inequality in an Age of Decline* (New York: Oxford University Press, 1980), pp. 202–203. Blumberg includes a wealth of examples from which we draw. Although he is perceptive in portraying the decline of consumer society, the analysis behind it is not especially cogent.

[4] Richmond *Times-Dispatch,* June 3, 1981, p. 9.

will be able to buy one without extra work, extra help from relatives, and sacrifice of other consumer desires.

Recent trends in the automobile industry indicate that a similar process is occurring there. For years, the purchase of a luxury, high powered automobile was an indicator of status in American society. But with the average car now costing nearly $9000 and the future price of gasoline unknown, Americans have had to restrain themselves. Fewer and fewer people are able to purchase a luxury car; indeed, fewer people are able to purchase any new car, at least as frequently as in the past. Used-car dealers complain that while they have no difficulty selling cars, they often have difficulty buying them because people now keep their autos longer. Many smaller used-car dealers purchase so-called junk cars and reconstruct them for eventual sale on the lot. By the late 1970s, almost all the domestic automakers were experiencing grave difficulties. The Chrysler Corporation was actually in danger of folding and it was only able to stay afloat with the help of a government bail-out.

While home buying, automobile purchasing, and interest rates on these items tarnish the American dream, the staggering performance of the economy was also reflected by general economic indicators. For instance, while productivity in the private sector grew by 3.2 percent per year from 1948 to 1965, the growth rate was only 1.1 percent per year from 1972 to 1978. The immediate causes of this decline are complicated and include a variety of domestic and international factors. We no longer have access to cheap and plentiful energy supplies. We are unable to redirect investment from low productivity to high productivity industries. We have many citizens who want to work in low productivity service industries and we find it difficult to replace deteriorating equipment in American plants.[5]

Explanations attempting to pinpoint reasons for this decline are normally dependent on the political allegiance of the commentator. Conservatives are fond of blaming what they consider the pampered American worker, excessively high taxes on corporate earnings, restrictions on investment, and government safety and health regulations which strangle business. Liberals suggest that the decline results largely from industry's lack of foresight and unwillingness to adjust to conditions. Regardless of the relative merits of either explanation, it is unlikely that America will be able to "reindustrialize" within the next few years.

We have not meant to suggest that everyone ought to have the opportunity to live in a luxury home or that everyone should be able to cruise the streets in a Lincoln Continental. It should be clear by now that our own position favors moderation in the consumption of goods and limited economic growth. Unlimited consumption and unrestricted growth are rarely consistent with decent human and environmental values. Our intention here was simply to highlight the problems confronting people who wish to purchase the standard kit of consumer society.

[5]See Lester Thurow, *The Zero Sum Society* (New York: Basic Books, 1980).

INTERNATIONAL PROBLEMS FOR CONSUMER SOCIETY

Students who attended American elementary schools 20 years ago often were taught geography as part of a social studies curriculum. Students learned, among other things, about America's resource base, about trade relations between the United States and other nations and about the principal resources of other countries. An important lesson taught in these conventional geography courses was that America was nearly a self-sufficient country. Students heard that we exported more than we imported, that we had huge reserves of many resources, and that we could purchase from friendly allies those resources we did need. Compared to the rest of the world, America appeared to be blessed with natural advantages.

A geography book written for an elementary student today could no longer make these assertions. Indeed, to depict present conditions accurately it would have to make a number of contrary statements. It would show the change over time in American imports and exports, it would note our dependency on other nations for many of our principal resources, it would speak about potential shortages of a number of key resources, and it would call attention to the emerging political consciousness in nations which are not themselves industrialized but possess large holdings of resources vital to the more prosperous nations. Since this is not a book on international relations, we cannot examine all the implications of these changing conditions. We do want to mention, however, the problems that dependence on foreign nations for resources, potential resource shortages, and the emerging political consciousness may pose for our present way of life.

The unpredictability of our resource supply in both price and availability has been most noticeable with respect to petroleum. Since the United States currently imports between 35 and 40 percent of its petroleum, our standard of living has become partially dependent on the oil-producing countries' willingness to sell us their product and to sell it at a predictable price. When they decide for one reason or another to hold back production or merely to raise prices, the United States experiences another round of inflation and, occasionally, social dislocation. And, as long as we remain committed to a petroleum-based economy, we will have little control over this situation.

We can already see how dependence on foreign oil to maintain our standard of living tailors the conduct of American foreign policy. Our efforts to promote a lasting peace in the Middle East have their roots not only in our desires to minimize violent conflict throughout the world, but in our economy's own need for a continuous flow of Mid-East oil. During the Carter administration, our reluctance to criticize Saudi Arabia for its human rights violations reflected our unwillingness to antagonize one of OPEC's most friendly nations. The Reagan administration's efforts to establish more cordial relations with Mexico is an implicit recognition that Mexico may become a major supplier of petroleum in the years to come.

Throughout the world, our political and strategic decisions are linked to our consumer appetites.

A second problem that international conditions pose for our way of life is that worldwide industrial growth may seriously deplete the supply of essential resources. We are not only using up resources at a fast pace on a worldwide basis, but we are also increasing our rate of use. Our long-term energy needs again provide the most vivid example of the problem. Currently, the industrial system of production is basically run by using nonrenewable energy sources. Many writers have begun to argue that our rate of use is fast outstripping the available supply and that long-term shortages are inevitable. For example, the political scientist William Ophuls maintains that "world supplies of fossil fuel, with the exception of coal, are not adequate to meet expected levels of demand much beyond the next century" and that America's own supply of fuels face "roughly the same future as the world's."[6]

Ophuls contends that a similar development is occurring with the raw materials used by industrial societies. He suggests that reserves of almost all our precious metals will be effectively exhausted within the next 50 to 100 years. Ophuls and others suggest that there are natural limits to industrial growth and to ignore these limits is dangerous. In the first place, the harm and disease caused by pollution can outweigh the benefits of greater production of consumer durables. More important, a short-term policy designed to produce more consumer goods may actually be jeopardizing the well-being of future generations.[7]

The third and perhaps most unsettling strain that international conditions may place on our way of life has been described by the political economist Robert Heilbroner. In a disturbing book entitled *An Inquiry into the Human Prospect*, he argues that anyone who might think that we can meet the challenges of the future without paying a fearful price ought to be told that "there is no hope." He maintains that we are currently spawning conditions in which nuclear terrorism may become a routine weapon used by poorer countries against richer nations in wars of redistribution.

Heilbroner reaches this conclusion by speculating about the effects of population growth in the non-industrialized world. He contends that population growth is likely to impose intolerable strains on many poorer nations, even if they are relatively successful with birth control programs. Cities will be overcrowded, land will be unavailable, and food will be scarce. In some instances, Heilbroner envisions nations sliding into anarchy where any semblance of civility is lost. He

[6]William Ophuls, *Ecology and the Politics of Scarcity*, (San Francisco: W.H. Freeman and Company, 1977), p. 87.

[7]Ibid., Chs. 2 and 3. For the initial and most controversial statement of this argument see Donella H. Meadows, et. al., *The Limits to Growth* (New York: Universe Books, 1972).

maintains that only "iron governments," those which are determined to ram change "down the throats of anyone" who resists may be capable of preventing a regression to anarchy and barbarism.[8]

Heilbroner predicts that the leaders of these iron governments will probably be acutely aware of the economic gaps between the richer and the poorer nations. He does not think that these leaders will look with forgiving eyes at the difference between the "first class" and the "cattle class" nations. They are likely to call for a more equal distribution of the world's wealth and, at a minimum, they will ask for more extensive aid packages.

Heilbroner does not believe that these requests are likely to be granted since governments generally do not spend more than token amounts on foreign aid. More important, people in the richer nations will be unwilling to alter their consumer lifestyles for the good of those whom they do not know. Heilbroner believes that we have become so addicted to our consumer needs that only an authoritarian government could cure the addiction.[9]

Yet he does not think that poorer nations will be left without any leverage in this situation. The spreading availability of nuclear weapons, in Heilbroner's mind, has introduced an entirely new element into the situation. He speculates that leaders or poorer governments will develop nuclear weapons, or will acquire them, and threaten to employ them against the richer nations. In fact, he imagines that they may well employ nuclear terrorism to achieve economic goals. Some writers have argued that in the foreseeable future it may be possible for a terrorist group to hold an entire city hostage. We may wake up one morning and hear that a nuclear bomb will devastate Chicago unless the demands of an international terrorist group are met. In the near future, a widening gap between some poorer nations and consumer nations may be a catalyst for a class war fought with the most terrifying of weapons.

The scenarios about resource shortages and international class war developed by Ophuls and Heilbroner are, in all likelihood, slightly exaggerated. We do have decades to develop alternatives to our present resource use and it is improbable that America will be threatened by Bolivia or Zimbabwe in the near future. But the doomsday nature of their warnings should not be a reason for neglecting the central truth in these forecasts. International conditions will put more and more pressure on the American consumer economy in upcoming years. As our resource use increases our dependence, we will find it impossible either to isolate ourselves from the rest of the world or to control it to our advantage.

[8]Robert Heilbroner, *An Inquiry into the Human Prospect* (New York: W.W. Norton and Company, 1980), pp. 37–45.
[9]Ibid.

RESTORING THE AMERICAN DREAM

Given our recent economic problems, it is not surprising that so many people have offered recommendations about how to overcome these difficulties. A central theme in Ronald Reagan's presidential campaign was the promise of a "great national crusade to make America great again." It has also been the concern of many authors who tell the public that we can bring prosperity to our lives regardless of social and political conditions. We want to examine the wisdom involved in Reagan's national crusade and the advice given in some self-help books as to how individuals might successfully combat the general drift of the American economy.

Making America Great Again

When Jimmy Carter was campaigning for president in 1976, he blamed Gerald Ford and Republican economic policies for the high level of unemployment and the high rate of inflation at that time. Carter promised that he would be a competent manager of the economy. He pointed to his experience in streamlining the government bureaucracy in Georgia and to his purported background as a nuclear engineer. He maintained that his election would finally give us a "government as good as the people." Jimmy Carter was a positive thinker.

Less than three months after taking office, however, Carter felt compelled to change his theme. Americans, he said, consumed too much energy. With or without good management, we faced difficult times and we were required to sacrifice. He admitted that the economy was not entirely under his control and now only promised to ensure that the burdens of hard times were distributed equitably. Advising us to lower our expectations, Carter proclaimed that he would manage scarcity for a wasteful citizenry.

Unhappiness with Carter's management of the economy became the principal theme of the 1980 election. Carter was repeatedly attacked by Ronald Reagan for following policies that raised the inflation rate while not reducing the level of unemployment. Reagan charged that Carter's policies were conceived in negative terms: that is, Carter emphasized regulation, taxation of business profits, and personal sacrifice. In contrast, Reagan portrayed *himself* as a positive thinker. He pleaded that if we only let individuals keep more of their income, removed the handcuffs from business and encouraged productivity instead of adjustment to scarcity, prosperity would return to American society. Asked in one of his debates prior to the election about what unpopular measures he would endorse as President, Reagan replied that he did not see any reason to endorse unpopular measures. Sound economic policy could restore prosperity without antagonizing any segment of the American population.

In many respects, Reagan's campaign was an effort to vindicate the consumer society. He first stated that he saw nothing wrong with a society devoted to increasing the amount of goods its citizens could purchase. In fact, Reagan's most telling charge against Carter was his assertion that we could not go the store and purchase "things" as cheaply as we could in 1976. Furthermore, Reagan argued that there were no valid reasons why America could not become an even more prosperous consumer society. Blaming almost all of our current ills on government regulation and government spending, Reagan maintained that unleashing business could restore the luster to the American dream.

Reagan's agenda for prosperity, however, is riddled with problems. The analysis itself is historically inaccurate because it misrepresents the history and purpose of government regulation. American conservatives normally portray government regulation of business as a plague that good businesses have opposed and always will oppose. This portrait is a gross distortion. Certain businesses have always favored government regulation (occasionally they sought it out) and still support it to this day. They favor regulation because it stabilizes an uncertain market situation and thus, in the long run, makes their profits more predictable.

The deregulation of the airline industry was opposed primarily by the large airline companies. The same is true today with deregulation of the trucking industry as the major opponents of deregulation include the large trucking concerns. At the very moment in 1981 when President Reagan was asking Congress to pass his budget cuts that would help to unleash business, the sugar industry was asking Reagan to implement price supports for the industry. To be sure, business is against many government regulatory programs. But it has rarely been opposed to regulation in general. Business has consistently favored those regulations which are profitable and opposed those which are not.

Reagan's proposals for restoring prosperity are misleading when these are presented with the implication that no one will be harmed by their consequences. To cite only the most obvious example, we will briefly comment on his proposals to reduce the federal budget. In principle, most people would like to cut the federal budget, just as most people are interested, in principle, in reducing their own budget. The problems arise when we begin to think about where the cuts ought to be made. Barring economic catastrophe, much of the federal budget is already fixed. A good portion of it is devoted to interest payment on debts, to unemployment compensation, to minimal care for the physically and mentally disabled, to pay salaries and retirement benefits of our military establishment, and to social security benefits for the elderly. President Reagan can make policy choices about the budget, but these are *choices* that will benefit some and harm others. Given the emphasis that Reagan has placed on increasing defense spending and reducing corporate taxes, social welfare expenditures and regulations that provide some minimal aid to the poor and the lower-middle class will have to be pared if overall federal spending is to be reduced.

This was made abundantly clear with the publication of Reagan's initial budget proposals. Poorer Americans will suffer because the reductions targeted for them will come primarily at the level of basic necessities with cuts in school lunch programs, food stamp benefits, and aid which helped to defray the cost of increased energy bills. Even the much ballyhooed savings that were to come to average Americans through the Reagan tax reduction are largely discriminatory. The recommended tax reductions will save the average middle-class family approximately $400 per year while it will save thousands for a person whose income is in the $100,000 bracket. But the savings to the middle-class family is, in part, illusory because it will necessarily be eaten up by the higher fuel prices that come with continued deregulation of the energy industry.

Reagan's misleading presentation of his program might be considered acceptable if we could actually believe that these temporary sacrifices would work to everyone's benefits in the long run. Unfortunately, this is not likely to be the case. An increase in corporate profits is unlikely to provide jobs for teenagers in the cities or to rebuild the deteriorating infrastructure of our urban areas. Nor is it clear that no one will be harmed by letting business off the leash. One of the reasons that it has been partially restricted in the past is that it has acted irresponsibly when left to its own designs. Unleashing business may well mean less effective safeguards for worker health and safety and greater destruction of the environment.

It is not even certain that unleashing business would promote the desired increase in investment and productivity. The economist Lester Thurow has noted that the American economy is not simply confronted by a crisis of investment in which businesses need tax reductions to purchase new materials and upgrade their equipment. Thurow argues that we have a crisis of disinvestment in which we do not know how to move from old, low productivity industries to new, high productivity industries. The problem here has very little to do with excessive government regulation. As Thurow points out, businesses are often willing to maintain a regular profit in a low-productivity industry rather than risk great losses in switching to a high-productivity industry. Similarly, workers are more interested in obtaining job security than they are in worrying about whether the job is in a low-productivity or high-productivity industry. Given the insecurity that pervades American economy, it would be surprising if things were otherwise.[10]

Ironically, one way this problem might be corrected is by more government intervention in the economy. If we had a full employment policy that guaranteed work to anyone capable of holding a job, the American work force might be disposed to consider matters such as productivity more seriously than it presently does. Furthermore, government can occasionally take the initial risk that private investors cannot afford or are unwilling to take. In the area of solar energy development, a large-scale government purchase of photovoltaic cells might permit these to be manufactured at a price that would make solar systems competitive with other energy sources. The transistor technology now available was the consequence

[10]Lester Thurow, *The Zero Sum Society*, Ch. 6.

of government investment. There is no reason why both our energy transition and efforts to make America more competitive on the world market cannot follow a similar path.

The practicality of the Reagan plan is likely to be further diminished by the planned increase in military spending. If this were to take place, the buildup from 1981 to 1986 would actually be three times as large as the military buildup during the Vietnam War.[11] There are a number of good ethical and strategic reasons for opposing the proposed new weapons systems. But at this point it is not even clear that the Reagan plan makes economic sense. The plan fails to do this because Reagan and his advisors simply assume that the weapons systems will be paid for by tax revenues generated by a productivity increase which is greater than any we have experienced during the past 40 years. However, if this miracle never materializes, Reagan will have committed the nation to an extraordinarily costly program without the funds to pay for it. The consequence will be another round of dislocation, with still higher levels of unemployment and inflation.

Prosperity Through Personal Effort

Americans have always been receptive to self-help books which instruct its readers how to perform a certain activity or how to reach a desired goal. Since Ben Franklin wrote *The Way to Wealth,* we have been especially receptive to books which chart the path to material riches. Lately, our bookstores and supermarkets have been stocked with advice on how individuals might become successful even if the general state of affairs is in decline. Without fail, these books exhort us to think positively about our personal future. At a minimum, we can make the American dream a reality in our own lives. We can "win through intimidation," we can get "power and use it," we can "become free in an unfree world," and we can learn how to "look out for number one."

The authors of these self-help books employ a common pattern of presentation. They begin by appealing to the reader's discontent. Are you unhappy? Do other people continually make you feel guilty? Do you feel that your worth is not appreciated by your boss? The authors are careful to emphasize that this discontent can be removed simply by changing the attitude you bring to the conduct of your life. For example, Robert Ringer writes that "you can be happier today than yesterday, twice as happy yesterday as you were a month ago. The degree of your happiness at any given moment will depend upon the rationality of your objectives and the success you have in obtaining them. The more rational you are, the easier they are to obtain."[12] The major part of these books usually consists of a simple

---

[11]Lester Thurow, "How to Wreck the Economy," *New York Review of Books,* May 14, 1981, pp. 3–8.

[12]Robert J. Ringer, *Looking Out for Number One* (New York: Funk and Wagnalls, 1977), p. 4.

formula which tells us how to act rationally and instructs how this formula can be applied to a variety of everyday situations.

The authors impress upon us the importance of caring only for ourselves and avoiding compassionate behavior. Everything else is said to be irrational. By acting self-interestedly, the authors contend that we achieve three kinds of liberation. First, there is liberation from economic subservience to others. By ruthlessly advancing up the corporate ladder and achieving financial security, we avoid the potentially humiliating effects of economic dependence. Second, by acting assertively and expecting people to return any favor that we might perform for them, we liberate ourselves from guilt feelings. We no longer will permit ourselves to be manipulated by other people. Third, by viewing the government's taxation powers as an unjustified evil, we free ourselves from the chains of patriotism and political compassion. We will realize that no one has a right to our money and will not feel responsible for the freeloaders who have been receiving our tax dollars.

Scratch the professed optimism of these self-help manuals and you discover a terrifying world view. While individuals are exalted for possessing the power to change their lives, the world in which all of us reside is described in overwhelmingly negative terms. The government is a thief, business competitors are eager to shaft us, and other human beings are merely obstacles to overcome. Revealingly, Robert Ringer, a self-professed apostle of freedom, thinks of his fellow human beings as nothing more than "weeds in the people store." While few authors of economic self-help books share Ringer's candor, the implication is nearly always the same: kindness, compassion, and friendship are worse than useless because the world only rewards those people who have purged themselves of traditional human values.

It is not uncommon for these authors to advise us to treat our lovers and spouses as we do any other "weed." Partners in a marriage are urged to draw up contracts with one another detailing their respective duties as if marriage is only a glorified business deal. Men are advised to be certain that their respective partner will be useful to their ambitions. Women are warned not to permit love to get in their way as they pursue money and power. Lurking behind such advice is a vision of personal relations in which everyone is a potential exploiter. The law of the struggle up the corporate ladder has been transferred to personal relations.

The popular success of these books stems from the appeal which the authors make to many of our deepest feelings. How many of us have not felt that the outside world is often an arena of mutual exploitation? How many of us have not occasionally felt that the people whom we love the most take advantage of this love to manipulate us? These are powerful feelings and can generate a need to respond in kind. If we acknowledge that life is a war and that only the ruthless can be assured of material success, we shall, at a minimum, keep the wolves away from the door.

The reason this advice has to be examined critically becomes apparent when we begin to think about issues that have been discussed throughout this book. Do we really find this way of living rewarding? Do we really want to live in a world in which everyone has to be constantly on guard? Do we want other people to relate to us as it is recommended that we relate to them? Such questions should lead us to be skeptical not only of the folk wisdom found on the paperback racks of drugstores, but of the pervasive notion that a consumer society can actually provide a high standard of living.

SHOULD THE DREAM BE RESTORED?

The great novelist Leo Tolstoy spent many of his later years writing fables and parables to instruct the Russian peasantry. After his success as a novelist, Tolstoy became a moralist who promoted a life of simple virtue and described the perils of living otherwise. Few of Tolstoy's parables contain the complex understanding of the human condition he exhibited in *War and Peace* and *Anna Karenina*. Yet many of these do convey the elementary wisdom about life which has been the message of good teachers throughout the ages.

One of Tolstoy's more interesting parables is entitled "How Much Land Does a Man Need?" The story begins when Pahom and his wife, good hearted peasants, are visited by Pahom's sister-in-law, the wife of a prosperous tradesman in town. While talking with her sister, the visitor disparages the country life of the peasants. She claims that Pahom's family does not live comfortably, dress elegantly, or attend the finest entertainments.

Under attack, Pahom's wife (whose name Tolstoy never discloses) defends the peasant life. She mentions that they have always had enough to eat, have fewer temptations than city people and are, in general, free from anxiety. Hearing his wife respond to her sister, Pahom thinks "It is perfectly true. . . . Our only trouble is that we haven't land enough. If I had plenty of land, I shouldn't fear the devil himself."[13]

The devil just happens to be sitting in Pahom's home at the time and, on reading his thoughts, decides to give Pahom the opportunity to purchase some land. Shortly thereafter, Pahom is able to scrape together enough savings and borrowings to buy 40 acres from a landholder who has suddenly put her acreage up for sale. The land is fertile and the harvest is plentiful. Tolstoy tells us that on Pahom's land "the grass that grew and the flowers that bloomed seemed to him unlike any that grew elsewhere."[14]

Some minor problems arise with the neighbors, however, and Pahom begins to think that more land and greener pastures are the answers. The plot of land with which he was once contented is now considered a "narrow hole" from which he

---

[13] Leo Tolstoy, "How Much Land Does a Man Need?" in John Bayley, ed., *The Portable Tolstoy* (New York: Viking, 1978), p. 507.

[14] Ibid., p. 509.

yearns to escape. Opportunity knocks again and Pahom takes advantage of a deal which nets him approximately 125 acres. But his new holdings are not located right next to each other and, after some time passes, Pahom thinks once more of acquiring choicer and more extensive holdings.

Pahom is ready to spend almost his entire worth on purchasing another piece of land when he meets a stranger who tells him about a magnificent land deal available in the province of the Bashkirs. According to the stranger, the land is extraordinarily fertile and because the Bashkirs are as "simple as sheep," the land "can be bought for almost nothing."[15] Pahom, who can hardly believe his ears, inquires about directions and immediately sets out for the land of the Bashkirs.

On arrival, Pahom meets the chief of the Bashkirs and asks how much the land will cost. The chief replies that it will cost him a 1000 rubles a day. Puzzled by the response, Pahom asks what kind of measuring unit a day is and how many acres does one contain. The chief tells him that "we do not know how to reckon it [the land] out. . . . We sell it by the day. As much as you can go round on your feet in a day is yours, and the price is one thousand rubles a day."[16] Pahom mentions that you can walk around a vast amount of land in a day, but the chief does not seem to care. He only tells Pahom that it will then be his. The one catch is that Pahom must return to his starting place by sundown. If he does not, he forfeits the one thousand rubles.

That night Pahom has a dream in which the devil is laughing at his folly. Although he wakes up in a sweat, he does not let the nightmare alter his plans to claim the land and he starts out from a designated spot shortly after daybreak. At first, Pahom intends to claim only an amount of land that will give him ample time to return by sunset. But as the morning proceeds, he lengthens the width of his path, saying to himself that there is sufficient time to return and that it would be a pity not to claim such fertile land. He repeats the process whenever he spies a choice piece of land outside his path, continuing to say what a pity it would be if he did not include it in his takings.

By mid-afternoon, Pahom has drastically altered his original route. He has tried to surround so much land that he has wandered far astray. Now he will have to hurry back if he is to arrive before sundown and not lose his money. Pahom begins to run, hoping to arrive at the spot from which he started before the sun vanishes. As he runs, Pahom realizes that he is not in good physical condition and "is seized with terror lest he die of the strain."[17] Yet he refuses to stop running and thinks that obtaining the land is worth the health risk. Moreover, Pahom believes that "they will call me a fool if I stop now."[18] Moments before sunset, Pahom arrives at the

[15]Ibid., p. 513.
[16]Ibid., p. 516.
[17]Ibid., p. 521.
[18]Ibid.

starting position. Yet he collapses on arrival. He dies before the villagers can even congratulate him on his accomplishment. After Pahom's servant digs a grave, Tolstoy concludes by telling us that "six feet from his head to his heels was all he needed."[19]

Tolstoy's parable is relevant to both the general themes of the book and the specific arguments of this chapter. He manages to illuminate in a few pages the major problems involved in making consumer acquisitions or material wealth the primary goal of life. He does this by showing how Pahom's single-minded pursuit of more land cuts him off from the values which permitted him to live simply and act decently. While all of us, of course, will not experience Pahom's fate, Tolstoy does imply that we experience a symbolic death or a death of the spirit by allowing so many important qualities to wither away if we follow Pahom's example.

As we have seen in Chapter 2, the American corporate structure continually strives to play on our fears and anxieties through such practices as advertising and the manipulation of fashion. There is always another skirt, another suit or another car that, as with Pahom, it would be a pity not to acquire. What begins as an effort to purchase some additional comfort and happiness becomes an end in itself, and one that is hardly questioned by people caught in its snares. It becomes difficult to acknowledge that the malaise which was not solved by purchasing one consumer item will not be remedied by purchasing one more.

Another way that pursuing economic success can be self-defeating is that by doing so we often attempt to deny that we are connected to other human beings. A person who makes a practice of only looking out for number one may eventually find that nobody else wants to have much contact with "number one." Such a strategy for living is unfortunate because loneliness and the inability to establish wholesome connections with one another are major problems today. Although this problem is not well publicized in the media, evidence of its dimensions is scattered throughout American culture. Psychiatric journals are filled with reports about otherwise successful people who come to therapists in order to discover why they are lonely and unable to relate well to other people. A good portion of our popular music industry catalogs the hopes, disappointments, and tribulations of people trying to establish connections with one another. Many American novelists have made loneliness and its problems the substance of their recent work. Kurt Vonnegut, for instance, has a successful presidential candidate in *Slapstick* campaign on the slogan that after his election Americans would be "Lonesome No More."

People who pursue economic success in a single-minded fashion often find, like Pahom did, that it requires a readiness to be mobile, to pack up and go. Consumer society requires not only physical mobility, but, more importantly, a kind of psychic mobility by which persons can shed attachments and obligations

[19]Ibid., p. 522.

they have made at one time. In the process, they frequently cut themselves off from friends, relatives, neighbors, and even their own past. This rootlessness can often hinder the formation of a secure personality. Perhaps one indication that Americans might be dimly aware of loneliness can be seen in the attention that was given to the television epic, *Roots*. The program appealed to many of the values that a consumer society finds dispensable: a sense of the past, a sense that we are connected to others, and a belief that our identity is formed, in part, by restoring the connections we have with the past and with other people.

Any effort to revitalize the American dream that does not acknowledge the existing economic problems is likely to have negative social consequences. If one believes that the level of inequality in America ought to be reduced, President Reagan's plan to unleash business has to be opposed because it is explicitly designed to increase it. As Michael Walzer has noted, the philosophy behind the plan seems to be "more poverty for the poor, more wealth for the wealthy." But even someone not keen about greater equality in America would be well advised to be wary about the ultimate effects of increased inequality. Rather than bringing new hope to Americans, it may well do the opposite. Greater inequality may heighten the general level of bitterness throughout society, increase distrust for government among members of less privileged groups and, most ominously, aggravate the already unacceptable level of violence in America.

The international consequences of attempting to build an ever more prosperous consumer society are not likely to be benign. In the first place, as we noted, such a policy might be terribly expensive for future Americans. If resource supplies are limited, we may face a grimmer future than most people have imagined. But even if the resource threat is successfully overcome, the strategy remains terribly risky. As our economy becomes yet more dependent on others' resources, America will naturally become more dependent on political events elsewhere. We will be compelled to form more entangling alliances and we will find ourselves embroiled in the local and regional disputes of the world's most volatile areas. In the long run, our resource dependence may require the use of American military force to maintain the flow of these needed supplies. In the process, the promises of consumer society will again be found illusory as personal gratification is sacrificed to military needs.

Our nation is presently confronted by a number of legitimate economic problems because American industry is not as competitive in the world economy as it could possibly be. But it is foolish to respond to these difficulties by only planning to re-create the American consumer paradise. The Reagan plan does not guarantee that productivity will actually increase tremendously. But it does use the real interests of the poor as collateral on the hope that an economic miracle will occur, the likes of which we have not witnessed in contemporary times. It also calls for a dangerous military buildup that cannot serve the cause of world peace. If this is what the American dream will be in the future, we shall undoubtedly continue to spend billions of dollars to get to sleep in the evening.

It is certainly reasonable that we try to run our economy more efficiently than we do today. But we need to take a broad and long-term view of what efficiency means. Economic efficiency is only meaningful within a political vision about American priorities. The type of efficiency which penalizes the poor, increases the long-term potential for wrenching resource shortages, and aggravates international tensions is a stark example of what the social critic C. Wright Mills called crackpot realism. An infinitely more sensible response would attempt to ensure that all Americans maintain a decent standard of living without mortgaging our future. Such a response would also prompt us to search for alternatives to the consumer life.

10

Democracy for America

An ethic of commitment does not require ever increasing affluence or prodigal expenditures of resources. Developing deeper relations with people and things does not demand great amounts of money, nor does reverential thinking or the creation of community or a deepened concern with past and future.

Daniel Yankelovich

The Ritz is a small neighborhood bar and grill in Richmond, Virginia. It does not take long for one to realize how inappropriate the name ''The Ritz'' is as a description of the clientele and the decor. The Ritz is anything but swank. The outside light which is supposed to read ''Restaurant'' has only said ''urant'' for the past three years because the burnt out bulbs have never been replaced. The walls of the Ritz are lined by cheap vinyl booths which have been patched and repatched to avoid the expense of purchasing new ones. And the shelves behind the bar are stocked with such vintage wines as Red Rocket and Boone's Farm. Even the stale beer odor—a smell common to many bars—seems worse in the Ritz than it does in other places.

The clientele of the Ritz appears to be a collection of losers and outcasts. There are a number of people who cannot find or hold a job. The patrons who are regularly employed are in low-paying, low-skill occupations. Some customers are castoffs from bad marriages and other relationships which soured. A few drink so heavily that they remind you of the people in country music songs who find their dreams at the bottom of a bottle. There is an occasional fight at the Ritz and Blackie the manager carries a large nightstick behind the counter to break up any fight before "they break up my place." There are few people reading this book who would want their mothers or fathers to be regulars at the Ritz; likewise there are few parents who would not be alarmed if their sons or daughters were regular patrons. A casual visitor might think that the legend which Dante placed above the Inferno, "Abandon All Hope Ye Who Enter Here," ought to be inscribed on the front door of the Ritz.

The Ritz is usually filled on Friday and Saturday nights. Some patrons are there to forget their jobs (or their lack of a job), but others have come for a "night out." There is no band, but a country music jukebox plays the latest tearjerkers of Loretta Lynn, Conway Twitty, and Crystal Gayle, along with a few rock and roll classics such as "Whole Lotta Shaking Goin' On" and "Great Balls of Fire." The small dance floor is usually packed also. The dancers sway together on the slow ones and shake with abandon to the fast ones. No one seems to care that hips, bellies, and thighs are a bit larger and not as fashionably covered as they are on the dance floors of the singles bars a few miles down the road.

What is so striking about the Ritz is how some of the customers who have never achieved much success in life can still pursue their dream of a better existence with hope and vigor on Saturday night. While their well-rounded bellies, misshapen thighs, and wrinkled foreheads betray many disappointments in life, they do not let these stand in the way of one more attempt to fulfill some of their deepest needs. It is clear that a few beers and a small dance floor is all that is needed to revive (at least temporarily) many of their hopes. The men and women ask each other to dance with respectful gestures and, on the floor, all take evident pride in the rhythmic movement of their bodies. Occasionally, you will see one of the patrons rouse someone lost in drink and drag him or her onto the dance floor. And though the drinker may go only under protest, you'll notice his or her entire body come alive after the first few movements.

There are probably hundreds of bars like the Ritz in the United States. However depressing these places might be, they also serve to remind us of the resiliency of the human spirit and the persistence of our desire to strive for a better life. Few Ritz patrons are so disgusted with their lives that they have given up completely. They still want to be respected (although this can sometimes lead to violence), they still want others to think of them as desirable, and a few still are hoping to find someone whom they can love. Many customers at places like the Ritz have been damaged so badly that they will never be able to experience fulfillment of their desires for anything more than a fleeting moment, yet it is a moving experience to watch how vigorously they pursue that moment.

In this book, we have argued that the major institutions of American society influence our everyday lives in a way that diminishes the quality of our existence. We have examined the how the economic system, the educational system, the media, and our political actors consider human beings to be simply consumers of goods and services. These institutions tend to impoverish our experience by defining the quality of life in consumer terms. In the previous chapter, we argued that it may be both impractical and dangerous for Americans to continue raising their expectations as consumers. In this concluding chapter, we suggest how we may respond creatively to our present difficulties so that we might also improve the quality of our everyday lives.

We first examine the personal resources we have to make positive changes. We suggest that most human beings resemble the patrons of the Ritz insofar as we have an enduring desire to enrich our lives and improve the current state of our existence. However, we do argue that our individual capacity for improving our lives is limited and that political activity is necessary to bring about widespread changes. How our democratic political tradition can be connected to some of the persistent desires of human beings is next discussed. We show how the democratic values of liberty and community are related to our individual desires to be free yet secure, powerful yet dependent. Some steps that might be taken to implement these values more fully are suggested. We speak about the importance of wealth distribution, the democratization of the work place, and experimenting with democracy in other areas of life as possible ways of renewing the vitality of American society. Rather than claim that these changes are imminent, we suggest a need to consider them more seriously than is the case now.

PERSONAL RESOURCES FOR CHANGE

Our attack on positive thinking as a method for solving personal problems might lead some people to believe that we think it is impossible for people to change their own lives by utilizing their personal resources. This is not the intended impression. We indicted the popular self-help manuals for encouraging the self-seeking behavior which is already excessive. While individuals do not possess an unlimited capacity to change their lives, they do have an inherent capacity to change and to grow. This capacity is limited, however, by many conditions over which individuals have little control.

It would be foolish to claim that political change must precede personal change, or vice versa. Obviously, certain people only get involved in politics after they have altered their personal priorities. We might think here of some American women who have become politically active after feeling unduly confined in their "traditional" role. Likewise, involvement in political matters can lead to a change in personal beliefs. People who become involved in struggles for political equality might become more sensitive to issues of unjustified inequality in their personal relations. If both methods of change did not exist, there would be little hope for reform of existing problems and injustices. Political change could not occur if it were dependent on every individual within a society first altering his or her own life.

On the other hand, unless some individuals begin to view matters differently, it is hard to imagine the development of any political reform movement.

In speaking about the personal resources for change in contemporary America, it is important to be attentive to those details that are normally considered trivial. For instance, if you asked a number of people to explain how they passed their day, the list would differ in specifics, from person to person, but most would relate the standard run of a day's external events. For example, they might list waking up, what they ate for breakfast, lunch, and dinner, how they traveled to work or school, and how they passed their evening before going to sleep. These would not be dishonest descriptions of how we spend our time, but they would be incomplete: for while we eat, work, and watch television, we are often engaged in what might be called internal activity. At breakfast, we may think about how much we enjoyed meeting a certain person the previous day. At work, we may fantasize that we have the nerve to tell the boss what we really think about some rule. Watching television in the evening, we may secretly identify ourselves with the exploits of our favorite hero.

When we examine the elements of our memories, daydreams, and fantasies, we find that a relatively constant set of themes occupy our thoughts. Few of us will find that our thoughts do not center on our desires for power, liberty, love, security, and sexual fulfillment. The particular manifestations, of course, are going to differ. Some women might fantasize about being the first female president, while others might want to be like Pat Benatar and sing loud rock and roll. We may want to be loved by different sorts of people: some of us worry about what close relations think, others may be more concerned with a person to whom they have never been introduced. Even our hates and desires to wield power maliciously will focus on different objects. Some may think about hurting the person we love, while others only daydream about gluing Howard Cosell's tongue to the roof of his mouth.

Anyone who watches an evening of television and its advertising will learn that those who operate the corporate economy do not think that these memories, daydreams, and fantasies are trivial at all. Most advertising, as we have seen, routinely makes two claims. The first and explicit claim concerns the quality of the product: buy brand X because it works faster, is more efficient, and is less costly than brand Y. The second claim is rarely verbalized in precise terms, but it is the obvious implication that purchasing the advertised product will fulfill a deep personal need. These claims do not speak to the inadequacy of comparable products but to our feelings of inadequacy or incompetency in getting what we want. A pervasive effort is thus made at the core of the American economy to connect our memories, daydreams, and fantasies with beer, cars, and deodorants.

We believe that the American economic order can never fully satisfy the needs and desires the system promises to fulfill. It cannot do this for at least two reasons. First, consumer goods can rarely be a fully satisfactory substitute for the variety of our intrapersonal and interpersonal needs. While the possession and use of consumer goods can provide a measure of power and liberty, it cannot provide a permanent sense of personal accomplishment, it cannot make a good friendship endure, nor can it maintain a rewarding marriage. Second, as we have noted previously, the very logic of the American economy prevents these desires from being fulfilled. No matter what we purchase today, we can be assured that a year from now we will be informed that our life is incomplete unless we make another acquisition. The system runs by perpetually generating anxiety and by continually seeking to undermine contentment with who we are and with what we have.

Our argument criticizing the American economic order should not be taken to mean that we believe every human desire can or should be fulfilled. Our wants cannot be fulfilled because our numerous desires are contradictory. Although we want to obtain power, we also enjoy being dependent on those people we respect. Though we claim to love liberty, we act in ways that place a higher priority on security than freedom. Or we profess to love a person deeply, then act in an opposite fashion. All our desires should not be fulfilled because some are anti-social in nature. Almost all of us have experienced aggressive urges that could potentially be translated into violence toward others. Similarly, some sexual urges occasionally overwhelm our sense of decency and lead us to be manipulative.

Since many desires are contradictory and some are socially unacceptable, we can never fulfill all of them. Our criticism of present-day American society is that it attempts to shape so many needs and desires into profit for the corporate sector. The effects of this tendency are harmful to us individually and to society at large. On an individual level, we have argued that following the advice of American corporations narrows the range of experience open to us and excessively limits our potential. Instead of tapping our talents and capacities, we regularly are advised to seek satisfaction through external goods. We do not believe that this has actually enhanced our happiness, but has only created a society where the experience of emptiness and loneliness is becoming more pervasive.

The constant focus on the self leads not only to a maze of contradictions, but to a moral absurdity as well. It is not unusual today to hear people speak of being obligated to themselves, of having a duty to themselves to perform certain actions. This ''ethic,'' promoted by the corporate economy, is ultimately destructive. Since the ethic has no external reference, it is impossible to determine which competing obligation to the self should be satisfied. People devoted to the self of the corporate economy will inevitably be disappointed when the pursuit of one goal precludes the attainment of another. Moreover, this ethic provides absolutely no basis for distinguishing those self-pursuits which serve the community and those which damage it.

This is one reason why American society performs such a poor job of constraining and sublimating our antisocial desires. The level of violence in our society can only be found acceptable by someone resolutely determined not to think about it. Not only are street crime and random violence at unacceptably high levels, but excessive amounts of white-collar criminally endangers safety, and the daily carnage on our highways is extraordinary. Moreover, it is difficult not to be disturbed with the manipulation of others encouraged in American society by the informal road to success in the corporate world, the media's fascination with legal and illegal gangsters, and the deference paid in America to those who have simply amassed fortunes.

The current system's inability to solve its problems keeps alive the possibility for positive change. Although the American economic system cannot provide happiness, liberty, and security in a genuine way, it does emphasize that these demands are rightfully ours. Given the emphasis which American society places on fulfilling our deepest needs, it should not be surprising that some of us criticize it when it does not meet these needs in a manner that is either individually rewarding or socially acceptable.

In fact, we would venture to propose that many of us do feel that American society does a poor job of meeting our individual needs in a socially responsible manner. There are only a few Americans who have not at one time been critical of consumer society. Many find commercials insulting and many believe that money cannot buy meaning and purpose in life. If our assumptions in this book are correct, many persons are dissatisfied with the educational system and are disturbed by the narrow range of employment options. We definitely want to organize our lives differently today, but we are ignorant of the steps that might be taken or the alternatives which could be created.

We can, to a degree, create a life outside of the existing system. We can be skeptical of what we hear, attempt to educate ourselves more broadly, and try our best with family, friends, and workers. People who can create an alternative life may be more fulfilled and certainly can serve as important models for the rest of us. Yet individual action can only be partially effective. We will always send our children to school and they will be exposed to a deluge of advertisements telling them what to expect from their parents. How do we manage to promote our beliefs when so much of society as it is organized attacks them? Here, of course, is where politics becomes critically important.

POLITICAL RESOURCES: OUR DEMOCRATIC TRADITION

Most Americans grow up hearing about the virtues of our ancestors and the wonders of democracy. We hear about George Washington's so-called unwillingness to tell a lie and Abe Lincoln's 3-mile walk to return some change to a customer who was overcharged at a store where Lincoln was clerking. We read in school about the noble struggles we have waged as a nation in the name of freedom, and we are informed about the benefits we receive because we live in a free society. If the efforts put forth by our families, schools, and media are not sufficient to impress us with our good fortune to be an American, special holidays are designed expressly for the purpose of celebrating America and Americanism.

As we become adults, we normally maintain much of the outlook about our nation we developed as children. Yet, for many of us, our positive evaluation of America becomes tempered by a dose of skepticism. We find fault with the system and its people. We complain about election choices, nod our heads in agreement with the assertion that there is no place for the little person anymore, and feel that all politicians are crooked. At times, even Washington and Lincoln do not escape our skeptical gaze. We hear that Washington was a spendthrift who ran up a huge expense tab as commander of the Continental Army and that Lincoln was a manic-depressive subject to fits of excitation and melancholy.

In much of this book, we have been skeptical of the claims made on behalf of American representative democracy by those who presently support the system. We noted how politics has been corrupted by the influence of corporate economics and showed how our options are shaped to make freedom difficult to obtain. We do not want to leave anyone with the impression that our criticism of American political life is intended to be a criticism of political activity itself. In fact, we believe that a much greater commitment to political activity is a prerequisite for reinvigorating American society so that the quality of our lives will actually improve.

While we do not believe that American politics functions in a genuinely democratic fashion today, we think that we ought to work to modify our society so that it begins to embody the principles of democracy to a greater extent. With respect to the arguments of this book, the significance of a more democratic orientation in American society is threefold. First, a society run according to democratic norms will recognize the conflicting needs and desires of the individuals who comprise the society. Second, a society run according to democratic norms will attempt to meet these needs and desires so that our dignity and potential is enhanced. Finally, a society run according to democratic norms may be able to transform our antisocial urges into socially acceptable behavior.

Democracy and Liberty

Almost every time we read or hear of a democratic political movement, we can expect to learn that the people involved claim that they have a right to more liberty than they have been granted. Prior to the American Revolution, Patrick Henry professed that he wanted "liberty or death." Thomas Jefferson justified the same revolution because of our "inalienable right to life, liberty, and the pursuit of happiness." In American society today, it is not uncommon to hear a seven- or eight-year-old child connect the events of everyday life with a presumed right to liberty. Told by an acquaintance or relative to be quiet, an American child may well refuse on the grounds that it is a "free country."

Our conception of liberty is usually a defensive one because we assume that liberty means freedom from arbitrary authority. We do not like anyone telling us to be quiet. The colonists revolted against the English because they felt that demands were being imposed that were not of their own choosing. Today, people who are concerned about liberty often justify their interest on similar grounds. In fact, conservatives and liberals often speak the same language, but simply point to different examples. We have mentioned Ralph Nader's efforts to protect us from the arbitrary authority of corporate America and we have discussed Milton Friedman's belief that individual freedom is threatened by government interference in the economic system.

Yet we want to be free from whimsical authority for reasons other than our fear about what those in power might do to us. Proper exercise of our liberty can help us become more mature and more competent. The nineteenth-century philosopher John Stuart Mill once addressed the question of whether the best form of government was that of the benevolent despot in which one person ran the affairs of the nation with an efficient yet kindly hand. Mill contended that it was not the most preferable form of government because it inevitably cramped individual development. He thought it was better to have a less efficient government than to have one in which people did not have a say about their politics. Mill suggested that it was preferable to have a society in which people made their own mistakes, than to have one in which they did not have the opportunity to go wrong.

There is an analog in our personal life which can help us make sense of Mill's notion. All of us are expected to listen to our parents and follow their direction during the first years of our lives. Eventually, however, a time comes when we no longer want to adhere to their rules and when parents themselves should expect their children to stake out their own path. This change is not only the consequence of fearing arbitrary authority, but stems from a belief that people are better off running their own lives. Parents are still to be respected, honored, and loved. But, after a certain time, they are not necessarily to be obeyed on every matter. They relinquish their authority so that children can become their own authorities and authors of their own lives.

Parents might occasionally make better decisions than their children, but we recognize the value of people making their own mistakes. We might think here of young men and women who move into their first apartment or rent their first home. Frequently, they are novices at household chores and home repairs. Yet they would rather have burnt dinners, leaky faucets and holes in their socks than to rely on help from relatives or friends. It would probably not be going too far to say that most of us believe that adults have an ethical imperative to control their own lives.

Given the connections we have drawn between our manner of organizing public affairs and our everyday lives, it should be easy to recognize how important political liberty is to our ability to control our lives. When we are told what to do and how to do something during most of our waking hours, we know that we are being treated more as a child than as a competent adult. A genuinely democratic society will attempt to maximize the time during the day and throughout our lives when we can legitimately employ our desire to have liberty. It is from this perspective that we have criticized many elements of contemporary American society: *for while we profess to maintain a system which encourages us to control our lives, we spend most of the day and much of our lives in an economic system whose operatives are encouraged to treat us as children.* Any effort to reform American society will have to recognize this and, as we shall argue later, attempt to extend our conception of democracy to the control and management of the economic arena.

Democracy and Community

While liberty is a very important value, there are limits to it. Few of us would want to have a legal and political system which condoned a murderer who defended his actions on the grounds that he was merely "doing his own thing." We would be dismayed if John Chancellor told deliberate lies on his evening newscast just to exercise his right to free speech. And if a hitchhiker to whom we were giving a lift informed us that he was an escapee from prison after being convicted of armed robbery, it would be unlikely that we would congratulate him on having regained his liberty.

Taken to extremes, liberty can be extraordinarily self-destructive. Most people have a few friends or relatives who use their liberty to hurt themselves. There are a number of people who drink or drug themselves into accidents or serious diseases. There are others among us who seem to choose a perfectly disastrous partner for all their intimate involvements. Finally, there are people who are so defeated by life that they decide suicide is the most appropriate use of their natural right to liberty. We may try to talk to these self-destructive people and reason with them to act differently, but we are reluctant to compel them by force when persuasion is unsuccessful.

At other times, most people think it is proper to limit liberty in a legal manner with official sanctions, because some people use their liberty to harm others as well as themselves. Americans have a common-sense understanding of this which is expressed in the saying that "your liberty ends where my nose begins." But drawing the line on this matter is rarely very easy. In practice, we never quite know where fists end and noses begin. What is perfectly innocent activity to one person may be considered socially unacceptable by another. An owner of an adult bookstore may feel that as long as there are shades on the windows and minors are refused entry, the owner is bothering nobody and meeting the wants of some members of the community. Yet the neighbors may feel quite differently and may claim that the store brings crime into the area, corrupts children, and lowers property values. Since democratic societies ought to take individual liberty seriously, drawing the line in these matters will be a perennial problem. Societies which do not cherish liberty can make these decisions more easily, yet most Americans would probably rather live with the problems that arise when we try to maintain both individual liberty and community rights.

It is important to note, however, that we often give up some of our liberty for reasons other than the concern we have about hurting others and getting harmed in return. Frequently, we voluntarily renounce our claim to full and complete liberty so that we might receive the benefits of establishing good relations with others. Persons who commit themselves to long-term involvements know that the benefits and security they will receive come at the cost of some measure of liberty. Partners who decide to become parents make a further renunciation of their liberty in order to experience the joys (and sufferings) that are the result of bearing and raising children. Indeed, many people would claim that without making such voluntary renunciations of our liberty, persons are apt to lead incomplete lives. We do not always want to be completely free. This is one of the reasons why we take families so importantly and why we, as we grow older, often choose to assume a series of responsibilities that reduce the range of our liberties. Many of us would find it somewhat pathetic to meet a 50-year old person who only wanted to ''fool around.''

Democratic values ought to encourage a similar process to occur in our communities. Specifically, democratic societies ought to encourage the citizenry to give up some free time to participate in political activity. Moreover, democratic values ought to encourage participation in which the good of the community is considered equal to or above our individual selfish desires. In return, people who act on behalf of the community good receive a number of benefits. By learning to make decisions with others about important matters, we may become more mature and competent persons. We can learn to be better listeners, to be sensitive to perspectives on life other than our own, and, ultimately, to become more well rounded ourselves. Furthermore, in a society where the common good is taken seriously, people can take pride in their collective accomplishments. They can defend their way of life not simply because they are ''free,'' but because they have used that freedom to create a society in which everyone respects what has been created in common. As in personal life, in a mature society we use our capacities to accomplish more than we can by merely ''fooling around.''

Unfortunately, present-day America provides little opportunity for us to practice this kind of politics. As we saw in Chapter 6, political participation is normally limited to periodic voting. Moreover, even that opportunity has been subject to a process of degradation so that candidates now use the techniques of public relations to market themselves as if they were competing bars of deodorant soap. Given this, we should not be surprised that a high proportion of Americans adamantly refuse to involve themselves with politics. We need, however, to think very deeply about how our democratic tradition might be reconstructed to meet the country's needs as we approach the end of the twentieth century.

POLITICS AND THE ECONOMY

We have continually noted the detrimental effects the corporate economy has brought to the quality of American life. These include the corruption of our politics, the degradation of work, the subversion of education's intellectual goals, and the effort to define people as merely mindless consumers. Given the influence of our economic arrangements, it is sensible to think that a politics which might eventually improve the quality of American life will have to challenge the assumptions of the corporate economy. This will not be a simple task because of the enormous powers held by powerful economic interests. To those interested in developing this challenge, three components of economic life will be relevant: (1) people interested in change will have to challenge the distributional consequences of our economic arrangements, (2) they will have to reform the organization of work life itself, and (3) they will have to challenge the prevailing ideas about what constitutes a worthwhile life.

The Politics of Distribution

Distributional issues pose inescapable questions if Americans are to deal responsibly with our economic difficulties. Yet distributional issues have an importance above and beyond the pragmatic considerations of the present. A more even distribution of wealth and income is important not only because of fears about what increasing inequality will mean for American society, but also because it is critical for creating a society that can enhance personal liberty while maintaining a degree of community spirit.

A society that encourages large economic inequalities is also likely to produce large discrepancies in personal liberty. In a decidedly unequal society, the measure of a person's wealth is apt to become the measure of that person's liberty. The practical liberties which the salary of a corporation executive brings are apt to be far greater than those of a secretary who works for the same corporation. Liberty is dependent not only on the formal economic creed, but also on the actual conditions of living and the choices really available to people. If society claims to promote liberty, but fosters huge disparities in income, it actually undermines its own premise for existing. It does not encourage liberty, but legal plunder instead.

A society that encourages vast disparities in income and wealth also promotes a manner of living in which the quality of life is typically rated high or low according to a person's standing on the economic ladder. Karl Marx maintained that the ruling ideas of every age are the ideas of the ruling class. This may not be precisely accurate, but it does point to a significant truth: our educational system, our media and others who help to shape public opinion will often support those who hold power. This may not take the form of explicit support for particular men and women who are ruling, but for the general ideas that have allowed them to gain power. One of the major arguments in favor of a more equal distribution of wealth is that power over an entire way of life may be taken away from the people who operate the economy.

There is also the possibility that redistribution can help create a greater commitment to communal norms than America now has. If economic disparities are lessened, there may be less reason for us to think that politics only consists of efforts to cheat people out of their tax dollars. As long as economic power remains so concentrated, it is difficult to believe that Americans will ever have a politics which sets personal interest aside in favor of the common good. Undoubtedly, redistribution would lessen the personal liberty of some people, but it is the kind of restriction that democratic societies ought to make. Redistribution would not immediately transform suspicious and distrustful people into open, considerate, public-spirited human beings. But it may be the precondition for allowing persons who want to be public-spirited to consider it a genuine alternative.

We should mention here that our notion of redistribution does not mean that everyone would become perfectly equal, but that the level of economic inequality would be vastly reduced. For instance, rules on income distribution could be drawn so that the highest income in America is not more than four times greater than the lowest. Redistributing wealth other than that acquired by income is a technically more complicated matter. Yet even here a tax system that was truly progressive and a planning process that was publicly controlled could gradually reduce wealth inequalities and still provide the funds that any economy needs for investment.

The Politics of Work

We have spoken about the importance of work in our lives, criticized its organization, and noted the lack of attention paid to the structure of work by mainstream political activists. Free enterprise conservatives do not recognize the coercion which marks work situations even when brute physical compulsion is not to be found. We criticized liberals for limiting their concern to unemployment and to safety at the workplace.

Most adults perform some work activity. In ideal form, it is simultaneously an expression of our freedom and of our commitment to the wider community. If we have freely chosen our occupation, we are said to have a vocation in life. In more traditional language, we have found our calling. Although this work activity should express our innermost talents, we also receive daily reminders of just how we are connected to others. In all likelihood, we would discover that we need other people to provide us with the tools or with some of the material of our activity. We would learn that other people help us with our work and still others distribute what we make. Using the language employed earlier in the chapter, work would be part of our ethical development.

Unfortunately, work is rarely organized in American society so that this is a realistic possibility for most people. As it currently stands, work is grim, routine and, for all too many people, sporadic. The first part of this characterization is not only true of assembly-line work, but is increasingly the case in white-collar jobs. A reorganization of work would be an integral part of a politics capable of providing us with more sustaining lives than is the case now. Most of us would prefer to see work as a calling and not only as an intolerable but necessary obligation. Let us be clear about our meaning. We are not simply exhorting people to change their attitude, to become robots who perform deadening tasks with a smile on their faces. We are suggesting that we think seriously about reorganizing the management of the work place and redefining the tasks involved in work.

Let us also be clear that we do not consider this a naive and idealistic goal. To be sure, it is impossible to have a society in which everyone pursues a genuine vocation. Some people will grow up not caring about future employment, others will not care about the jobs they are performing, and more than a few people will have sidelines and avocations to which they devote more energy than they do to their regular jobs. There is no reason, however, why we cannot extend the principle of equal opportunity to include the notion that everyone ought to have equal opportunity to have a calling. This would require something more than equal opportunity in education. It would require work to be organzied in such a way that people can enlarge their skills and participate in decision making. The work place could be viewed as a school of continuing education, a school in which late learners are not penalized for what happened on college entrance exams. The skeptics are correct when they argue that not everyone would use this opportunity and that all work has boring moments. But they are mistaken when they trot out these obvious truths to justify not providing the opportunity for people to perform cooperative and democratic work.

The Politics of Frugality

We have criticized the notion that a high standard of living ought to mean that we consume a great quantity of goods. We have further argued that the primary goal of politics ought not be simply to promote affluence. But while our attacks have been directed at existing habits and living politicians, the origins of our ideas are actually embedded in the original structure of American democratic politics. The democratic criticism of consumerism had its origins with the Puritans who settled New England. It was most fully developed; however, by the eighteenth-century Americans who fought the War of Independence against Great Britain.

The eighteenth-century Americans drew on a body of thought which portrayed England as a nation which had once been free, but had unfortunately failed to protect its liberty. In the colonists' minds, English virtue had been corrupted by a system of bribery among public officials and by an emphasis on luxury among the populace. In contrast, the colonists depicted themselves as thrifty, hard-working, devotees of liberty. When the British imposed various commercial sanctions on the colonies, a number of Americans responded with a hearty "So what." Some saw the British refusal to ship their goods across the Atlantic as an "act of kind providence" which ensured that Americans would not become enslaved to the consumer trifles of another nation. By the 1770s, colonial doctors were even warning that English tea was bad for your health. Devotion to acquiring consumer goods was commonly thought to enslave the individual. If it was not really bad for your health, it was surely no exaggeration to note how harmful it was to liberty.[1]

After the Revolution, a number of Americans worried that the citizenry was falling into the habits which had ruined the British. Americans had gone on a spending spree, purchasing items of luxury from foreign merchants. Warnings were issued from various quarters and all carried a similar message: unless Americans could restrain their multiplying desires for consumer purchases, the Revolution would have been fought in vain. It was said that pursuing economic luxury would reinstate our servile dependence. Since so much of our trade was with England, writers were warning that England was accomplishing by means of foreign trade what it failed to achieve by military means.

In the course of 200 years, the connection between frugality in personal life and democratic liberty has been all but severed in mainstream American political life. As American capitalism developed, especially in the late nineteenth and early twentieth century, the distinction between a democratic society and a luxurious society was blurred. Indeed, the merchants of luxury clothed themselves in the garb of democracy by claiming that they were bringing the consumer goods of the upper classes to the masses. From this, only a short step was required to equate the possession of consumer goods with a person's worth in life.

While critics of luxury went underground, they did not disappear entirely from American life. Many fine novelists in the 1920s and 1930s expressed dissatisfaction with the quality of life in capitalist America. Others, like F. Scott Fitzgerald, felt a tension similar to that which people frequently experience today. Fitzgerald was fascinated with the power of money, the people who were attracted to it, and the dreams it could temporarily purchase. On the other hand, Fitzgerald felt compelled to portray in his novels the corruption at the core of the rich and their inability to fulfill their deepest needs by relying on the power of their money. Recently, Americans who have been concerned about environmental quality and people worried about the political effects of our resource dependence have issued criticisms of consumer society which implicitly draw on this older legacy.

If our argument about the tendencies of consumer society to narrow the range of available experiences makes sense, it might also be sensible to refashion the

---

[1]See Bernard Bailyn, *The Ideological Origins of the American Revolution* (Cambridge: Harvard University Press, 1967) and Edmund S. Morgan, *The Challenge of the American Revolution* (New York: W.W. Norton and Company, 1976) for interesting expositions of this point.

democratic criticism of luxury in line with our times. This is not to say that we should avoid pleasure or sleep on a bed of nails. Rather we need to become aware of the problems in both our personal lives and the political order when we define ourselves primarily as consumers. In doing so, we will not be acting in an un-American manner, but will be reviving one of the most powerful democratic traditions that we have.

IS THERE ANY HOPE?

In conjunction with reforms of the economy, a truly democratic politics would make changes in other significant areas of life. Yet one of the most important difficulties facing us is that we hardly know how to talk about changes in our politics that could move us in a more democratic direction. Given the pervasiveness of large-scale bureaucracy, the apparent complexity of government in a technological era, and the apathy of the populace with respect to politics, these changes appear difficult to imagine. At the moment, we do not even have a significant body of utopian thought that has imagined the details of a new society, let alone actually have created one. Obviously, we want to know how an educational system would operate, to what use various media would be put, and how community affairs might be run differently in a democratic society. Without this information, any talk of revitalizing American society tends to seem more wistful and nostalgic than possible.

We cannot pretend to have solved these problems as much of this work has been critical in nature. We hope our readers do not see this criticism as purely a negative activity. Admittedly, we have not given a "positive" evaluation of America. Yet by pointing out connections between our public order and unnoticed everyday experiences our criticism serves a positive purpose. We think it is a positive gain if people can relate their life options (or lack thereof) to the stated and implicit social priorities of American society. We believe that this is ultimately more constructive than another look at the "good side" of America.

Criticism can also serve a positive purpose if it leads to experimentation. People who think that our arguments make sense may well go beyond any recommendations we could make in creating new forms of life more attuned to democratic principles. They might bring changes to the educational system or they might establish educational oportunities outside the school setting. Alternative uses for various media and, in communities, alternative ways of promoting more communal and cooperative activities might be developed. These experiments with democracy may, of course, be dismal failures, but failures can also be valuable learning experiences.

In many ways, America is proceeding in a direction precisely contrary to that which we have recommended. Rather than promising to extend democracy, we have a president pledged to unleashing business. We see more college students who feel that they have no other alternative than to major in business administration. We have a media culture that appears intent on fostering mindlessness throughout America. And we have an increasing number of intellectuals who believe that America's problem is that we have too much democracy.

President Reagan is a fitting symbol of the state of American politics. The election of an ex-movie actor extremely adept at image manipulation merely epitomizes the trend of making politics into an adjunct of public relations. As in many other areas of American life, the folksy and genial style of the president tends to disguise the strong power relationships. He eats jellybeans and speaks of restoring hope to the average person while endorsing policies that allow corporate America to become more powerful. His attack on government as the source of our problems helps to deflect attention away from the problems generated by business activity.

Given this trend, there is good reason to be pessimistic about the future of American politics. There is almost sufficient reason for people to maintain that they are fed up with politics and to refuse to become involved. Yet the reasons for giving up are not quite convincing. They ignore the reality that changes, occasionally dramatic changes, do occur in the political world. They also ignore, as we mentioned throughout the book, the problems that arise in our lives when we make a habit of submitting to things as they are.

There is perhaps one sense in which this book has itself been overly pessimistic. While we have tried to give an accurate portrayal of central tendencies in American life, we have not always given full consideration to the cracks in the structure we have described. In each chapter, we could have given examples of individuals, groups, or movements that have opposed the dominant tendencies in American life. Nowhere has this opposition achieved complete success and not all aspects of it are equally valuable, but some of it surely deserves mention.

Many individuals have consciously rejected the basic assumptions of consumer society. Despite the insistent pleas of advertisers, they refuse to tie their identities to the world of commerce. We see this rejection not only in people who live on the fringes of American society but in average citizens who believe that the values of family, friendship and community are more important than the values of the corporate economy. We also see it in students and teachers who act as if school is something more than a personnel agency for the economy and try to form a genuine community of people interested in knowledge.

An alternative vision of work life also is beginning to emerge. Some people who have come to see their work as inherently unsatisfying have accepted a lower material standard of living in exchange for work that will allow them to pursue more enduring values. We can find these people in bikeshops, bookshops, restaurants, and small farms in rural areas. More importantly, a belief in the importance of creating democratic and cooperative work is slowly gaining a foothold in this country. A number of firms have found it necessary to improve the quality of work life simply to get workers to perform at a rate profitable for the company. The

Campaign for Economic Democracy, based in California, has recently helped to elect mayors in two mid-sized cities in that state. Various versions of worker self-management operating in other nations are being critically and seriously examined. And even some unions are beginning to test the waters of worker participation.

There are also hopeful signs in the media. Public radio and television have provided news programs like *All Things Considered*, the *McNeil-Lehrer Report*, and *Bill Moyers' Journal* which offer news coverage clearly superior to the offerings of the mass media. Despite financial difficulties, the critical press survives so that a person willing to spend the time can still find critical outlooks on American society by reading *Dissent, democracy, Mother Jones, The Nation* and *In These Times*. Moreover, cable television has the potential to initiate a substantial media democratization. Its products are thus far unimpressive, consisting mainly of more sports and movies; yet it represents an untapped potential for media reform.

None of these hopeful signs will be meaningful in the long term if they do not find a common political expression. A new political party, the Citizens party, did emerge on the left in 1980. In its first effort, however, the new party performed poorly at the polls. Whether it or any party on the left can become a significant force in American politics is yet to be determined. It is clear what the Citizens party or any party on the left will have to do if they are to be effective forces. *People who desire to change the priorities of American society will have to show ordinary citizens how their lives have been diminished by the workings of the corporate economy. They will have to show how the concerns and values of ordinary Americans have been neglected and destroyed by the priorities of the corporate economy.* This will be a formidable task and the most optimistic we could be is to say that success would come after a long and difficult struggle.

The reason for making this effort not to accept things as they are was explained very well by the late folksinger Phil Ochs. Known as a protest singer, Ochs was especially opposed to the use of American military force abroad and to racism and civil rights violations at home. Songs like "I Ain't Marching Anymore," "Cops of the World," and "Here's to the State of Mississippi" vividly expressed the dissatisfaction with the direction of American life that was prevalent during the 1960s in some circles of American society. But Ochs was more than just a protest singer, for some of his songs revealed that he was a person capable of deep introspection. He could explain his own purposes as a writer as clearly as he could criticize American society.

In one of his introspective songs, a ballad titled "When I'm Gone," Ochs spoke about his reasons for being a folksinger and a critic of American society. He explained that he was a folksinger because it was a calling that enabled him to live with integrity. He sang his songs because these permitted him to "live proud enough to die." Moreover, Ochs even implied that his efforts could, at least momentarily, overshadow the activity of the social order against which he protested. Although his only weapons were his voice and an acoustic guitar, he maintained that he could occasionally sing "louder than the guns."

One does not have to be an aging hippie or even someone who shared Phil Ochs' ideology to realize that his song did express what is commonly recognized as a psychological truth. People who make the effort to live with integrity and commitment have a richer existence than men and women whose lives are one long compromise and who continually submit to things which they know in their hearts are not right. It is not always an easier life for we may have to suffer, as Ochs admitted, "from the pains" of our integrity. Yet how we live in youth and middle age determines whether our last years are filled with the consolations of old age or with terror at having lived dishonestly.[2]

There is no reason to be foolishly optimistic about the state of America today. The problems we face are profound. The resources which we have been able to muster against these problems have been, at least to this point, meager. Yet we ought not to be foolishly despairing either. To despair of making our lives better ignores the desire that many of us share to do exactly this. It is a desire to be found even in the outposts of society like the Ritz bar. It also ignores the truth that a life without hope can hardly be worthwhile.

Throughout this book, we have tried to point out the connections between our everyday lives and the American social and political order. Much of what we have done is to point out how this order effects the options we have in our everyday lives. We have demonstrated this by reference to our typical experiences in school, at work, and watching the media. Our hope for the future lies in the possibility that we might see how the improvement of our everyday lives is tied to the change of our political order. It would be a change designed to make the virtues of democracy a living reality in American life. Such a change might enable more of us to live "proud enough to die."

[2]Sadly, Phil Ochs himself eventually became so troubled after having his throat damaged by an attacker that he committed suicide. Fortunately, a songwriter has a calling in which his life work will outlive the memory of how he actually dies.

Selected Bibliography

Anyone who wishes to explore the themes of this book in more detail should find the following works useful.

BOOKS

Arlen, Michael J. *Thirty Seconds*. New York: Farrar, Straus & Giroux, 1979.

Bailyn, Bernard. *The Ideological Origins of the American Revolution*. Cambridge: Harvard Univ. Press, 1967.

Barnet, Richard, and Muller, Ronald. *Global Reach*. New York: Simon & Schuster, 1975.

Barnouw, Erik. *A History of Broadcasting in the United States*. New York: Oxford Univ. Press, 1966, 1970.

————. *The Sponsor*. New York: Oxford Univ. Press, 1978.

Berry, Wendell. *The Unsettling of America*. New York: Avon Books, 1977.

Blumberg, Paul. *Inequality in an Age of Decline*. New York: Oxford Univ. Press, 1980.

Bowles, Samuel, and Gintis, Herbert. *Schooling in Capitalist America*. New York: Basic Books, 1976

Braverman, Harry. *Labor and Monopoly Capital*. New York: Monthly Review Press, 1975.

Callenbach, Ernest. *Ecotopia*. New York: Bantam, 1977.

Carnoy, Martin, and Shearer, Derek. *Economic Democracy: The Challenge of the Eighties*. White Plains, N.Y.: M.E. Sharpe, 1980.

Cicourel, Aaron, and Kitsuse, John. *The Educational Decision-Makers*. New York: Bobbs-Merrill, 1963.

Crawford, Alan. *Thunder on the Right: The New Right and the Politics of Resentment.* New York: Pantheon, 1980.

Crouse, Timothy. *The Boys on the Bus.* New York: Ballantine, 1972.

Davis, David Howard. *Energy Politics.* New York: St. Martin's Press, 1978.

Dickstein, Morris. *Gates of Eden: American Culture in the Sixties.* New York: Basic Books, 1978.

Doctorow, E.L. *The Book of Daniel.* New York: Random House, 1971.

Dolbeare, Kenneth M., ed. *American Political Thought.* Monterey: Duxbury Press, 1981.

Edelman, Murray. *The Symbolic Uses of Politics.* Urbana: Univ. of Illinois Press, 1964.

Edwards, Richard. *Contested Terrain.* New York: Basic Books, 1979.

Epstein, Edward. *News From Nowhere.* New York: Vintage, 1974.

Ewen, Stuart. *Captains of Consciousness.* New York: McGraw-Hill, 1976.

Fitzgerald, Frances. *America Revised.* Boston: Little, Brown, 1979.

Friedman, Milton. *Capitalism and Freedom.* Chicago: Univ. of Chicago Press, 1962.

Friedman, Milton, and Friedman, Rose. *Free to Choose.* New York: Harcourt, Brace Jovanovich, 1980.

Galbraith, John Kenneth. *The New Industrial State.* New York: New American Library, 1979.

Gans, Herbert. *Deciding What's News.* New York: Random House, 1979.

Garson, Barbara. *All the Livelong Day.* Garden City, N.Y.: Doubleday, 1975.

Gilder, George. *Wealth and Poverty.* New York: Basic Books, 1980.

Gitlin, Todd. *The Whole World is Watching.* Berkeley: Univ. of California Press, 1980.

Glazer, Nathan, and Kristol, Irving, eds. *The American Commonwealth.* New York: Basic Books, 1976.

Goodwyn, Lawrence. *The Populist Movement.* New York: Oxford Univ. Press, 1979.

Gosz, Andre. *Ecology as Politics.* Boston: South End Press, 1980.

Graber, Doris. *Mass Media and American Politics.* Washington, D.C.: Congressional Quarterly Press, 1980.

Gutman, Herbert G. *Work, Culture and Society.* New York: Random House, 1966.

Halberstam, David. *The Powers That Be.* New York: Knopf, 1979.

Harrington, Michael. *The Accidental Century.* New York: Macmillan, 1965.

———. *Decade of Decision.* New York: Simon & Schuster, 1980.

———. *The Other America.* New York: Penguin Books, 1971.

Heilbroner, Robert. *An Inquiry into the Human Prospect.* New York: Norton, 1980.

Henry, Jules. *Culture Against Man.* New York: Vintage, 1965.

———. *Essays on Education.* New York: Penguin Books, 1971.

Hodgson, Godfrey. *America in Our Time.* New York: Vintage, 1978.

Holsworth, Robert. *Public Interest Liberalism and the Crisis of Affluence.* Cambridge, Mass.: Schenkman Publishing, 1981.

Illich, Ivan. *Deschooling Society.* New York: Harper & Row, 1970.

Kantor, Rosabeth Moss. *Men and Women of the Corporation.* New York: Bsic Books, 1978.

Karabel, Jerome, and Halsey, A.H., eds. *Power and Ideology in Education.* Fair Lawn, N.J.: Oxford Univ. Press, 1977.

Kasson, John F. *Civilizing the Machine: Technology and Republican Values in America, 1776–1900.* New York: Penguin Books, 1976.

———. *Amusing the Million*. New York: Hill and Wang, 1978.

Katz, Michael. *School Reform: Past and Presdent*. Boston: Little, Brown, 1971.

Kearns, Doris A. *Lyndon Johnson and the American Dream*. New York: New American Library, 1977.

Koch, James. *Industrial Organization and Prices*. Englewood Cliffs, N.J.: Prentice-Hall, 1980.

Kristol, Irving. *Two Cheers for Capitalism*. New York: Basic Books, 1978.

Lang, Kurt, and Lang, Gladys. *Politics and Television*. Chicago, Quadrangle Books, 1968.

Lasch, Christopher. *The Culture of Narcissism*. New York: Norton, 1978.

———. *The World of Nations*. New York: Knopf, 1973.

Leiss, William. *The Limits to Satisfaction: An Essay on the Problem of Needs and Commodities*. Toronto: Univ. of Toronto Press, 1976.

Levitan, Sar, and Taggart, Robert. *The Promise of Greatness*. Cambridge: Harvard Univ. Press, 1976.

Lovins, Amory B. *Soft Energy Paths*. New York: Harper & Row, 1977.

Maccoby, Michael. *The Gamesman*. New York: Simon & Schuster, 1976.

Macpherson, C.B. *The Life and Times of Liberal Democracy*. New York: Oxford Univ. Press, 1977.

Malcolm X. *The Autibiography of Malcolm X*. New York: Ballantine, 1973.

Mander, Jerry. *Four Arguments for the Elimination of Television*. New York: Morrow, 1978.

Marx, Leo. *The Machine in the Garden*. New York: Oxford Univ. Press, 1964.

Miliband, Ralph. *The State in Capitalist Society*. New York: Basic Books, 1969.

Minow, Newton, and Mitchell, Lee. *Presidential Television*. New York: Basic Books, 1973.

Miroff, Bruce. *Pragmatic Illusions: The Presidential Politics of John F. Kennedy*. New York: McKay, 1976.

Morgan, Edmund. *The Challenge of the American Revolution*. New York: Norton, 1976.

———. *The Meaning of Independence*. New York: Norton, 1978.

Morris, William. *News From Nowhere*. London: Routledge and Kegan Paul, 1970.

Nasaw, David. *Schooled to Order*. Fair Lawn, N.J.: Oxford Univ. Press, 1979.

Nieburg, H.L. *Culture Storm*. New York: St. Martin's Press, 1973.

Nixon, Richard. *RN: The Memoirs of Richard Nixon*. New York: Warner Books, 1979.

Noble, David. *America By Design*. New York: Oxford Univ. Press, 1979.

O'Connor, James. *The Fiscal Crisis of the State*. New York: St. Martin's Press, 1973.

Ophuls, William. *Ecology and the Politics of Scarcity*. San Francisco: W.H. Freeman, 1977.

Paletz, David, Pearson, Roberta, and Willis, Ronald. *Politics in Public Service Advertising on Television*. New York: Praeger, 1977.

Patterson, Thomas E., and McClure, Robert D. *The Unseeing Eye*. New York: G.P. Putnam's Sons, 1976.

Pfeffer, Richard. *Working for Capitalism*. New York: Columbia Univ. Press, 1977.

Podhoretz, Norman. *Breaking Ranks*. New York: Harper & Row, 1979.

———. *The Present Danger*. New York: Simon & Schuster, 1980.

Polanyi, Karl. *The Great Transformation*. Boston: Beacon Press, 1944.

Ravitch, Diane. *The Great School Wars, New York City, 1805–1973*. New York: Basic Books, 1974.

Real, Michael. *Mass Mediated Culture.* Englewood Cliffs, N.J.: Prentice-Hall, 1977.

Reich, Charles. *The Greening of America.* New York: Random House, 1970.

Ritzer, George. *Working: Conflict and Change.* Englewood Cliffs, N.J.: Prentice-Hall, 1977.

Rodgers, Daniel T. *The Work Ethic in Industrial America, 1850–1920.* Chicago: Univ. of Chicago Press, 1974.

Roszak, Theodore, *The Making of a Counter Culture.* New York: Doubleday, 1970.

———. *Person/Planet.* New York: Anchor Press, 1978.

Sampson, Anthony. *The Seven Sisters.* New York: Bantam Books, 1975.

Schell, Jonathan. *The Time of Illusion.* New York: Knopf, 1976.

Schlafly, Phyllis. *The Power of the Positive Woman.* Westport, Conn.: Arlington House, 1977.

Schlozman, Kay, and Verba, Sidney. *Insult to Injury.* Cambridge: Harvard Univ. Press, 1979.

Schumacher, E.F. *Small is Beautiful.* New York: Harper & Row, 1973.

Scitovsky, Tibor. *The Joyless Economy.* New York: Oxford Univ. Press, 1976.

Sennett, Richard, and Cobb, Jonathan. *The Hidden Injuries of Class.* New York: Vintage, 1973.

Sigal, Leon. *Reporters and Officials.* Lexington, Mass.: Heath, 1973.

Silberman, Charles. *Crisis in the Classroom.* New York: Vintage, 1971.

Simon, William. *A Time for Truth.* New York: McGraw-Hill, 1978.

Slater, Philip. *The Pursuit of Loneliness.* Boston: Beacon Press, 1970.

Steinfels, Peter. *The Neo-Conservatives.* New York: Simon & Schuster, 1979.

Stobaugh, Robert, and Yergin, Daniel. *Energy Future.* New York: Random House, 1979.

Stretton, Hugh. *Capitalism, Socialism and the Environment.* Cambridge: Cambridge Univ. Press, 1976.

Tawney, R.H. *The Acquisitive Society.* New York: Harcourt, Brace Jovanovich, 1955.

Terkel, Studs. *Working.* New York: Pantheon, 1974.

Thurow, Lester. *The Zero Sum Society.* New York: Basic Books, 1980.

Tocqueville, Alexis De. *Democracy in America.* New York: Doubleday, 1967.

Tuchman, Gaye. *Making News.* New York: Free Press, 1978.

Tucker, Robert W. *The Inequality of Nations.* New York: Basic Books, 1979.

Veblen, Thorstein. *The Theory of the Leisure Class. New York: Penguin Books, 1979.*

Walzer, Michael. Radical Principles: Reflections of an Unreconstructed Democrat. New York: Basic Books, 1980.

Whyte, William H. *The Organization Man.* New York: Simon & Schuster, 1956.

Winn, Marie. *The Plug-in Drug.* New York: Viking, 1977.

Wood, Gordon. *The Creation of the American Republic.* Chapel Hill: Univ. of North Carolina Press, 1969.

Yankelovich, Daniel. *New Rules,* New York: Random House, 1981.

Zaretsky. Eli. *Capitalism, the Family and Personal Life.* New York: Harper & Row, 1976.

ARTICLES

Apple, Michael, and King, Nancy. ''What Do Schools Teach.'' *Curriculum Inquiry* 6 (1977): 341–57.

Bagdikian, Ben H. "Congress and the Media: Partners in Propaganda." *Columbia Journalism Review,* January 1974, pp. 3 – 12.

Berman, Marshall. "Buildings Are Judgments on 'What Man Can Build'." *Ramparts* March 1975, pp. 33ff.

———. "Sympathy for the Devil: Faust, the Sixties, and the Tragedy of Development." *American Review 19,* January 1974, pp. 23 – 75.

Bogart, Leo, "Is All This Advertising Necessary?" *Journal of Advertising Research,* October 1978, pp. 17 – 30.

Boyte, Harry, "Populism and the Left." *democracy,* April 1981, pp. 53 – 66.

Burawoy, Michael. "Towards a Marxist Theory of the Labor Process: Braverman and Beyond." *Politics and Society* 8 (3 – 4), 1978.

Cagan, Elizabeth. "Individualism, Collectivism and Radical Educational Reform." *Harvard Education Review* 48 (2), May 1978, pp. 227 – 266.

Clark, Burton R. "The Cooling Out Function of American Higher Education." *American Journal of Sociology* 65, May 1960, pp. 569 – 576.

Clark, Kim B., and Summers, Lawrence. "Unemployment Reconsidered." *Harvard Business Review,* November – December 1980, pp. 171 – 179.

Cohen, David, and Rosenberg, Bella. "Functions and Fantasies: Understanding Schools in Capitalist America." *History of Education Quarterly,* Summer, 1977, pp. 113 – 138.

Corrigan, Richard. "There's Not Much Left for Production from the $227 Billion Windfall Profits Tax." *National Journal,* February 22, 1980, pp. 314 – 316.

Dahl, Robert. "On Removing Certain Impediments to Democracy." *Political Science Quarterly,* Spring 1977, pp. 1 – 20.

Dreeben, Robert. "The Contribution of Schools to the Learning of Norms." *Harvard Education Review,* Spring 1967, pp. 211 – 237.

Epps, Garrett. "Two Cheers for the '70's." *The Washington Post Magazine,* February 25, 1979, pp. 8 – 15.

Friedman, Robert. "Try American Capitalism Today." *Columbia Journalism Review,* May 1976, pp. 7 – 12.

Gintis, Herbert. "Education, Technology and the Characteristics of Worker Productivity." *American Economic Review,* May 1971, pp. 266 – 279.

———. "Toward a Political Economy of Education: A Radical Critique of Ivan Illich." *Harvard Education Review,* February 1972, pp. 70 – 96.

Gitlin, Tood, "Prime Time Ideology: The Hegemonic Process in Education." *Social Problems,* February 1979, pp. 251 – 266.

Greenbaum, Joan. "Division of Labor in the Computer Field." *Monthly Reivew,* July – August, 1976. pp. 40 – 55.

Heilbroner, Robert. "The Demand for the Supply Side." *The New York Review of Books,* June 11, 1981, pp. 37 – 41.

Hogan, David. "Education and the Making of the Chicago Working Class, 1880 – 1930." *History of Education Quarterly* 19(3) (Fall 1978): 227 – 270.

Holsworth, Robert D. "Recycling Hobbes: The Limits to Political Ecology." *The Massachusetts Review,* Spring, 1979, pp. 9 – 40.

Howard, Robert. "Second Class in Silicon Valley." *Working Papers Magazine,* September/October 1981, pp. 21 – 31.

Husock, Howard. "The High Cost of Starting Out." *The New York Times Sunday Magazine,* June 7, 1981, pp. 47 ff.

Karabel, Jerome. "Community College and Social Stratification." *Harvard Educational Review,* November 1972, pp. 521–562.

Kasun, Jacqueline. "Turning Children into Sex Experts." *The Public Interest,* Spring 1979, pp. 99.

Katz, Michael. "The Origins of Public Education: A Reassessment." *History of Education Quarterly,* Winter 1976, pp. 381–408.

Katzman, Nathan. "TV Soaps: What's Going On?" *Public Opinion Quarterly,* Summer 1972, pp. 200–212.

Kirkpatrick, Jeane. "Dictatorships and Double Standards." *Commentary,* November 1979, pp. 40–54.

Kopkind, Andrew. "The "Unwritten Watergate Story." *More,* November 1974, pp. 6–12.

Kuttner, Bob. "Growth with Equity." *Working Papers Magazine,* September/October 1981, pp. 32–42.

Lasch, Christopher. "The Good Old Days." *The New York Review of Books,* February 10, 1972, pp. 25–26.

———. "Inequality and Education." *The New York Review of Books,* May 17, 1973, pp. 19–24.

———. "Democracy and the Crisis of Confidence," *democracy,* January 1981.

Lowinger, Paul. "Health Information During a Week of Television." *New England Journal of Medicine,* 1972, p. 516.

Lydenberg, Robin. "The Rhetoric of Advertising." *Michigan Quarterly* Review, Winter 1978, pp. 77–92.

Marglin, Stephen. "What Do Bosses Do: The Origins and Functions of Hierarchy in Capitalist Production." *Review of Radical Economics,* Summer 1974, pp. 60–112.

Marin, Peter. "The New Narcissism." *Harper's,* October 1975, pp. 45–56.

Moynihan, Daniel. "The Presidency and the Press." *Commentary,* March 1971, pp. 41–52.

Nader, Ralph. "Business Crime." *The New Republic,* September 9, 1967, pp. 7–8.

———. "We're Still in the Jungle." *The New Republic,* July 15, 1967, pp. 11–12.

Orr, David. "U.S. Energy Policy and the Political Economy of Participation." *Journal of Politics,* November 1979, pp. 1027–56.

Orr, David, and Hill, Stuart. "Leviathan, the Open Society and the Crisis of Ecology. *Western Political Quarterly,* December 1978, pp. 457–469.

Powers, Ron. "Eyewitless News." *Columbia Journalism Review,* May 1977, p. 17–25.

Robbins, Thomas, Anthony, Dick, Doucas, Madeline, and Curtis, Thomas. "The Last Civil Religion: Reverend Moon and the Unification Church," in Irving Louis Horowitz (ed.), *Science, Sin and Scholarship: The Politics of Reverend Moon and the Unification Church,* Cambridge, MIT Press.

Robinson, Michael J. "Television and American Politics: 1956–76." *The Public Interest,* Summer 1977, pp. 3–40.

Rossiter, John R. "Does Advertising Research Affect Children?" *Journal of Advertising Research,* February 1979, pp. 49–54.

Samuelson, Robert J. "The $100 Billion Mistake—Is the 'Windfall' Revenue Estimate Too

High?'' *National Journal,* April 26, 1980, pp. 677−680.

Schiller, Bradley. ''Welfare: Reforming Our Expectations.'' *The Public Interest,* Winter 1981, pp. 55−65.

Scott, Bruce R. ''OPEC, The American Scapegoat.'' *Harvard Business Review,* January/February, 1981, pp. 6−32.

Staines, Graham, and Quinn, Robert P. ''American Workers Evaluate the Quality of Their Jobs.'' *Monthly Labor Review,* January 1979, pp. 3−13.

Stark, David. ''Class Struggle and the Transformation of the Labor Process.'' *Theory and Society,* January 1980, pp. 89−130.

Stockman, David. ''The Wrong War? The Case Against a National Energy Policy.'' *The Public Interest,* Fall 1978, pp. 3−44.

Thero, Susan. ''Billions to the Poor for Fuel Bills, But Not a Penny for Transportation.'' *National Journal,* May 17, 1980, pp. 811−813.

Tuchman, Gaye. ''Objectivity as a Strategic Ritual.'' *American Journal of Sociology,* January 1972, pp. 660−680.

Walzer, Michael. ''Politics in the Welfare State.'' *Dissent,* January/February 1968, pp. 26−40.

Weaver, Paul. ''Is TV News Biased?'' *The Public Interest,* Winter 1972, pp. 57−74.

Williams, Raymond. ''Base and Superstructure in Marxist Cultural Theory.'' *New Left Review* 82 (1973): 3−16.

Wolfe, Tom. ''The 'Me' Decade.'' *New York Magazine,* August 26, 1975, pp. 28−39.

Wolin, Sheldon. ''The State of the Union.'' *The New York Review of Books,* May 18, 1978, pp. 3−8.

Wray, J. Harry. ''Comment on Interpretations of Early Research into Belief Systems.'' *Journal of Politics,* November 1979, pp. 1173−81.

———. ''Rethinking Responsible Parties.'' *Western Political Quarterly,* December 1981.

Wynee, Edward A. ''What Are the Courts Doing to Our Children?'' *The Public Interest,* Summer 1981, pp. 3−18.

Index